TERRY JONES'
BARBARIANS

Terry Jones is best known as a member of Monty Python, but he has also written four books on medieval England – *Chaucer's Knight*, the highly acclaimed *Who Murdered Chaucer?*, *Crusades* and *Terry Jones' Medieval Lives*, which accompanied a major television series he presented in 2004. He is the author of several children's books including *Fairy Tales and Fantastic Stories*, *The Knight and the Squire* and *The Lady and the Squire*. Terry has also directed several feature films – *Monty Python and the Holy Grail*, *The Life of Brian*, *The Meaning of Life*, *Personal Services*, *Erik the Viking* and *The Wind in the Willows*.

Alan Ereira has worked as an award-winning producer and writer of history programmes on radio and television for over 40 years, and has collaborated with Terry for ten years on a number of historical films. His previous books include *The People's England*, *The Invergordon Mutiny*, *The Heart of the World* and (with Terry Jones) *Crusades* and *Terry Jones' Medieval Lives*.

TERRY JONES'
BARBARIANS

TERRY JONES & ALAN EREIRA

BBC BOOKS

937.06
Jone

This book is published to accompany the television series *Terry Jones' Barbarians* produced by Oxford Film and Television for BBC Television and first broadcast on BBC2 in 2006.

First published in 2006
This edition published in 2007 by BBC Books, an imprint of Ebury Publishing

10 9 8 7 6 5 4 3

Ebury Publishing is a division of the Random House Group Ltd.

The Random House Group Ltd Reg. No. 954009

Addresses for companies within the Random House Group Ltd can be found at www.randomhouse.co.uk

A CIP catalogue record for this book is available from the British Library.

The Random House Group Ltd makes every effort to ensure that the papers used in our books are made from trees that have been legally sourced from well-managed and credibly certified forests. Our paper procurement policy can be found at www.randomhouse.co.uk

ISBN: 978 0 563 53916 2

Commissioning editors: Sally Potter and Martin Redfern
Project editor: Cameron Fitch
Copy editor: Esther Jagger
Designer: Martin Hendry
Maps by HL Studios, Long Hanborough, Oxon
Picture researcher: Caroline Wood
Production: David Brimble

Set in Fairfield Light
Printed in Great Britain by CPI Cox & Wyman, Reading, RG1 8EX
Colour separations by Dot Gradations, Wickford, Essex

CONTENTS

PREFACE

It took some nerve to write this book and the TV series associated with it. It embraces over 700 years of history on three continents, and involves us striding into the territory of many dedicated and highly impressive scholars.

But it's been a bit of an obsession. We first proposed a TV series on this subject to the BBC in 1997 and have been coming back pretty much every year. And for some reason it's a subject that stirs the passions. What other TV project would have four grown men shouting angrily in an office over the significance of a gerundive in a line of Tacitus?

Terry Jones' Barbarians is about all those peoples whom the Romans wrote off as uncivilized, but it's also a chance to take a look at the Romans themselves from an alternative point of view – from the point of view of the people they trashed. And as such it fits into a thesis we've been banging on about in *Terry Jones' Medieval Lives* and in Terry's radio series *The Anti-Renaissance Show*. That thesis is that we've all been sold a false history of Rome that has twisted our entire understanding of our own history – glorifying (and glossing over) a long era of ruthless imperial power, celebrating it for the benefit of Renaissance tyrants and more modern empires, and wildly distorting our view of the so-called 'Middle Ages' and of the peoples whom Rome crushed and who were then blamed for its fall. Oh yes, and it includes a few measured comments on the Church while we're at it.

We are certainly not experts in the field, and we are indebted to the many real scholars and historians who have allowed us to pick their brains and stomp all over their patch in our inevitably heavy boots. Many thanks to all of them for being so tolerant and generous with their advice. We should particularly like to thank Dr Walter Pohl for his helpful comments, Dr Peter Heather for taking the time to explore answers to our occasionally obsessive questions, Dr Hartmut Ziche and, above all, Professor Barry Cunliffe, whose kindness in carefully steering us away from some real mistakes, and whose unfailing and discreet enthusiasm for the project, have been of enormous help. To all these people: our apologies.

We owe a huge debt of gratitude to the TV production team, especially Nick Kent of OFTV, who managed to get the BBC and the History Channel to sign up to the project and watched over it with a fatherly eye; to David McNab, the series editor; to the producer/directors Rob Coldstream and David Wilson (who had to master a vast amount of material and wrestle with us in the heat of pseudo-academic passion); and to the production assistants and researchers Clare Lynch, Susannah Davis and Sarah Veevers.

If you treat this book as a Lego construction, take it apart and reassemble it in chronological order, you will find a story that goes from the first stirrings of Rome around the fifth century BC through to the last Roman emperor nearly 1000 years later. But there will be odd-shaped gaps, and a number of left-over pieces scattered around the floor. This isn't a history of Rome, and the narrative here is a different one from the others that have been written.

There are, of course, hundreds of books in English covering the period, but no general look at it from a non-Roman perspective. The 'barbarians' of the early period, through to the first century AD, have been written about in books specifically on individual societies – mostly Celts and Germans. For the later period, the general reader has had to browse among a series of huge narratives written in the shadow of Gibbon's great *Decline and Fall of the Roman Empire*. The people whom the Romans called Barbarians are either on the periphery of the main story, or come into it as invaders.

But we're looking at the world they created and inhabited, and it's Rome that is the intruder, or, later, their sometime host, sometime prey. Our interest in Rome lies less in what these people did to the Empire than in what the Empire did to them. And since 'they' are actually the people who created the world we live in, this becomes quite literally a question of 'What did the Romans ever do for us?' The answer, as you will have already figured, is not usually very nice.

So what we have constructed here is not a chronological journey through the Empire's history. We have, instead, chosen to survey the non-Roman world in four sections.

In Part One the world of the Atlantic Celts is traced from its fullest flowering in the first century BC through to its final destruction by Roman armies 200 years later. We then look at the failure of the

Roman state in Celtic territory during the third century, and the steady breakdown that led to the re-emergence of a separate Atlantic world in the old Celtic lands.

Part Two is about German territory (in which we include Dacia) and the Germans. So we look at the way in which the Germans resisted Roman occupation in the first century AD, the great civilization of Dacia, which Rome extinguished in the second century, and then the Goths and their attempts to integrate themselves into the Empire in the fourth and early fifth centuries.

In Part Three we turn to people who regarded the Romans as the Barbarians – the Greeks (who in the early period saw all outsiders as Barbarians, and found that the Romans took the same view of them) and the Persians – a 'barbarian' society that posed a successful military challenge to Rome and long outlived the Western Empire. To tell the Greek story we go back to the early fourth century BC, and for the Persians even further back, another 100 years, in an epic sweep that ends, for our story, with the arrival of the Huns in Persia nearly 800 years later.

So far we have looked west, north and east. Part Four of the book takes us south, into Vandal Africa, with a narrative entirely set in the fifth century AD. But this is where we look at the Christian revolution and its impact on the very idea of 'barbarian', as well as on the Barbarians themselves, and also at the quite extraordinary reign of Attila the Hun, who probably (and quite inadvertently) did more to effect a transfer of power in the West from Empire to Church than anyone else.

There's quite a lot that may come as a surprise: the sophistication of Celtic engineering and mathematics, the highly developed religious philosophy of Dacia, the fact that the Greeks were evidently on the edge of an industrial revolution, the comfort of life in Vandal villas, Attila's remarkable 'Iron Curtain' between his kingdom and the Roman Empire. And much more besides.

So welcome to history from a different point of view.

BARBARIAN TIMELINE

A crude and somewhat primitive timeline of events covered in this book, but it may provide a sense of chronology to help you through the narrative.

c.576 BC	Reign of Cyrus I, King of Persia begins
c.550 BC	Great age of religious philosophy – Pythagoras and Zalmoxis (and Buddha)
522 BC	Reign of Darius I, King of Persia begins
486 BC	Reign of Xerxes I, King of Persia begins
406 BC	Syracuse–Carthage war
c.390 BC	Brennus' Celts attack Rome
336 BC	Alexander 'the Great' becomes king of Macedonia
330 BC	Persepolis destroyed
324 BC	Alexander dies
305 BC	Rhodes–Macedon war
282 BC	Colossus of Rhodes erected
279 BC	Celts attack Greece
212 BC	Romans take Syracuse
168 BC	Rome controls Greece
164 BC	Rhodes–Rome treaty
146 BC	Romans raze Corinth
c.70 BC	Reign of Burebista, King of Dacia begins
59 BC	Caesar appointed Protector of the Gauls
55, 54 BC	Caesar to Britain
53 BC	Vercingetorix victory: Battle of Harran
52 BC	Fall of Alesia
49 BC	Caesar invades Rome: civil war
44 BC	Caesar assassinated; Burebista assassinated
42 BC	Sack of Rhodes
27 BC	Octavian (Augustus) becomes first emperor
12 BC	Rome occupies Germany
AD 9	Varus' defeat
AD 14	Tiberius becomes emperor
AD 17	Germanicus' Triumph
AD 41	Claudius becomes emperor

AD 42	Cunobelin dies
AD 43	Invasion of Britain
AD 54	Nero becomes emperor
AD 60	Revolt of Iceni
AD 69	Vespasian becomes emperor, captures Rome
AD 81	Domitian becomes emperor
AD 87	Reign of Decebalus, King of Dacia begins
AD 98	Trajan becomes emperor
AD 105	Rome takes Dacia
AD 117	Hadrian becomes emperor
AD 196	Albinus proclaimed emperor; Septimius Severus loots Persia
AD 218	Elegabalus becomes emperor
AD 222	Alexander Severus becomes emperor; reign of Ardashir I, King of Persia begins
AD 235	Start of 50-year period when 49 people are proclaimed emperor
AD 241	Reign of Shapur I, King of Persia begins
AD 244	Gordian III killed
AD 259	Postumus sets up Gallic Empire
AD 260	Shapur I captures Valerian
AD 267	Zenobia declares her son emperor
AD 270	Aurelian becomes emperor, abandons Dacia
AD 272	Aurelian defeats Zenobia; Shapur I dies
AD 273	Aurelian reconquers Gallic Empire
AD 284	Diocletian becomes emperor, divides Empire and Maximian rules West
AD 286	Carausius makes Britain independent
AD 297	Constantius retakes Britain
AD 309	Shapur II crowned in womb
AD 312	Constantine captures Rome
AD 324	Constantine takes Byzantium, sole emperor
AD 325	Council of Nicaea
AD 337	Constantine I dies
AD 350	Huns attack Persia
AD 358	Shapur II resolves Hun problem
AD 363	Julian defeated and killed by Shapur II
AD 364	Valentinian I becomes emperor; Valens becomes emperor in East

AD 375	Valentinian I dies; Valentinian II becomes emperor in West; Huns in Dacia; Goths cross Danube and convert to Christianity
AD 378	Valens killed at Hadrianople; Theodosius I becomes emperor in East
AD 391	Arianism and paganism outlawed
AD 392	Valentinian II killed
AD 394	Battle of Frigidus: Eugenius defeated; Theodosius I becomes sole emperor
AD 395	Theodosius I dies; Alaric rebels; Empire permanently divided into East and West
AD 401	Alaric attacks Italy; Vandals in Alps
AD 406	Vandals, etc., cross Rhine
AD 407	British proclaim Constantine III emperor
AD 408	Stilicho killed; Alaric's first siege of Rome
AD 410	Alaric's 'sack' of Rome
AD 411	Vandals in Spain
AD 412	Murder of Hypatia
AD 417	Visigoth Kingdom of Aquitaine; Visigoths attack Spain
AD 425	Vandals take Cartagena and Seville
AD 428	Gunderic dies; reign of Gaiseric, King of Vandals begins
AD 429	Vandals move to Africa
AD 434	Attila and Bleda rule Huns
AD 439	Vandals take Carthage
AD 441	Huns attack Balkans
AD 444	Death of Bleda
AD 447	Attila attacks Constantinople
AD 451	Huns invade Gaul
AD 452	Huns invade Italy
AD 455	Vandal 'sack' of Rome
AD 476	Last Western emperor deposed
AD 477	Gaiseric dies
AD 489	Ostrogoths take over Italy
AD 496	Clovis converts to Catholicism
AD 507	Franks conquer Visigoths
AD 526	Death of Theodoric
AD 533	Byzantine conquest of Africa
AD 535	Byzantine conquest of Ravenna

Introducing the Goodies and Baddies

WHO WERE THE BARBARIANS?

Nobody ever called themselves 'barbarians'. It's not that sort of word. It's a word used about other people. In fact, it's a term of otherness. It had been used by the Ancient Greeks to describe non-Greek people whose language they couldn't understand and who therefore seemed to babble unintelligibly: 'Ba ba ba'. The same word, *Barbara*, appears in Sanskrit, the language of ancient India, meaning 'stammering, gibbering' – in other words, alien.

The Romans adopted the Greek word and used it to label (and usually libel) the peoples who surrounded their own world.

Once the term had the might and majesty of Rome behind it, the Roman interpretation became the only one that counted, and the peoples whom they called Barbarians became forever branded – be they Spaniards, Britons, Gauls, Germans, Scythians, Persians or Syrians. And of course 'barbarian' has become a by-word for the very opposite of everything we consider civilized. In contrast to the Romans, the Barbarians were lacking in refinement, primitive, ignorant, brutal, rapacious, destructive and cruel.

The Romans kept the Barbarians at bay as long as they could, but finally they were engulfed, and the savage hordes over-ran the Empire, destroying the cultural achievements of centuries. The light of reason and civilization was virtually snuffed out by the Barbarian hordes who swarmed across Europe, annihilating everything the Romans had put in place, sacking Rome itself and consigning Europe to the Dark Ages. The Barbarians brought only chaos and ignorance, until the Renaissance rekindled the fires of Roman learning and art.

It's a familiar story, but it's codswallop.

The unique feature of Rome was not its arts or its science or its philosophical culture, not its attachment to law, its care for humanity or its sophisticated political culture. In fact, in all these areas it was equalled or even surpassed by peoples whom it conquered. The unique feature of Rome was that it had the world's first professional army. Normal societies consisted of farmers, hunters, craftsmen and traders. When they needed to fight they relied not on training or on standardized weapons, but on psyching themselves up to acts of individual heroism. Seen through the eyes of people who possessed trained soldiers to fight for them, they were easily portrayed as simple savages. But that was far from the truth.

We actually owe far more to the so-called 'barbarians' than we do to the men in togas. And the fact that we still think of the Celts, the Huns, the Vandals, the Goths, the Visigoths and so on as 'barbarians' means that we have all fallen hook, line and sinker for Roman propaganda. We are still letting the Romans define our world and our view of history.

In the last 30 years, however, the story has begun to change. Archaeological discoveries have shed new light on the ancient texts that have survived, and this has led to new interpretations of the past. We now know that the Roman Empire brought much of the development of science and mathematics to a grinding halt for about 1500 years, and that a great deal of what was known and achieved before Rome took over had to be relearned and rediscovered much more recently.

Rome used its army to eliminate the cultures that surrounded it, and paid its soldiers with the wealth it took from them. It 'Romanized' these conquered societies and left as little record of them as possible. The truth is that much of what we understand to be 'Roman civilization' was plundered from the Barbarian world. The Romans conquered with swords, shields, armour and artillery that were copied from the people they fought; their cities were built with the loot from the wealthier cultures that surrounded them; and as for the famous Roman roads, well, read on ... Sadly, many of the engineering and scientific achievements of the Barbarian world were destroyed so completely that, even when evidence of them turned up, it was either disbelieved or the achievements attributed to the Romans themselves. Now, however, we are beginning to realize that the story of a descent from the light of Rome to the darkness of Barbarian dominion is completely false.

Of course, it was thoughtless of the Celts not to leave us anything much in the way of written records – they should have known that the lack of books putting forward their own propaganda would weight the evidence firmly in favour of the Romans. But even so, we shouldn't believe everything the Romans tell us. Here, for example, is Julius Caesar's considered opinion about elks. Elks, the great statesman and general informs us, are

> destitute of horns, and have legs without joints and ligatures; nor do they lie down for the purpose of rest, nor, if they have been thrown down by any accident, can they raise or lift themselves up. Trees serve as beds to them; they lean themselves against them, and thus reclining only slightly, they take their rest; when the huntsmen have discovered from the footsteps of these animals whither they are accustomed to betake themselves, they either undermine all the trees at the roots, or cut into them so far that the upper part of the trees may appear to be left standing. When they [the elks] have leant upon them, according to their habit, they knock down by their weight the unsupported trees, and fall down themselves along with them.[1]

This interesting piece of zoological observation was solemnly repeated by the Greek geographer Strabo[2] and the encyclopedist Pliny the Elder.[3] It seems to be a confusion with an identical story about elephants told by Aristotle, and which, having also been repeated by Strabo, became part of the 'standard truth' about elephants right into the late seventeenth century, when Sir Thomas Browne complained that, even when people could see the animals perfectly clearly, and watch them kneel and stand, the determination to cling to the security of classical authorities made them deny what was in front of their own eyes.[4]

Just as people were prepared for centuries to deny that animals had knees even when they could see them, Western society's enthusiasm since the Renaissance for all things Roman has persuaded us to see much of the past through Roman eyes even when contrary evidence stares us in the face. Of course, we now have a better working knowledge of elks than Julius Caesar had, but when it comes to Barbarians we still tend to accept his estimate of them – the estimate of a conqueror with an agenda to push.

But once we turn the picture upside-down and look at history from a non-Roman point of view, things start to look very different. For example, the Roman depiction of the Vandals gave us the term 'vandalism', and yet, as we shall see, the Vandals were highly moral, educated, literate and often a lot more civilized than the Romans.

The sacks of Rome by the Goths and Vandals were not great acts of destruction. The Goths destroyed only one building, the Vandals none at all. Both were armies of Christians. But the Roman Empire itself had already adopted a particular form of Christianity – Catholicism – and, being Rome, it was trying to impose this form of the religion on everyone else.

The Catholic Church triumphed, and – again in the great Roman tradition – did all it could to remake people and history as it wanted them. The Church decided which documents would survive and which would not: all our sources come to us from medieval Catholic copyists. So again, our picture of the past has been given to us in a very particular way.

This book is an attempt to reconsider the vast numbers of European and Asian peoples who have been written off as the villains of history – the Barbarians – and, at the same time, to re-evaluate those paragons of civilization: the all-conquering Romans.

WHO WERE THE ROMANS?
WELL, THEY WEREN'T BARBARIANS

Because the word 'barbarian', as we use it, is essentially a term that the Romans used to describe those who weren't Roman, we have to start with Rome. The Romans had a very clear concept of themselves. They called it *Romanitas* or 'Roman-ness'. It meant using the Latin language, respecting Latin literature, obeying Roman law and tradition, and even following the custom of having three names. Everyone else, everyone foreign, was a Barbarian and was to be feared.

Oddly enough, fear seems to have played a key role in the history of Rome, and despite the might and power of the Romans, there is something curiously desperate about their whole story. It's almost as if the grandeur of Rome was born of paranoia and desperation. Another odd thing is that the major event in Roman history that kicked off this paranoia may never have happened at all – it may just have been a legend. But true or false, the great Roman historian Livy (59 BC–AD 17) wrote it down, and his account became the standard historical text for every Roman ever afterwards. This was where Romans learned to fear the Barbarians.

THE STORY OF BRENNUS

In the late fourth century BC, when the city of Rome was beginning to dominate central Italy, a community of very different people crossed the Apennines from Gaul and settled on the Adriatic coast between what are now the towns of Rimini and Ancona. They were called the Senones, and they founded a town called Senigallia. Unfortunately, it turned out to be a great place for a beach holiday but not much use agriculturally. Their search for a better spot wasn't easy – other Celts had already bagged the best places. So, in 390 BC, the Senones' warriors turned up at the gates of Clusium (modern Chiusi, in Tuscany), 'strange men in thousands … men the like of whom the townsfolk had never seen, outlandish warriors armed with strange weapons'.[5] Clusium didn't seem as well protected as the other places they'd tried, so these fearsome newcomers demanded they be given better land on which they could settle.

The inhabitants of Clusium appealed to Rome to help them negotiate, and the Romans duly sent three brothers from the Fabii family to act as arbitrators. According to Livy, when the Roman envoys asked the Celts what gave them the right to demand land from the people of Clusium, 'the haughty answer was returned that they carried their right in their weapons, and that everything belonged to the brave'.[6]

The Fabii brothers were young, arrogant and not the most tactful negotiators in the world. They were, according to Livy, 'envoys of a violent temper, more like Gauls than Romans'. In fact it was the Celts who seemed to have the greater respect for international law. When the talks broke down, the Fabii brothers joined the townsmen in fighting the Senones; one of the brothers, Quintus Fabius, even killed one of the Celtic chieftains. As both Livy and another historian, Plutarch, observed, it was 'contrary to the law of nations' for a negotiator to take arms to support one side against the other. The Senones were rightly outraged and decided to send their own ambassadors to Rome to complain.[7]

Unfortunately, the Fabii brothers belonged to a very powerful family, and when the Senate referred the matter to the people of Rome the brothers' actions were endorsed and – to make matters worse – the Fabii were heaped with honours. The Celtic ambassadors warned the Romans that there would be repercussions and then withdrew to Clusium. There it was decided to teach these upstart Romans to respect international legalities in future. According to Plutarch, the army, under the command of Brennus, marched the 80 miles from Clusium to Rome in a highly orderly manner: 'Contrary to expectation, they did no injury as they passed, nor took anything from the fields; and, as they went by any city, cried out that they were going to Rome; that the Romans only were their enemies, and that they took all others for their friends.'[8]

This 'strange enemy from the ends of the earth' then smashed the Roman army and swarmed through the city, burning and looting. Many Romans fled, and those who did not took refuge on the Capitoline Hill. Brennus and his army laid siege to them for six months, but finally agreed to withdraw in return for 1000 lb of gold.

Three hundred years later, Livy narrates the horror and the shame of that event, which was to haunt the Roman psyche for eight centuries: 'Insult was added to what was already sufficiently disgraceful, for the weights which the Gauls brought for weighing the metal were heavier than standard, and when the Roman commander objected the insolent Barbarian flung his sword into the scale, saying "Vae Victis" – "Woe to the vanquished!"'[9] Actually, what really seems to have got up Livy's nose was the fact that the Celts had been bought off so cheaply. Imagine, he writes, 1000 lb of gold as 'the price of a nation soon to rule the world'!

At the time, according to Livy, the Romans seriously considered abandoning their city. But they decided instead to rebuild it, and never again to be put in the shameful position of being the vanquished. The legend of Brennus became one of the motors driving Roman expansion. Out there were Barbarians, terrible savages, and Rome needed to strengthen its frontiers. Not just strengthen them, but push them away, further and further away, until eventually there would be no place left for Barbarians unless they had been thoroughly Romanized. From now on Rome would follow the doctrine of pre-emptive strikes to subdue all the peoples on its frontiers and thus make the Roman world safe from otherness.

Although we no longer believe that there are quadruped mammals without knees we still accept the Roman view of their world, in which the word 'barbarians' goes together with 'hordes'. They painted a picture of themselves as civilized people whose Empire held at bay a world inhabited by incoherent tribes of violent savages.

The Roman legend begins with the story of Romulus and Remus, two lost babies who were suckled by a she-wolf. The Romans did not see that as a charming story; they meant to show that they had imbibed wolfish appetites and ferocity with their mothers' milk. It's time to ask what the world would be like if, instead of feeding them, the wolf had eaten Romulus and Remus. What if there had been no Rome?

What if there had been only Barbarians?

PART I

THE CELTS

I
UNEARTHING THE CELTS

There was once a town called Alesia, in what is now central France. It was here that the French Celts, the Gauls, under their charismatic leader Vercingetorix – whose enduring memorial is, of course, his reincarnation as the French comic-book hero – made their last concerted stand against Julius Caesar's legions. There is another monument to him: it is a huge statue of the Gallic hero, pensively looking over the remains of his city ... except that the city he looks over isn't Gallic – it's Roman, with a theatre, temples and basilica. The town that Vercingetorix would have known has been squashed flat.

A few miles away, an archaeological museum celebrates the famous siege that was his downfall. The great, dominating exhibit is a reconstruction of the siege works built by Julius Caesar. Everywhere we look, the Celtic story has been buried under the heavy stones of Roman history.

The Romans imposed their mark all over Europe. Remains of aqueducts, amphitheatres, walls and roads carry their own message. Signs of the native cultures that inhabited the provinces before the Romans arrived are much harder to see, and it's all too easy to assume that these societies were vastly inferior and were replaced by Progress and the superior civilization of Rome.

Part of this annihilation was deliberate policy. The Romans had learnt their lesson from the occupation of Brennus and his Celts in 390 BC, and that lesson was a simple one: woe to the vanquished! Might is right and military power is the only international law. The Romans had no problem demolishing whatever stood in their way.

But part of it was also acculturation: the Roman world possessed such mass that its gravity simply drew satellite cultures into its own orbit. In the Barbarian world, the rich and influential saw financial and political advantage in seeking Roman support, and began adopting Roman habits and building styles as signs of status. Some who were not so rich no doubt also longed to join the party. In this way, those who opposed Roman domination, and who tried to defend the traditional values of their own people, faced a double enemy: the one without and the one within. The parallels with the modern world are not hard to find.

The net result was a cultural eclipse that has made the real ancestors of modern Europe, the ancient Celts, hard to trace. Their place in history has been usurped by the might of the Roman Empire, and it is only recently that Celtic civilization has begun to be rediscovered. And it's not at all what anyone expected.

CELTIC ROOTS

The Celts didn't all think of themselves as Celts, any more than they thought of themselves as Barbarians. Some did. Julius Caesar tells us that the inhabitants of central France called themselves Celts. But we now apply the term to many more peoples than would have seen themselves as 'Celtic' in Caesar's time.

Indeed, historians have recently begun to regard the word with dark suspicion, and with some reason.[1] The term 'Celtic', in the way we understand the word today, was not coined until 1707, when a Welsh antiquary and naturalist by the name of Edward Lhuyd used it to identify Irish, Welsh, Cornish and Breton as a distinct group of languages.

Before that date, no inhabitants of the British Isles would have dreamt of calling themselves 'Celtic'. But this does not mean that Lhuyd was barking mad; there was an identifiable and cohesive culture that existed over a large area of Europe, and even if those people who shared that culture were unaware of it at the time, it seems as reasonable to supply them with a group identity (now it has been recognized) as it is to refer to the people of the Stone Age as 'Stone Age people', even though they would undoubtedly have regarded themselves as 'modern man'.

But before we go any further we need to rid our minds of the Mediterranean world-view, in which the warm centre of the universe

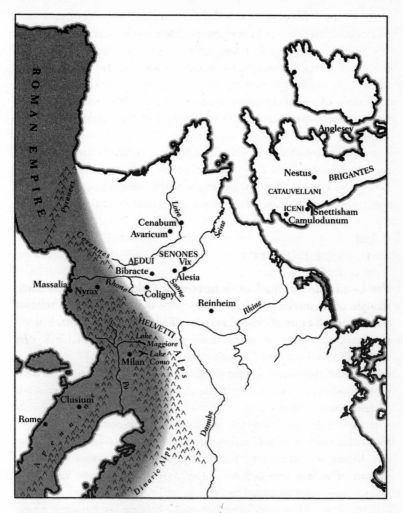

The labels on the map include: ROMAN EMPIRE, Anglesey, Nestus, BRIGANTES, CATAUVELLANI, ICENI, Snettisham, Camulodunum, Pyrenees, Cevennes, Cenabum, Avaricum, Loire, Seine, AEDUI, SENONES, Vix, Bibracte, Alesia, Massalia, Nyrax, Rhone, Saône, Coligny, Reinheim, Rhine, HELVETTI, Lake Maggiore, Lake Como, Alps, Milan, Po, Clusium, Danube, Rome, Apennines, Dinaric Alps.

The World of the Atlantic Celts

is the sunny Med and a place like the Orkneys would be regarded as the end of the earth – a remote and inhospitable hinterland on the fringes of knowledge. That may have been how the Romans saw it, but the Celtic world – the world as the Celts themselves saw it – wasn't necessarily like that at all.[2]

Human communication in early times tended to evolve around water. The seaways and the rivers were the natural means of travel, especially when transporting heavy goods. Being a sea, the Mediterranean formed one such network of communication, but so too did the Atlantic seaboard of Europe. Rather than being a series of far-flung places on the fringe of the civilized world, the settlements of the Atlantic coast represented a network of interlinked societies.

This network goes back a very long way. As far back as the fourth millennium BC, polished stone axes made of diorite (magma that has solidified beneath the earth's surface) from central Brittany were being manufactured and distributed on a massive scale. And radiocarbon dating has shown that the megalithic monuments of the Atlantic coastal region owe nothing to Mediterranean inspiration. It seems that there were closely related belief systems concerning the cosmos and death operating over this area from time immemorial, and that Portugal, southern Brittany, Ireland and the Orkney Isles were all centres of innovation that practised similar art and architecture.

In the past, the assumption was always that mass migrations of people accounted for the spread of such similarities, and that Celtic culture was carried by invading migrants from central Europe. More recently, however, archaeologists have suggested that cultures often spread via short sea voyages and river journeys, linking scattered and perhaps disparate communities in a network of trade and communication.

Back in prehistoric times, the Atlantic seaboard demonstrated a 'stunning display of shared culture'.[3] Neck ornaments made of gold mined in Ireland show up in Cornwall, Normandy and Brittany; neck-rings from southern Iberia are found in Brittany, northern Britain and Northern Ireland. It is our good fortune that these peoples had a rather odd habit: they were very keen on throwing a lot of their most valuable possessions into bogs and lakes or burying them in the ground. Whatever their reasons for such a flamboyant waste of resources, it does mean that we have some record of their world. Moving into the Iron Age, the common culture of the Atlantic coast becomes even more evident in the form of offerings of swords, shields and spears that demonstrate a shared value system and sometimes exhibit similarities of design.

So the culture and languages that we now designate as 'Celtic' might not have been brought to western Europe by invaders from the east, but may have been indigenous to the Atlantic seaboard. In other words, the Celts' origins may lie in the coastal network of the Atlantic.

But rivers too were important routes of cultural transmission. That is why Celtic identity was also strong in west central Europe – in the regions north of the Alps, supplied by the great rivers Danube, Rhine, Rhone, Saone, Seine and Loire. We just don't know which way the flow went.

We do know that from around 440 BC Celts from the Danube region started to cross the Alps and settle in northern Italy around Lakes Como and Maggiore. They also made a settlement in what is now Milan. Perhaps not surprisingly, our knowledge of the Celts improves as they begin to make contact with the thoroughly literate world of Classical antiquity.

HOW BARBAROUS WERE THE CELTS?

Much of our view of Iron Age Celts comes more from the Greeks than the Romans.[4] Plato lumped them together with a whole lot of other Barbarians who were warlike and enjoyed getting totally legless. Binge drinking is a constant theme in descriptions of Celts over the next 800 years. Diodorus Siculus ('the Sicilian'), writing in the first century BC, depicts the Celts as prototype lager louts – 'wine wallies' might be the more appropriate term. 'They are,' he tells us, 'exceedingly addicted to the use of wine.'[5] They don't water it down as Greeks do, and they drink until 'they fall into a stupor or a state of madness'.[6] Sound familiar?

Obviously the Celts weren't the sort of chaps any self-respecting Greek would invite around for dinner: 'They look like wood-demons, their hair thick and shaggy like a horse's mane. Some of them are clean-shaven, but others – especially those of high rank – shave their cheeks but leave a moustache that covers the whole mouth and, when they eat and drink, acts like a sieve, trapping particles of food.'[7]

What particularly shocked the conservative patricians of the Classical world was the vulgar way the Celts dressed: 'The Gauls display a ... love of ornament. They wear golden collars round their necks, and bracelets on their arms and wrists, and those of any status have garments dyed and embroidered with gold.'[8] It's easy to imagine the sober Romans in their plain white togas tut-tutting at all that foreign frippery! It was all evidence of a serious moral failing that would inevitably reveal itself in battle: 'This lightness of character makes them intolerable when they conquer, and fills them with panic when things go wrong.'[9]

On the other hand, they weren't to be treated too lightly – after all, they were head-hunters who went around 'hanging the heads of their enemies from their horses' necks on their return from battle, and then nailing them up on their gates for people to see'.[10]

What's more, they were big! The Britons (whom Classical writers distinguish from the Celts) were particularly tall. Strabo saw them with his own eyes: 'I myself, in Rome, saw mere lads towering as much as half a foot above the tallest people in the city,' he states in some awe, but then hastily adds that there is no need for short but handsome Romans to envy them because apart from their height 'they were bandy-legged and presented no fair lines anywhere else in their figure'.[11]

The Celts were also wildly aggressive and easily provoked: 'The entire race ... is warlike, passionate, and always ready for fighting ... Anyone can enrage them when, where, and under whatever pretext he pleases ... ' It sounds as if Celt-baiting must have been a regular Roman pastime. But on second thoughts, perhaps not: there were a lot of them! 'Their power lies both in the size of their bodies and also in their large numbers.'[12]

Strabo, writing as he was in the first century BC, displayed a distinct nervousness about the Celts that is lacking in the earliest commentaries. Some 400 years before, his fellow Greeks didn't seem to have anything to fear from the Celts. Hellanicus of Lesbos, a historian of the fifth century BC, described them as 'practising justice and righteousness'. In the next century the historian Ephorus described them as using 'the same customs as the Greeks' and being on very friendly terms with them.

All that changed in 279 BC, when Celts from the lower Danube launched a massive attack on Greece. We don't really know why the Celts became more aggressive, if that is indeed what happened, but perhaps those 'large numbers' that Strabo talked about indicated an exploding population that forced the Celts to search for new territory. Or perhaps it was simply a cultural change. There seems no doubt that during this time some Celtic societies developed an heroic culture based on a warrior elite. Courage and honour became crucial, and gave the Greeks plenty to admire. Strabo praised their sense of duty to each other: 'Their frankness and simplicity lead them to form mobs easily, everyone feeling indignant at what looks like injustice to his neighbour.' But in the end this simplicity meant they could be defeated by a superior civilization: 'They are simple and not malicious. If provoked, they rush in crowds to the fight, openly and without any caution; and thus are easily vanquished by those who employ strategy.'[13]

Perhaps not surprisingly, the Greeks began to sentimentalize the struggle of the Celts. The concept of the Dying Gaul became a theme of Greek sculpture, in which a well-muscled heroic youth with a golden torque around his neck gracefully expires from a sword-thrust. The Romans copied several of these in marble; a Dying Gaul is on show today in the Capitol.

The attitude of both Greeks and Romans appears somewhat patronizing, but then why not? After all, the Celts were in every way inferior, with poorer technology, fewer skills and less science and understanding. To us, looking through the hindsight of history, it seems inevitable that Rome should have triumphed against these brave but backward people.

But it wasn't like that. It wasn't like that at all.

CELTIC MILITARY TECHNOLOGY

In Roman eyes the Celts may have lacked battle strategy, but their arms and equipment were in no way inferior to the Roman army's. In times past some of the Celts may have charged naked into battle, but by the first century BC they had become master armourers.

When the Gallic chieftain Vercingetorix inflicted on Caesar his first military defeat in 53 BC, you might – if you were simply judging by appearances – have had a problem knowing who was who on the battlefield. There were chaps in Roman helmets, but they weren't the Romans – they were the Gauls. The Romans were the ones in bronze hats with rather cute ponytails. They later copied the sturdier design of the Gallic helmet, with its characteristic cheek-guards.

And then again, the Celts had better shields than the Romans. 'They have man-sized shields,'[14] wrote Diodorus Siculus, 'decorated in a manner peculiar to them. Some of these have projecting figures in bronze skilfully wrought not only for decoration but for protection.' (Perhaps the first example of offensive decor?) The Romans were quick to adopt the Celtic style of shield and make it their own. They also copied a variety of Celtic weapons and adopted the Celtic names for them. The Latin for a light spear, *lancea*, was taken from the Gauls of Spain, the Celtic word *materis* became the Romans' word for a javelin, and *gaesum*, meaning a long javelin, was also borrowed from the Celts.

When the Romans got to Britain they found another technological advance: chariots. It may seem odd to those of us brought up on *Ben Hur* that the Romans should have been surprised by chariots on the battlefield, but that was the case. It was the skill with which the Britons operated their chariots and the use they made of them that most impressed Caesar:

> The way they fight with their chariots is this: they start by driving all over the battlefield hurling their javelins and generally the terror created by the horses and the noise of the wheels is enough to throw the enemy's ranks into disorder … Thus they combine the mobility of cavalry with the staying-power of infantry; and by daily practice and training they become so proficient that, even on a steep slope, they are able to control the horses at full gallop, and to check and turn them around in a moment. They can run along the chariot pole, stand on the yoke, and get back into the chariot as quick as anything.[15]

All this was entirely new to the Roman troops: Caesar goes on to say that his men were 'dismayed by the novelty of this mode of battle', and that he was forced to retire from the field.

War chariots had been used long ago in the Near East, but had been replaced by cavalry. Roman chariots were either heavy, lumbering vehicles used for parades, or ultra-lightweight, specialized race vehicles. The Britons, however, had made significant design improvements and, as Caesar notes, had thoroughly mastered the art of using them. Yet despite the evidence, horse-drawn chariots are an essential part of the myth of Roman superiority. Collins' *English Dictionary*, for example, defines 'chariot' as 'a two-wheeled horse-drawn vehicle used in ancient Egypt, Greece, Rome etc ... ' The Britons don't get a mention. And yet it was actually the Celts who were leaders in the development of wheeled transport.

The grave goods included in burials are a good sign of what mattered to people, and rich Celtic burials sometimes included a wagon and a huge jar for holding drink. For example, there's a tomb-chamber at Hochdorf in south-west Germany, dating from about the fifth century BC. The dead man fits Strabo's description of the Celts as big, powerful warriors – he's 6 feet 2 inches tall – and he lies on a huge bronze couch beneath walls hung with fabrics. He must have been a formidable warrior – except that there are no weapons in here except a dagger. The grave contains only a huge cauldron for mead, drinking horns and a wagon that takes up almost half the chamber.[16]

The Romans seem to have adopted their wheeled transport from the Celts. At any rate, that's what the linguistic evidence suggests. Although the earlier inhabitants of Italy, the Etruscans, did have wheeled vehicles, the wheel rims were fragile – they were made by joining sections together with dowels. The Celts invented a way to make the whole rim out of a single piece of heat-bent wood. In Asia, iron was fastened to the rim to strengthen it, but the Celts' skill with iron-work allowed them to shrink a complete iron tyre on to the wheel, making it even stronger and more reliable.[17] So the Latin word for a two-wheeled cart, *carpentum*, was imported from the Old Celtic. It survives in modern English as 'carpenter'. And a whole raft of other words for different kinds of carriages and wagons entered the Latin language from Celtic: *carruca, carrus, essedum, reda, petorritum, covinarius, plaustrum*.

Even the Latin for horse, *caballus*, seems to have come from the Celtic, giving us eventually the English words 'cavalry' and 'cavalier'. And, as the *coup de grâce*, the Latin word for a league, *leuca*, originated with the Celts.

WHO BUILT THE ROADS?

So how come the Romans built roads and the Celts didn't? Well, the answer is simple. The Celts did build roads. We know about them only because of ones that have survived in locations where no Roman road was put on top. These Celtic roads were made of wood and laid across bogland into which they have sunk over the centuries and thus been preserved.

As usual, the 'Romans-were-greatest' version of history made the earlier roads invisible until very recently. One of the best-preserved Iron Age roads is at Corlea in Ireland, but it was not until the 1980s that people realized how old it is. It was known locally as 'The Danes' Road', and generally assumed to be of the Viking period or later. It wasn't until the timbers were submitted for tree-ring dating that the truth emerged: they were cut in 148 BC.

But the really startling thing is that wooden roads built the same way and at the same time have been found right across Europe, as far away as northern Germany. The Celts, it seems, were sophisticated road-builders, and the construction of these wooden roads was no mean feat of engineering. Oak planks were laid on birch runners, and they were built broad enough for two carts to pass each other. What's more, Celtic road-building is not necessarily predated by that of the Romans. The first Roman road was the Appian Way, built in 312 BC, but the so-called 'Upton Track' in South Wales, a wooden road laid across the mudflats along the Severn estuary, dates back to the fifth century BC.

And now we call Roman roads 'roads', and the surviving Celtic roads 'causeways' or 'trackways' – not roads at all, just some Barbarian track.

THE FALLACY OF TEXTS

One of the main reasons why we tend to see Celts as 'barbaric' and Romans as 'civilized' is that we have so much written material in Latin and virtually nothing in Celtic. No Celtic books, poems, works of science or literature have survived from the Iron Age (by which we mean before being taken over by Rome). But that is in itself misleading because hardly any Roman texts have survived either. We don't have Latin manuscripts from the time of Caesar: the oldest surviving text of Caesar's *Gallic Wars* was copied out 1000 years later.

The Catholic Church originally devoted itself to stamping out paganism – the one remaining bronze statue of a pre-Christian emperor, Marcus Aurelius, survived only because the image was mistakenly thought to be that of a Christian. Pope Gregory the Great (540–604) tried to suppress the works of Cicero and is said to have burnt all manuscripts of Livy that he could lay hands on.[18] But monks in monasteries did painstakingly copy out the writers that they approved of. That's how we know about Roman authors. Even then, only fragments survived of those medieval manuscripts, to be recopied in later centuries.

We would know even less if it hadn't been for the Irish. There seems to have been a flight of intellectuals from Gaul to Ireland in the fifth century AD, during the invasions of the Goths and Huns, and these people may well have taken their books with them. They arrived in a society that was by now Christian, but where the Church was Celtic, not Roman Catholic. This Irish Church was far more comfortable with paganism, and was more interested in preserving knowledge than in destroying it. Irish monasteries were centres of book-copying untroubled by much religious censorship, and wherever Irish missionaries set up new foundations (near Genoa in 613, near Constance in 614, at Péronne in 650) 'they founded libraries which included manuscripts of classical authors'.[19]

To a considerable extent, then, we owe the survival of Latin authors to Celtic monks. And their intellectual roots lay deep in the pagan Celtic world. The Iron Age Celts had a class of professional intellectuals known as Druids, who evidently had a power that extended over the whole of society. As religious authorities, Druids could walk between armies and order them to lay down their arms. They moved freely between Gaul and Britain (and probably other parts of the Celtic world). As the guardians of literature and of historical, medical, scientific and religious knowledge, they received education and training for 20 years because there was a great deal to master.

It's true that a lot of the knowledge was not to be written down, so Celtic literature was purely oral. The Druids insisted on that. Caesar thought that they did so partly because 'it generally occurs to most men, that, in their dependence on writing, they relax their diligence in learning thoroughly, and their employment of the memory'.[20] But the Druids could and did write for more mundane purposes, and 'in almost all other matters, in their public and private transactions, they use Greek characters'. Archaeologists have found many thousands of inscriptions in Celtic languages from the years before Julius Caesar. The alphabet used is sometimes Latin, sometimes Greek, and sometimes their own alphabet, called Ogham.

It's not surprising, given the attitudes of monks in Ireland, that this is the one place where extensive Celtic literary material has survived. Unlike Roman Catholic monks, Irish abbots saw their job as being to engage fully with the local communities, and saw no reason to cut themselves off from the society around them – even if it never did grasp Christian ideas of family morality. A Catholic monk shaved the crown of his head, a Greco-Roman sign of slavery, to symbolize his submission to the rules. An Irish monk shaved the front of his head, as the Druids had done, to show that he was carrying on an old tradition of religious and intellectual authority.

This unique breed of monks not only copied out pagan Roman authors but also preserved Celtic memories in law books and books of tales. Obviously this material needs to be approached with some caution, and not only because we can't be sure how relevant it is to the rest of Europe. But there are collections of literature such as *The Book of Leinster*, written out in the twelfth century, which contain stories set in the pagan Celtic world and whose details show that they are clearly drawn straight from that time. For example, they describe warriors going into battle in chariots, leaving the battlefield with the heads of their slain enemies attached to the shafts of the chariot and riding back with these grisly trophies. We believe that really happened because it is described by Greek writers such as Diodorus Siculus, but these Irish monks didn't read any Greek texts. Their knowledge came from the oral tradition, and they were writing it down.

Illiterate Barbarians, you might think, would have quite primitive laws, mostly along the lines of 'You touch-a my car, I smash-a your face'. Yet the Irish monks have left us with a body of Celtic law that reveals an astonishing level of sophistication. Unfortunately, it has hardly been studied at all.

We know about Irish Celtic law from a collection of texts known as the Brehon Laws, named after the Brehons or *brithemuin* ('judges') who took over the legal functions of the Druids after the conversion of Ireland to Christianity. These laws were written in poetic form, obviously shaped by the bardic tradition, from the seventh century AD.

Roman law and Celtic law were fundamentally different because they served the needs of fundamentally different societies. Roman law is primarily concerned with the power of the *paterfamilias* (the head of the family, the only person who really counts in the law) and his rights over property and when doing business. The Brehon Laws are concerned with the duties of clan members on land that is owned not by individuals but by groups, with the rules of hierarchy and the obligations of the whole community to its members. They have been regarded with deep suspicion for a long time because of their provenance, because the text is from Christian times, and because they are written as poetry. This is an excellent example of the pro-Roman bias in Western culture: the fact is that Roman law is not much better attested than Celtic law. We just like to think it is.

Roman law was completely forgotten in medieval Europe until a copy of the sixth-century law code of the Emperor Justinian was found in Italy in 1070. On the basis of that document, law schools developed, beginning with the University of Bologna, which was founded in 1088. The graduates of these places served princes and merchants, so by the middle of the sixteenth century Europe saw itself as being ruled by Roman law. But this Roman law was actually nothing like the law that governed the Roman Empire; not only was the text that medieval scholars were using different from the original, but it was in any case that of a later, Byzantine law code created by a reforming emperor.

All that we actually know about the Roman law that held sway in Europe comes from a second-century textbook by someone called Gaius, and until the nineteenth century most of what was known of its contents came from a summary in the law code of a Visigoth king, Alaric II, written in 506. In 1816 a full text was found on a sixth-century manuscript, but it was a palimpsest, which means that it had been washed out and Christian texts written over it. This was standard practice in the medieval Church, partly because parchment was expensive, but mainly because it was a practical way for Christianity to replace the pagan past. It was a deliberate holy act of destruction.

Fortunately for us the destruction was imperfectly carried out, so much of the book could still be read. But that's a rather flimsy foundation for the widespread belief that Roman law survived robustly through the ages. It could be said that we have far better evidence for Celtic law, but we just don't pay it any attention. Instead, we have been encouraged to believe the second-century BC Roman historian Polybius, who said that the Celts had 'no knowledge whatsoever of any art or science.'[21]

In fact, it looks as if Polybius didn't know much about the Celts. They had art, manufacturing, literature and law. And most astonishing of all is the evidence that they used serious mathematics.

THE COLIGNY CALENDAR

This readiness to give credit to the Romans for their technological advances, while ignoring the achievements of the Celts, is nowhere better illustrated than in the strange case of the Coligny Calendar. Although discovered in the late nineteenth century, this astonishing device – conclusive evidence of Celtic mathematical sophistication – lay neglected and unrecognized throughout most of the twentieth century.

In 1897 a man digging in a field outside the small town of Coligny in east central France unearthed 153 fragments of bronze covered in Celtic words that referred to phases of the moon and feasts. When the jigsaw was finally assembled the archaeologists found that they had an early Celtic calendar, although no one could understand how it worked. It would be almost 100 years before anyone realized just what a staggering find this was: it was a discovery that would revolutionize our understanding of the Celts and their intellectual achievements.

In 1989 a young American scholar by the name of Garrett Olmsted became interested in the calendar. Now as luck would have it, Olmsted was not only a Celtic scholar, but also happened to be a mathematician and a systems engineer – exactly the right combination of skills to crack the code.

Calendars are tricky things. Each month should start at a new moon, but at the end of a year of 12 lunar months, there are nearly 11 days left over. And neither a month nor a year lasts an exact number of days. Olmsted demonstrated that these Barbarians had calculated a calendar system that allowed them to start each month at the new moon – the lunar calendar – without their festivals losing their exact place in the seasons – the solar calendar.[22] He concluded that the calculation system used was in advance of anything else devised for many centuries.

The maths involved is pretty overwhelming, but the belief that the Celts were intellectually unsophisticated was so strong that French archaeologists at first refused to publish Olmsted's work and he had to publish in Germany. The equation 'barbarian = unsophisticated' is one that has blinded us to the significance of many 'barbarian' objects, and that will be a constant theme of this book.

If you want to know what happens if you can't do these complicated calendar maths, take a look at the Romans. Their calendar was so hopeless that by the first century BC they were out by about three months. The siege of Vercingetorix's army at Alesia began on 25 June, but according to the Romans it was taking place in September.

Their calendar was such a disaster that a few years later the Romans abandoned the whole idea of trying to link their months to the new moon. Julius Caesar commissioned a Greek astronomer to work out a new calendar for Rome – all it had to do was get the same date in the same spot in the season each year. To make it start right he had to begin with a year of 445 days, which is why that year was called the *annus confusionis*. The Celts must have been falling about.

And even the new Julian calendar didn't work all that well. It had to be further messed around with at the end of the sixteenth century to produce our modern calendar, which, according to Olmsted, is no better than the one the Celts were using.

THE IRON-MASTERS OF EUROPE

It is only now that historians are beginning to reassess the sophistication of Celtic science and engineering. From early times the Celts were the iron-masters of Europe. A Celtic smith was regarded as a magician, a man who could take a lump of rock and transform it into a magical new substance – a cunningly worked steel blade sharp enough to cut through bronze or ordinary iron. When St Patrick was preparing to combat paganism in Ireland he supposedly composed a prayer, 'St Patrick's Breast-Plate', which included the lines:

> I invoke today all these virtues Against every hostile merciless
> power … Against the spells of women, and smiths, and
> druids, Against every knowledge that binds the soul of man.

The spells of smiths are right up there with the most powerful magicians of all, women and Druids. The science of metal-working was a secret and mysterious art, and the Romans were not as well informed about it as the Celts – not just in the matter of weapons, but in peaceful applications too.

The Celts' mastery of metal technology also enabled them to develop sophisticated arable farms. We know they had iron ploughshares in Britain from about the fourth century BC because in a shrine at Frilford on the River Ock, near Abingdon in Oxfordshire – a site that was occupied from about 350 BC – an iron ploughshare was found under one of the central pillars where it had been buried, perhaps as a votive offering. It's a fair guess that the temple was one of the first buildings to be erected, and that the iron ploughshare was offered at the time its foundations were laid.[23]

The Celts' use of metal even allowed them to invent a harvesting machine. The Roman historian Pliny, writing in the first century AD, provides the only written account of the device: 'On the vast estates in the provinces of Gaul very large frames fitted with teeth at the edge, and carried on two wheels, are driven through the corn by a team of oxen pushing from behind.'[24] The Romans named it the *Gallic vallus*. Historians didn't believe it could be true until bas-relief sculptures were discovered that apparently show just such a contraption. It was a sort of comb on wheels that beat off the ears of corn and deposited them in a container rather like the grass-box of a lawn-mower. A replica was built and tested in the 1980s.[25] There seems to be no trace of it after the third century AD, and the work of harvesting became back-breaking labour with a scythe until the machine was reinvented in 1831.

Simpler Celtic tools stayed in use. The Celts improved the way wooden handles were fixed to iron blades. As a result, the spades and sickles, forks, axes and scythes used by Iron Age Celtic farmers are little different from the tools we use today.

Our improved appreciation of Celtic technology over recent years is due in particular to the experimental archaeology developed at Butser Ancient Farm in Hampshire. Here techniques that were once scorned have been put to the test in the most practical ways possible, with the result that we have often had to revise our estimate of Celtic expertise. The Ancient Celts, it turns out, knew what they were doing.

Perhaps the simplest example of this re-evaluation of ancient technology is the way they stored the harvest. For many years, archaeologists had been puzzled by the presence of grain and other dry goods buried in holes in the ground. It seemed to fly in the face of common sense to suggest that burial could keep food dry and fresh. Yet when the technique was tested, to everyone's surprise it seemed to work. What happens is that the grain on the outer part of the storage pit, which is in contact with the damp walls, germinates, using up the available oxygen and releasing carbon dioxide. This creates an anaerobic environment in which the grain will remain in perfect condition for some time.

CELTIC TOWNS

It's been easy to underestimate Celtic technological achievements because so much has vanished or been misunderstood. The same goes for the Celtic way of life in general. The way they lived has disappeared under an avalanche of Roman stone and propaganda. Just as we call

Roman trackways 'roads' and Celtic ones 'trackways', we call Roman settlements 'towns' and Celtic ones 'hill-forts', or give them a Roman name, 'oppida'. That's the power of spin; the word *oppidum* was used by Caesar to mean a defended settlement. If he had ever written about Jerusalem, we'd probably call it a hill-fort.

Language isn't the only thing that has hidden the Celts' urban civilization from us. Their towns were simply wiped away by the Roman conquest, either disappearing under arable land or being replaced by Roman buildings. Roman towns were constructed on a different principle; they were above all administrative centres and places for the collection of taxes. A Roman town was based on two main streets crossing each other at right-angles, and its heart was a set of public buildings that represented the authority of the Empire, instantly recognizable as Roman. These included temples, basilicas, baths and often amphitheatres. Since Celtic towns didn't look like that, and existed for a different purpose, it has taken us a long time to recognize them.

The Celtic world was a place of trade, and Celtic towns were trading centres, often closely connected to mining operations. The assumption that Celts lived in primitive huts is a bit of a mistake; even away from the towns, they often had quite substantial houses. A Gallic farmhouse, for instance, was often a large, rectangular, two-storey building, whose interior sometimes consisted of a single grand room and sometimes of many different chambers.

In Britain an older tradition of round houses from the Atlantic coast culture seems to have survived into the first century BC. But these could be surprisingly sophisticated. At Chysauster Ancient Village, on the Land's End peninsula in Cornwall, there are remains of stone houses with thatched roofs built around a courtyard. The floors were of stone and – surprise, surprise – they had under-floor plumbing! How barbarian is that?

Celtic builders were held in high esteem and commanded professional status. In Irish tradition a master builder was called *Ollamh* – which survives as the modern Irish word for 'professor'. He was highly paid and would receive an annual retainer. And such men earned it. Celtic builders were capable of remarkable ingenuity and skill. Perhaps the clearest demonstration of their expertise is the *crannog*, a timber-framed circular house, built on an artificial island in the middle of a lake or estuary or on marshland. Boulders were sunk until they broke the surface of the water or bog, and timbers were then combined with the stones to form a foundation. The houses could be anything up to 50 feet in diameter.

From the second century BC, Celtic trade grew substantially, and so did the size and number of towns. Some of them were very large. One of the largest was Manching in southern Germany. It was the capital of the Vindelici, and boasted city walls 5 miles in circumference. It was probably burnt by the Romans in 15 BC.

The most spectacular of all Celtic towns lies also in southern Germany, between Stuttgart and Ulm. Unfortunately, the site has not been properly excavated and the name of the city is still unknown, but the walls enclosed an extraordinarily huge conurbation covering more than 6 square miles. Just for comparison: the Aventine Wall that surrounded Rome in the first century AD enclosed just a quarter of that.

One Celtic town that is currently being excavated is Bibracte, situated on a hilltop in central France. The inhabitants minted their own coins from the third century BC to 50 BC – first in gold and then in silver, with the same value as the Roman *denarius*. It was an important place – we know that because Caesar tells us it was; in fact he chose to stay there during his conquest of Gaul while he was writing up his account of it. The manuscript was rushed to Rome for public readings – it was all part of Caesar's PR campaign to make himself Mr Big in his home town. And that used to be all we knew about Bibracte. The town quite simply disappeared and became farmland and forest. But now archaeologists have been uncovering facts about Bibracte that fit into the new picture of Celtic society as a dynamic, literate and Europe-wide trading culture with a strong financial base, using money to go shopping.

What has emerged is evidence of a substantial town with a bustling high street of workshops and shops based on trade in iron goods from the nearby mines, making and selling tools, jewellery and enamelled decorative items. They were also working in glass, making beads and bracelets, and minting coins right down to the level of small change. Each shop had its own warehouse cellar. The town covered

330 acres and was divided into specific zones. There were craft and religious centres, and the aristocratic residential area contained very attractive houses.

Towns such as Bibracte were connected to trade routes that reached as far afield as Africa and China, but most of their trade was with the Roman world, and both Rome and the Gauls were doing very nicely out of the arrangement. Obviously you don't do this kind of business by relying on phoney weights and shouting 'Vae victis!' at your customers – it's all a very far cry from the Celts of Brennus.

II
THE LOOTING OF GAUL

When one considers all the fabulous wealth of Rome, it might seem odd that the Romans should have wanted to go to all the trouble of conquering the impoverished Barbarian nations that bordered their Empire. Of course there was always the imperative of homeland security and the doctrine of pre-emptive strikes pushing them to attack before they were attacked themselves. But could there have been another reason too?

Around the middle of the first century BC the Gallic chieftain Vercingetorix issued a series of gold coins bearing his name and an idealized portrait, possibly modelled on Alexander the Great's father, Philip of Macedon. Apart from the absence of a moustache on Vercingetorix (despite Diodorus Siculus' assertion that all the upper-class men wore them), the most striking thing about the coin appears when one compares it to a Roman gold coin of the same date.

Because there aren't any. The Romans didn't have enough gold to make gold coins. Not until they'd conquered Gaul. That's where the gold was.

CELTIC GOLD

The Celts had actually imported the idea of coinage from the Greeks before the Romans did. The Insubrean Celts in northern Italy were minting their own coins 50 years before the Romans caught on to the idea. And different communities and princes continued to mint coins of gold and silver from the fourth century BC onwards. By the time of Caesar, of course, the Romans did have coins, but they were silver or bronze. There had been occasional issues of gold coins, but they had stopped by Caesar's time; Rome simply did not have the gold. But the Gauls did, and they were minting it.

Until quite recently, historians did not realize that Gaul was so wealthy. It was believed that the Gauls acquired their gold by selling slaves to richer peoples, probably in the eastern Mediterranean. But it is now known that the Gauls' gold came from hundreds of mines.[1] Béatrice Cauuet, who has excavated many of them, estimates that they must have produced nearly 70 tons of the stuff. Gold mines 100 feet deep have been found in the Dordogne, with fully lined galleries that used Archimedes screw pumps to keep them from flooding. This contrasts dramatically with old beliefs about pre-Roman Gaul. The mine works are so well engineered that they were assumed until recently to be Roman. Well, obviously you couldn't imagine wild, moustachioed Barbarians doing this sort of thing.

Miners, by the nature of their business, cannot produce food for themselves, so they have to rely on an infrastructure of agriculture and trade to support them. This means that any large-scale mining operations require a complex and sophisticated social organization to sustain them.

This was no simple tribal society, but a complex world of specialized industry supplying gold ingots to mints and jewellery-makers hundreds of miles away – for about 300 years. And, of course, the Celts had absolutely no inhibitions about showing off all this gold they produced. Doing so was part of their culture: the men as well as the women sported lots of glitz – gold torques around their necks, gold arm-bands and gold bracelets, gold brooches, gold clasps and gold rings – even tunics embroidered and decorated with gold.[2]

In Roman eyes, the Celts weren't impoverished savages eking out a subsistence; on the contrary, they must have appeared irritatingly wealthy. Which probably explains a lot: in particular, why the Romans became so interested in the world of the Celts.

CAESAR INVADES GAUL

One thing we can be certain about is that Julius Caesar wasn't interested in taking over Gaul for the sake of getting to know the natives better. Caesar was an ambitious 40-year-old senator looking for a way to relaunch his faltering career. By 61 BC he had incurred debts worth 25 tons of silver,[3] and was dependent on a billionaire backer called Crassus for his survival. He desperately needed cash to pay off his debts, and a military adventure to boost his career. It was to be Gaul that provided him with the opportunity for both, and a Gaul who gave him the excuse.

The Gaul's name was Diviciacus, and he'd been the leader of the Aedui. When his brother deposed him in a coup, he fled to Rome and tried to persuade the Romans to reinstate him.

They treated Diviciacus as an exotic figure, and he was happy to play along with it. He clearly knew how to mind his table manners because he was invited to all the best houses. He was even asked to address the Senate, and caused a sensation by appearing dressed as a warrior and leaning on his shield. But there was no enthusiasm in Rome for a military adventure. People refused to believe his assertions that his brother was a dangerous warmonger.

Until Caesar saw his opportunity. Diviciacus began claiming that his wicked brother was involved in a plot by another Celtic people, the Helvetii, to 'obtain possession of the whole of Gaul'.[4] Most Romans would have said, 'So what?', but Caesar managed to turn this into an 'imminent threat' to Rome itself. The Helvetii lived in the Alps, and if they moved west into what is now central France, the wild Germans would obviously take over their lands and then threaten Italy.[5] Playing it up for all he was worth, Caesar persuaded the Senate to give him the job of 'Protector of the Gauls'. In 59 BC he was appointed to this position for five years. In the years that followed nearly 1,000,000 Gauls, maybe one-sixth of the whole population, would be killed by his armies.[6] Some protection! Some Protector!

But then why should Caesar be concerned about protecting a bunch of Barbarians? His goal was personal power, and to achieve it he had an extraordinary military machine at his disposal. Thanks to a complete reform of the army by his uncle Marius, Rome had the only full-time professional army in the world, with standardized wages, armour, weapons, equipment, tactics and benefits.

The Gauls, on the other hand, were farmers and traders who could come together for military action only for short periods, after very limited training, before having to return home and take care of their families. The only way they could sustain any military effectiveness was by displaying all those qualities that defined them as Barbarians – a readiness to engage in passionately shared committment, a willingness to switch instantly into fighting mode, and a pride in personal heroism regardless of personal risk.

Caesar knew that while his legions might possibly lose a battle, they just needed to stay in the field to win any possible war. All he needed was an excuse, and here was an exiled Gallic chief providing him with a ready-made one. Caesar announced that he was being forced to invade Gaul (now under his protection) because the Helvetii had started to over-run the territory of the Aedui: 'About 15,000 of them had crossed the Rhine: but then these wild and savage men had become enamoured of the lands, refinement and the abundance of the Gauls, so that more were brought over, until there were now as many as 120,000 of them in Gaul.'[7] So he marched north and slaughtered them. It was a glorious victory and boosted Caesar's image back in Rome no end.

But there is something fishy about Caesar's story. He says that, after the battle, his men found documents in the remains of the Helvetii camp. These 'wild and savage men' had drawn up a complete census 'name by name' in Greek characters

> of the number which had gone forth from their country of those who were able to bear arms; and likewise the boys, the old men, and the women, separately. Of all which items the total was:

Of the heads of the Helvetii	263,000
Of the Tulingi	36,000
Of the Latobrigi	14,000
Of the Rauraci	23,000
Of the Boii	32,000
The sum of all amounted to	368,000

> Out of these, such as could bear arms, [amounted] to about 92,000.[8]

So they were literate and could do maths. So could Caesar. He did his own census 'of those who returned home', and calculated there were 110,000. In other words, over 250,000 of these people had disappeared – most of them presumably killed or enslaved. A small price to make them pay when your aim is to rule the world.

But the real point about these figures is that the Helvetii certainly don't sound like a random mob of savages, and indeed they weren't. They were trying to migrate. The whole thing was highly organized and controlled – the census they had carried out was designed to make sure everyone got fed and housed. What's more, they'd asked Caesar for permission to pass through Roman territory. He refused, and when they took another route, he said they were invading the Aedui.

It was a stitch-up. Caesar's account of what happened was as misleading as possible. And he now had his claws into Gaul: he had begun a campaign that would bring him both enough wealth to pay off all his debts and enough glory to make him the conquering hero of Rome. Vast numbers of Gauls became his personal property, sold off in Roman slave markets; and, according to Suetonius, he ended up with more gold than he knew what to do with, and offered it for sale at 25 per cent off. And then there was all the rest of the plunder.[9]

According to Plutarch, Caesar's armies not only killed a million people, they enslaved a million more. If the total population was six million, that means Caesar's 'protection' had taken out a third of them. It may be safe to assume that he was more interested in protecting the Gauls' resources than their lives, and that, like the Helvetii, he had 'become enamoured of the lands, refinement and the abundance of the Gauls'.

His savagery was spectacular: in 55 BC, when two groups of Germans dared to attack a Roman camp, killing 74 Romans, he massacred every man, woman and child – by his own estimate there were 430,000 of them.[10] The Senate decreed a celebration of the genocide, but this was too much even for some Romans. Cato the Younger was so outraged that he demanded Caesar be handed over to the Germans![11]

Having gone too far, Caesar then spent a couple of years restoring his reputation by being the first Roman general to cross the Rhine and invade Germany, and by being the first to cross the sea and invade Britain, which, for the ordinary Roman, was 'outside the known world'.[12]

At the end of the summer of 53 BC, Caesar withdrew to Italy, leaving various garrisons scattered around the occupied territory but not necessarily in control. His five years as 'Protector' were coming to an end, and he was still not out of the woods. On the day his term of office ended he would not only lose command of his legions in Gaul; he would become vulnerable to any charges of illegality or corruption his enemies might want to bring for actions carried out during his conquests. And he was not short of enemies in Rome who understood very well what he had been up to. The only thing that could save him was an emergency – and the Gauls (God bless them!) provided it.

VERCINGETORIX AND THE GAULS' LAST STAND

The warrior Vercingetorix had been kicked out of his own territory by his uncle and the elders, who opposed his ideas of fomenting rebellion and standing up to Rome. Nevertheless, he succeeded in forming an army and taking command of his people, the Arverni. He then began to prove himself a charismatic leader, and managed to do something that no other Gallic leader had been able to do: he created an anti-Caesar alliance, and was able to impose his authority over a coalition army drawn from the diverse peoples of Gaul.

In fact, that's what his name means. It's not a name but a title, made up of two Gallic words, *ver* meaning 'over' and *cengetos* meaning 'warriors', and one Latin word, *rex*, the king. Over and over again we will find great 'barbarian' leaders, from Vercingeto-rix in the first century BC to Ala-ric and Gaise-ric over 400 years later, bearing names that are actually Latin titles of royalty.

The uprising was actually started by people called the Carnutes, who slaughtered the Roman tradesmen and their families who had settled in the town of Cenabum (Orleans). But then Vercingetorix attacked and destroyed the Roman winter garrisons. A revolt was just what Caesar wanted. He force-marched his army across the Cevennes, which at that time of year were 6 feet deep in snow. The Gauls, thinking the mountains impassable in such weather, were taken by surprise, and over the next weeks Vercingetorix suffered a series of defeats.

He was, however, clearly a remarkable leader, for he retained his authority and summoned a council at which he announced that he and his fellow Gauls must fight this war in a completely different way from normal. Instead of meeting the Romans head-on, they would simply starve the enemy out. The Gauls would attack foraging parties, and, what is more, they would burn towns and villages where provisions were stored so that the Roman army would have nothing to live on. The burning of the towns would also give those Gauls who did not want to join in the rebellion nowhere to retreat to, and they would be forced to come and fight.

The council unanimously approved this advice, and no fewer than 20 towns were destroyed by fire in one day. Caesar tells us that conflagrations were seen wherever you looked. There was one town, however, that the local Gauls were loath to put to the torch: Avaricum – modern-day Bourges. The locals pleaded with Vercingetorix in the council not to burn one of the most beautiful towns in all Gaul. Against his better judgement, the Gallic leader allowed them to defend the place.

The result was a disaster: the Romans were able to breach the defences and, in revenge for the massacre at Cenabum, they put to the sword 40,000 men, women and children. Perhaps 800 escaped to Vercingetorix. Ironically, this catastrophe probably boosted Vercingetorix's reputation as a wise war leader, since he had been so firmly opposed to the plan that led to it.

THE CRUSHING OF THE GAULS

Vercingetorix now marched his army into his home territory, pursued by Caesar and no fewer than six legions plus some auxiliaries from the Aedui – a pay-off for the Romans having reinstated Diviciacus as their leader. Nevertheless, the Gauls were able to drive the Romans off in their first battle, and, by Caesar's own estimate, 700 Romans were killed, including 46 centurions. Vercingetorix's reputation was now at its height, and other people started to join the revolt. The Aedui rebelled against their Roman-backed king, and they too joined the

revolt. What's more, a mass vote at the general council confirmed
Vercingetorix as overall commander of the Celts. He now assembled a
formidable army with 15,000 cavalry – outnumbering Caesar's. They
all swore that 'that no member of the cavalry who had not twice ridden
through the enemy's army, should ever again be received under a roof
or be allowed to see his children, parents or wife'.[13] Tough stuff.

But Caesar had secretly recruited a large number of German
cavalry, and these gave him an unexpected edge. When the Gauls
attacked, they were repulsed and retreated to Alesia, some 30 miles
west of modern Dijon.

Caesar pressed home his advantage, and prepared to starve out
this fortified town. Today there is a hugely impressive re-creation of
his siege-works at the Archeodrome just south of Beaune. Here you
can really sense what Rome brought into the world – the marriage of
rational thought, engineering ability and political authority with military power, to take over and civilize the savage peoples that
surrounded them.

Caesar dug one ditch 20 feet deep and another two ditches 15
feet deep, one of which he filled with water diverted from the nearby
river. He also built a rampart some 11 miles around, surmounted by a
wall with watch-towers at regular intervals. Spikes were fixed on top
of the wall so that the enemy would not be able to climb it.

But before Caesar could finish his siege fortifications, with their
ditches and booby-traps, Vercingetorix sent out his cavalry by night
through the gaps that still remained. Their orders were to ride to every
part of Gaul and raise an army to come to his rescue. If they failed,
'80,000 chosen men would perish with him'.[14] It was the kind of emergency that brought out the best in Celtic solidarity. A council of all
Gaul was convened with amazing rapidity, and an extraordinary army
of 320,000 assembled to go to the rescue. The Gauls were finally
acting as a single political entity.

So Caesar then built a second, identical, circuit around the first
one, consisting of 14 miles of walls and ditches, to defend his own
besieging army from the vast relief force that he knew was on its way.
But the men inside Alesia didn't know whether or not it was coming.
They began to despair as their food ran out. As a last resort, they
expelled all the non- combatants from the town. Old men, women and

children were forced into the no man's land between Alesia's own wall and the Roman fortifications. Here they pleaded with the Romans to take them in and make them slaves or whatever, so long as they were given food. But Caesar refused to let them through his gates. Vercingetorix dared not readmit them because as soon as he opened the gates, the Romans would burst through. The result, presumably, was that they stayed in no man's land and perished, though Caesar makes no mention of their fate.

And when the relief force did arrive, the Roman fortifications proved too strong. Day after day the Gauls hurled themselves at the blockaders' defences, but without breaching them. After five days of fighting, Vercingetorix decided he could no longer watch his people dying. According to Caesar, he gave up his authority and had himself handed over. Plutarch described how he put on his most colourful armour, had his horse carefully groomed and rode out of the city and right up to Caesar. He then rode in a circle around the Roman general, dismounted, removed his own armour and surrendered himself at Caesar's feet.

Vercingetorix was taken to Rome and imprisoned in a dungeon, the Tullianum, for five years. He was eventually taken out to be put on display in a 20-day celebration of Caesar's victories. The savage Barbarian, having been shown to the crowd, was put to death by strangulation. By this time Caesar, thanks to Vercingetorix's most useful revolt, had become rich enough, powerful enough and popular enough to take over Rome.

The heroic statue of the Gallic leader that stands outside Alesia was put up by a French emperor, Napoleon III, to celebrate French national pride. Vercingetorix stands proud, unbowed, the tribal leader who represents a way of life about to be extinguished. He stares out over the ruins of the Roman settlement built over his town, and the obliteration of his world.

Nothing more than a Barbarian.

III
CELTIC WOMEN AND THE GREAT BRITISH REVOLT

There she stands, right next to the Houses of Parliament in London, larger than life and twice as 'orrible, the Barbarian Queen herself – Boadicea as we learnt to call her, or Boudica as she was known to the Celts. She became known as 'Boadicea' to millions of British school-kids because two people got it wrong. First of all, the Roman historian Tacitus recorded her name with two 'c's as Boudicca. Then, in the Middle Ages, a copyist compounded Tacitus' original error by misreading the 'u' as 'a' and the second 'c' as an 'e'. So Boudicca became Boadicea.

In any case, that wasn't her name. As with so many 'barbarian' leaders, what we take for a name was a sobriquet, like 'The Sun King' for Louis XIV of France. *Buideac* is a Celtic word, meaning 'victorious'. Which just goes to show that you can't even believe what you read on monuments – especially if they're right bang outside the Houses of Parliament.

But whatever she called herself, Boudica was an affront to everything any decent Roman stood for: a female who was not only assertive and dominating, but a warrior and a leader. 'A terrible disaster occurred in Britain. Two cities were sacked, eighty thousand of the Romans and of their allies perished, and the island was lost to Rome. Moreover, all this ruin was brought upon the Romans by a woman, a fact which in itself caused them the greatest shame.'[1] The idea of women going to war alongside men was monstrous to the Romans. As for actually leading men into battle – well! That was such a perversion of the natural order of things that it hardly bore thinking about, at least if you were a Roman male.

ROMAN MATRONS

There was a strong Roman belief that it was a moral evil for a woman to wield power. To the Romans it was one of the clearest signs of the difference between civilization and barbarism. The symbols of Roman womanhood were enshrined in the Temple of the Vestal Virgins in Rome. The Vestals were brides of the city – the guardians of the sacred flame that had to be kept burning in the public hearth of the temple. If the flame went out, it was believed, disaster would strike Rome. The Vestal Virgins were also guarding the purity of Roman womanhood. Chosen between the ages of six and ten, they served for 30 years. If, during that time, they broke their vow of chastity, the Romans had a simple cure for their sexual drive – the women were walled up to die of starvation.

As regards the rest of the female sex, no woman in the Roman world could be head of a family or exercise control (*potestas*). She had no political status, no vote, couldn't hold political office or – heaven defend us – join the army. The famous orator Cicero explained that 'our ancestors established the rule that all women, because of their weakness of intellect, should be under the power of guardians'. There was no legal validity to anything any Roman woman did unless a man had approved it.

So Roman women, whether daughters, wives or slaves, were under the total control of the man who headed the household, the paterfamilias. 'Who's the daddy?' was an important question in Rome. Dio Cassius narrates a story of how Julia Domna, wife of the emperor Septimius Severus (AD 193–211), was shocked by the apparent openness with which Celtic women chose their husbands and lovers. She declared that it showed a complete lack of moral scruple.

The wife of the British chieftain to whom she uttered this opinion responded with some spirit: 'We Celtic women obey the demands of Nature in a more moral way than the women of Rome. We consort openly with the best of men but you, of Rome, allow yourselves to be debauched in secret by the vilest.'[2] No wonder Barbarian women exercised such a powerful hold on the imagination of Roman men. They were wayward, powerful, dangerous and – perhaps – erotic. It was the asso- ciation of Celtic women with barbarism that persuaded the

Senate to decree in AD 40 that prostitutes should make their hair blonde – the colour the Romans associated with the Celts. It was the eroticism, how-ever, that persuaded ladies at the highest level of Roman society to put on blonde wigs.

Women were not supposed to run things. Of course, there were occasions when women such as Nero's mother, Agrippina, did hold power in Rome. But it was not something the Romans were at all comfortable with, and Roman writers subsequently tried to poison her memory with scorn and venom.

CELTIC WOMEN

In Celtic society, women were in a completely different position. 'Barbarian' households were not owned by the head of the family, and women did not become their husband's property the moment they married: they retained their own integrity and their own money. Whatever property or wealth the two partners brought to the marriage was jointly owned, and whoever survived the other took the lot.

Caesar, to whom we are indebted for this information, also adds that in Gaul husbands had the power of life or death over their wives and that the wife could be tortured if the husband died in suspicious circumstances. Otherwise, as Strabo notes, even married women could lead lives remarkably independent of their husbands. And they could perform the role of head of the family, as a 'curse tablet' found in Bath makes clear – it cites a certain Veloriga as the head of her family. Hundreds of these tablets, in which Britons request the gods to deal with people who have stolen from them or mistreated them, have been found there, and they show that British women owned property and engaged in business dealings.

What we know of Celtic law comes from the Irish Brehon Laws, the rules of a legal system of self-help without courts or police, and which depended on communal respect. These laws respect individuals more than property, treat contracts as sacred, impose duties of hospitality and protection to strangers, and assume that women have equal property rights to men and can divorce.[3]

It seems certain that these laws are of great antiquity. They list 14 grounds on which a woman can demand a divorce, including being treated badly in public by her husband and being beaten by him. Beating your wife, if you were Roman, was about as significant as breaking your crockery: she was property. In these Celtic law codes a wife has the same rights as anybody else, so if she was beaten, there were fines and tables of compensation. In addition, the woman was entitled to a divorce and could take back all the property she had brought into the marriage. She was then free to marry again.

In Rome, rape was not a crime against a woman, but an injury to her male guardian, an offence against his property. In the Celtic world, if a woman was raped she was entitled not only to personal compensation but also to revenge.

When the Romans invaded the Celtic lands of Galatia (in modern Turkey) in 189 BC they captured a chieftain's wife by the name of Chiomara. A centurion raped her and, when he discovered her high rank, had the gall to send a ransom note to her husband. An exchange was arranged, and agents from her people came and handed over the money. However, as the centurion took an affectionate leave of her, Chiomara signalled to one of her compatriots to cut off his head. She took the gruesome object home with her, as Celtic warriors tended to do, and threw it at her husband's feet. He was appalled at this truce-breaking: 'Woman! Good faith is a fine thing!' To which Chiomara replied: 'Yes, but it is even better that only one man who has slept with me should remain alive.'[4]

Unlike Roman women, Celtic women could exercise power in their own right, and queens are known throughout the Celtic world. For example, one leader of the Scordisci, who founded what is now Belgrade, is recorded as being a woman by the name of Onomaris (which may mean 'Mountain Ash').[5] And around 231 BC, Polybius tells us, a certain Queen Teuta led her people against the Greeks of Epiros. When Rome sent ambassadors to intervene it may be that they found negotiating with a woman distasteful and made no attempt to hide it. At all events they seem to have thoroughly put the queen's nose out of joint, for, according to Polybius, she 'gave way to a fit of womanish petulance' and had them assassinated on the way home.[6]

Celtic women participated in political and public life in a way that was an affront to the Roman concept of decency. Plutarch, for example, records that the Volcae in northern Italy sent female

ambassadors to negotiate with the Carthaginian general Hannibal in
the fourth century BC: 'In their treaty with Hannibal they wrote the
provision that, if the Celts complained against the Carthaginians, the
governors and generals of the Carthaginians in Spain should be the
judges; and if the Carthaginians complained against the Celts, the
judges should be the Celtic women.'[7]

The archaeological record provides plenty of evidence of women
buried in such style and with such a wealth of grave goods as to suggest
that they were most likely rulers. One such woman was buried at Vix,
in the Burgundy region of France. She died, aged about 35, around 480
BC. When the grave was opened up in 1952 it proved to be one of the
most spectacular archaeological finds of the twentieth century.

Whoever the woman was, she was clearly a powerful and important figure, judging from the opulence of her grave goods. They
included one of the largest mixing bowls for wine, known as 'craters',
to have survived from antiquity, along with other valuable utensils. The
crater is significant because hosting feasts with huge quantities of alco-
hol was a central feature of leadership. The woman herself was adorned
with magnificent jewellery made of gold, bronze, amber, lignite and
coral, and on her skull was a fabulous gold torque of extraordinary
craftsmanship. Her body had been placed on a highly decorated
wagon.[8] The funeral must have been a spectacular statement of her
power; crowds would have seen her body taken to the grave on a
horse-drawn bier and watched the ceremony in which the hearse was
dismantled, the wheels placed along the sides of the grave, and the
great crater brought in – probably filled with wine for the funeral feast.

Another Celtic woman, who had been buried with a chariot and
with grave goods of comparable quality in the fourth century BC, was
discovered at Reinheim, just south of Saarbrücken on the German-
French border. The fact that she was buried with a chariot suggests
that she had been a war leader. She too was surrounded by a fabulous
hoard of jewellery.[9]

Powerful women existed at the bottom of the Celtic social scale
as well as at the top, and a grudging admiration for these women
sometimes peeps through the text of the Roman writers. Diodorus
Siculus informs us: 'The women of the Celts are nearly as tall as the
men and they rival them also in courage.' Of course, he might have

been trying to diminish the stature of Celtic men, but it was a common Roman view that it was part of the un-naturalness of Celtic society for their women to be even fiercer than the men.

A fourth-century AD Roman soldier by the name of Ammianus Marcellinus seems to have lumped Celtic women in the same category as the clichéd mother-in-law joke:

> A whole troop of foreigners would not be able to withstand a
> single Celt if he called his wife to his assistance. The wife is
> even more formidable. She is usually very strong, and has
> blue eyes; in rage her neck veins swell, she gnashes her
> teeth, and brandishes her snow-white robust arms. She
> begins to strike blows mingled with kicks, as if they were so
> many missiles sent from the string of a catapult. The voices
> of these women are formidable and threatening, even when
> they are not angry but being friendly.[10]

Marcellinus, the last capable historian to write in Latin, saw active service in Gaul, so he could have based his observations on personal experience. Perhaps as a young, rather intellectual army officer he got short shrift from the local fishwives, who didn't want boy soldiers telling them what to do. Nevertheless, he was impressed by their hygiene: 'All Celtic women, with equal care, keep neat and clean.'

It was the way that Celtic women broke into the male preserve of warfare that was most alien – most barbarous – to the Roman observers. A bemused Tacitus notes that the Celts had no objection to being led by a woman: 'In Britain,' he writes, 'there is no rule of distinction to exclude the female line from the throne, or the command of armies.' In fact, when the Romans invaded Britain in AD 43, part of the island was ruled by a married woman who was queen over her own husband. She was Cartimandua, Queen of the Brigantes, a federation of peoples occupying most of the north-east of England.

BRITISH COLLABORATORS

Cartimandua ('Sleek Pony') was no patriot and freedom fighter. She was quite happy to betray her fellow countrymen to the Roman occupiers and to call in Roman troops to put down resistance – even when it was being organized by her own husband. Naturally, she enjoyed a long and prosperous reign: Tacitus describes her as 'flourishing in all the splendour of wealth and power'. But then, perhaps we are being too hard on her. Cartimandua was merely continuing in the proud tradition of British chiefs who had long been taking the Roman shilling. In fact, British collaboration with the Roman super-power went back almost a century – perhaps longer.

Strabo, writing shortly after Caesar's conquest of Gaul in the first century BC, remarks that there is no need to invade Britain since many British chiefs are already only too happy to play ball with the Romans:

> Some of the chieftains there, after procuring the friendship
> of Caesar Augustus by sending embassies and by paying
> court to him have not only dedicated offerings in the Capitol,
> but have also managed to make the whole of the island
> virtually Roman property. Further, they submit so easily to
> heavy duties, both on the exports from there to Celtica
> [Gaul] and on the imports from Celtica ... that there is no
> need of garrisoning the island.[11]

In the years since Caesar had visited the island and made some of the local rulers into Roman clients, many well-to-do Britons had fallen in love with the Roman lifestyle. For instance, at Calleva (modern Silchester) excavations by archaeologists from Reading University have revealed styli and graffiti with writing in Latin, and quantities of pottery imported from France and the Mediterranean.[12] At the same time some of the traditional round buildings were rebuilt as rectangular, and the streets were organized on a grid, like Roman towns – even though the civic buildings were still timber-framed with wattle-and-daub infill, and thatched instead of tiled. At least these Celts were upwardly mobile.[13]

Of course, not everyone was equally enthusiastic about the Romans. For example, of the two British kings in the south-east whom Rome recognized as allies, Cunobelin, King of the Catuvellauni, was less pro-Roman than Verica, King of the Atrebates. It may be significant that Cunobelin's coins depicted barley, for British beer, while

Verica's depicted grapes, for Roman wine. Cunobelin, however, played a smart game, and was able to keep the Romans sweet while at the same time reducing the kingdom of their ally, Verica, to a rump.

Unfortunately for Verica, Cunobelin died in AD 42, and his two sons, Togodumnus and Caratacus, were by no means as enthusiastic about paying the taxes on trade that recognition by Rome demanded. They were also less prepared to observe the niceties of diplomacy. They promptly over-ran much of Verica's kingdom, and probably another, until they controlled most of southern Britain. They refused to act as clients of Rome, and when Verica fled there they had the nerve to demand his extradition!

This direct challenge to Rome put the Emperor Claudius on the spot. If he stood by and let these two British princes cock a snook at the might of Rome, he would look weaker and feebler than, as an elderly, stuttering, scholarly man, he already seemed to many Romans.

What is more, although there had always been sound financial arguments against invading Britain, the discovery of silver lead ore in the west of the country had recently destroyed those arguments. This was a huge bonus: the silver would revitalize the Roman currency, and the lead would make pipes for plumbing and glassware for the table, and glaze an awful lot of Roman pots. The invasion would be self-financing. Finally, Claudius had two new legions on the Rhine that needed to be employed. Here was his chance to win respect as emperor and to make money. He really had no alternative. In AD 43 he launched his attack.

Of the two trouble-makers who had triggered this Roman invasion, Togodumnus surrendered, but Caratacus fought on from Wales. When he was finally overwhelmed he fled north in AD 51 to seek political asylum with Cartimandua and the Brigantes. But that was a terrible misjudgement because Cartimandua did not share his politics. She had already formed an alliance with the occupiers and had no intention of doing anything to jeopardize her position with Rome, which was her only means of keeping control over her people. And so it was that when Caratacus came to her for protection, she coolly trampled over all the laws of hospitality (an important thing for the Celts) and had him and his family bound in chains and handed over to the Romans.

However, the story of this remarkable British warrior king didn't end there. Caratacus and his nearest and dearest were all taken to Rome, where things didn't go as they usually did for a captured enemy. His fame as a valiant resistance hero, holding out against all the odds and the might of Rome, had preceded him. And although he and his family were put on public display in chains and paraded through Rome, Caratacus was allowed to address the Emperor and make a dignified and eloquent appeal for clemency: 'If you want to rule the world, does it follow that everyone else welcomes enslavement? ... Were I to have been at once delivered up as a prisoner, neither my fall nor your triumph would have become famous. My punishment would be followed by oblivion, whereas, if you save my life, I shall be an everlasting memorial of your clemency.'[14] It worked. Caratacus was pardoned and he and his family lived out the rest of their lives in high esteem in Rome.

Meanwhile, the dreadful Cartimandua was quarrelling with her consort, Venutius. When he tried to raise an insurrection, she cheerfully called in the Roman army to put him in his place. However, the two of them patched things up and carried on as a married couple until Cartimandua took up with her husband's armour-bearer, Vellocatus. Not surprisingly, Venutius used this as an excuse to get another rebellion going. Cartimandua called in the Romans again, but this time the Brigantes' resistance proved too strong and the Romans were forced to retreat, along with the queen and her lover. What happened to them after that is not recorded.

But the story of Cartimandua demonstrates very clearly the power and independence of Celtic women in stark contrast to their Roman counterparts. In Britain, at this period, a high-ranking woman could occupy a position of major political power, negotiate with the Romans, sign treaties and rule over not just her own people but a whole federation. Moreover, she could choose her own lover and divorce her husband as she saw fit.

QUEEN BOUDICA AND THE ICENI

All of which brings us back to Boudica, Queen of the Iceni – a formidable figure: 'In stature she was very tall, in appearance most terrifying, in the glance of her eye most fierce, and her voice was harsh; a great mass of the tawniest hair fell to her hips; around her neck was a large golden necklace; and she wore a tunic of divers colours over which a thick mantle was fastened with a brooch. This was her invariable attire.'[15]

Boudica was the wife of Prasutagus, the King of the Iceni, who controlled the region roughly corresponding to modern Norfolk. Tacitus refers to him as 'Prasutagus, king of the Iceni, famed for his long prosperity'. He sounds like a sort of Celtic King Midas, and the impression that the Iceni rulers were extremely well-off has been reinforced in recent years by a remarkable discovery.

In August 1990, Charles Hodder was wandering around a field in the village of Snettisham with his metal detector when he stumbled on something. Digging down, he found a Celtic bronze container. It held scrap metal, which was odd. He called in the British Museum, who discovered that it was a dummy: there was a real treasure under a false floor below the container. Eventually they found 12 treasure-pits. The treasure had been very carefully stowed in each one, with the most precious item always on top. And this treasure was absolutely fabulous.

What had been found was, in effect, a set of bank deposit boxes, presumably a ritual deposit containing the greatest riches of the Iceni royal family. These golden torques, of incredibly high quality, staggered historians, who had not imagined that such wealth existed in Britain at that time. There were coins in the hoards that dated to about 100 years before Boudica, but these finds were inside a 20-acre enclosure ditch that had been filled in around the time that she was alive.[16]

It is the most valuable archaeological find ever made in Britain, and it was an indication that, once Rome had reopened Britain for business, there was money to be made there. To help with the Romanization of the south-east, the Emperor Claudius had made huge loans to favoured local leaders; so did the court of his adopted son Nero. But whereas Claudius may have been doing it for political ends, Nero and his courtiers saw it as a money-making scam.

The Roman elite was well aware that a decent rate of interest was at least as effective a way of milking Barbarians as demanding 'tribute', and large loans were pushed on to the leading families. The standard rate was 1 per cent a month. The philosopher Seneca, Nero's 'tutor' (in effect his guardian), convinced that he was on to a good thing, 'had lent to the islanders 40,000,000 sesterces that they did not want'.[17] Forty million sesterces was enough to pay for a legion for 40 years. The Snettisham treasure shows why he had thought his money was secure. Some of this money – maybe all of it – must have been a personal loan to the King of the Iceni, perhaps secured on his crown jewels. Prasutagus was a collaborator with the Romans from his shoes upwards. Whether or not he was actually installed as king by the Romans, he seems to have used the money that Rome put at his disposal to build himself up as a major figure.

Excavations at Thetford in the 1980s revealed a hilltop enclosure that was suddenly transformed by a huge building project at about the time of the Roman conquest. It seems to have become a ceremonial site containing a single substantial circular building, probably two storeys high. There was metal-working in another new enclosure, maybe a mint or jewellery workshops, but no one seems to have lived there. It was, quite obviously, a very expensive and lavish royal centre. The archaeologists were puzzled by evidence of an enormous number of great wooden pillars around the enclosure, and concluded that they were a huge artificial sacred grove of oak trees. Perhaps this was a Romano-British version of a Druid centre.[18]

Prasutagus was clearly, as far as the Romans were concerned, the acceptable face of Celtic rule. He seems to have flourished in the post-invasion state. Moreover, he was allowed to keep his kingdom free of Roman control until his death, whereupon it was supposed to be subsumed into the Roman system. Tacitus tells us that in order to get round this imposition, Prasutagus thought up a cunning ruse. He 'made the emperor his heir along with his two daughters, under the impression that this token of submission would put his kingdom and his house out of the reach of wrong'.[19] But when he died, in AD 59, Boudica took over. And here there was a problem.

Boudica was now the head of the royal household, a situation mean-ingless in Roman law. Under Celtic law, she could be the legal guardian of her daughters and responsible for any debt. But under Roman law a woman could not be a guardian,[20] and a law passed just a few years earlier, in AD 46, stated that she could not take on responsibility for someone else's debt.[21] The Romans would have to have their money back.

As a philosopher, Seneca wrote lofty essays about forgiving injuries and overcoming evil with good, about the universal brotherhood of man and the obligation to universal benevolence. But that didn't amount to a hill of beans when it came to the bottom line. Cancelling Third World debt was not exactly Seneca's style. He and Nero called in the loans, and Boudica, to put it bluntly, couldn't pay. Or wouldn't pay. So Nero confiscated her whole kingdom and sent in the bailiffs.

Which is where the flogging and raping came in. Tacitus sounds decidedly pro-Celt as he narrates what happened: '[Prasutagus'] dominions were ravaged by the centurions; the slaves pillaged his house, and his effects were seized as lawful plunder. His wife, Boudica, suffered the humiliation of being beaten; her daughters were raped, and the Icenian aristocracy were stripped of their titles and inheritance.' Rome's proud legend of its own history began with a mass rape, when the Romans – essentially a gang of criminals and outlaws – seized the women of another town, the 'Sabine Women', to make themselves some babies. The rape of Boudica's daughters was the most ruthless demonstration that, under Rome, women were deprived of power and were the property of men.

'All the chief men of the Iceni,' Tacitus goes on, 'as if Rome had received the whole country as a gift, were stript of their ancestral possessions, and the king's relatives were made slaves.'[22] Nor was the contempt of the Romans for the rights of their Barbarian subjects limited to the Great and Good. The meanest of Roman soldiers felt that whatever the British had once possessed was now theirs for the taking, and their behaviour shocked Tacitus to the core: 'It was against the veterans [retired soldiers who were granted conquered peoples' land] that their [the Britons'] hatred was most intense. For these new settlers in the colony of Camulodunum [Colchester] drove people out of their houses, ejected them from their farms, called them captives and slaves, and the lawlessness of the veterans was encouraged by the soldiers, who lived a similar life and hoped for similar licence.'[23]

Matters now came to a head.

THE DEATH OF THE DRUIDS?

The Druids were the political backbone of Celtic society. Roman sources tell us that they were not just religious practitioners, but also the supreme judges of the Celtic world, with an authority that transcended all political boundaries. According to Caesar, writing 100 years earlier, their cult started in Britain[24] and from there spread to Gaul. The area around what is now Chartres was its centre. But by the time Caesar had done his business in Gaul, the centre of Druid activity was focused back in the little island of Anglesey, off the north coast of Wales.[25]

Claudius had already tried to stamp out the Druids in Gaul.[26] Now the Romans decided on surgical removal of the heart of Celtic resistance by destroying the Druids in their fastness – deep in their most sacred territory. Of course, the Romans claimed there were sound humanitarian grounds for doing so, since the Druids – horror of horrors! – still practised human sacrifice. Whether or not this is true is a much-contested issue. But we do have the earlier evidence of Poseidonius (c.135–50 BC), who actually travelled in Celtic Gaul and Iberia and was a reliable eye witness to the Celtic way of life at that time. We don't know whether he actually witnessed human sacrifice, but there is no reason for him to have made it up – after all, he admired the Celts and wanted to present them as noble savages. His account is convincingly detailed:

> [The Druids] have an especially odd and unbelievable
> method of divination for the most important matters. Having
> anointed a human victim, they stab him with a small knife in
> the area above the diaphragm. When the man has collapsed
> from the wound, they interpret the future by observing the
> nature of his fall, the convulsion of his limbs, and especially
> from the pattern of his spurting blood.[27]

These are not Poseidonius' own words because no copy of his *Histories* has survived, but they are reported by Diodorus Siculus, who was writing later in the same century. Diodorus has his own less enthusiastic take on the Celts: 'It is in keeping with their wildness and savage nature that they carry out particularly offensive religious practices. They will keep some criminal under guard for five years, then impale him on a pole in honour of their gods – followed by burning him on an enormous pyre along with many other first-fruits. They also use prisoners of war as sacrifices to the gods.'[28]

Mind you, the Romans were fine ones to complain about human sacrifice. Livy and Plutarch record three occasions, in the years 228, 216 and 113 BC, when two pairs of Gauls and Greeks, a man and a woman each, were buried alive in the Forum Boarium. And of course Vestal Virgins who broke their vow of chastity suffered the same fate. Not only that – when it came to taking human life on an industrial scale, who could hold a candle to the Romans? They had no scruples about crucifying rebel slaves in their thousands, or throwing criminals into the arena to be torn to pieces by wild animals for the gratification of the crowd.

But the high moral ground was a good standpoint from which to attack the core of Celtic identity. And that is how, in AD 60, the major part of the occupying Roman forces came to be gathered on the Menai Strait, facing across to Anglesey.

> On the shore stood the opposing army with its dense array of armed warriors, while between the ranks dashed women, in black attire like the Furies, with hair dishevelled, waving brands. All around, the Druids, lifting up their hands to heaven, and pouring forth dreadful imprecations, scared our soldiers by the unfamiliar sight, so that, as if their limbs were paralysed, they stood motionless, and exposed to wounds. Then urged by their general's appeals and mutual encouragements not to quail before a troop of frenzied women, they bore the standards onwards, smote down all resistance, and wrapped the foe in the flames of his own brands. A force was next set over the conquered, and their groves, devoted to inhuman superstitions, were destroyed. They deemed it indeed a duty to cover their altars with the blood of captives and to consult their deities through human entrails.[29]

That's when the balloon went up.

BOUDICA'S REVOLT

The uprising led by Boudica was an eruption of fury and outrage by a coalition of British peoples. It is said that she amassed an army of some

100,000 fighters. Dio Cassius gives a figure of 120,000 and later ups it to 230,000. Its first target was the hated colony at Camulodunum.

Nero had done the Britons the favour – nay, honour – of setting up a temple there to his adoptive father, Emperor Claudius, who had supposedly become a god by dying. Here wealthy Brits were forced to act as priests and, to add insult to injury, to pay for the rituals they were supposed to perform. Tacitus noted that this temple 'was ever before their eyes, a citadel, as it seemed, of perpetual tyranny'. And with imperial arrogance the army had neglected to put up any defences around Camulodunum. It was a sitting duck.

If the colonists there had been worried when they first heard of the uprising, their confidence was further shattered by a series of evil omens. First, the statue of victory in the town centre toppled over for no reason at all and turned its back to the enemy, as if fleeing from them. Then ' ... women excited to frenzy prophesied impending destruction,' wrote Tacitus. 'Ravings in a strange tongue ... were heard in their Senate-house; the theatre resounded with wailings, and in the estuary of the Thames men saw the image of an overthrown town; even the ocean took on the colour of blood, and, when the tide ebbed, human forms were seen on the sand.'[30] It was enough to send the most hard-bitten veterans into a panic. They appealed to the administrator – or Procurator, to use his Roman title – Catus Decianus for assistance, but all he did was despatch a mere 200 soldiers, and even they weren't properly equipped.

If those soldiers felt they'd drawn the short straw, they were right. The siege lasted a bare two days. Before the final attack, all the soldiers retreated to the temple for shelter. But it didn't do them any good. Before torching the town, the rebels hauled them out and took them to a sacred grove where they were slaughtered to a man. Talk about Barbarians! Did they turn it into a public performance, as the civilized Romans did when there was slaughtering to be done in the circus? They did not! That was what made them Barbarians – they had no sense of showbiz.

Except when it came to a nice fire. Dig a 10-foot-deep hole anywhere in the middle of Colchester and you hit a layer of charcoal. This is the residue of a big, big fire – the one that Boudica and her followers lit with the town of Camulodunum as its fuel. The statue of

Claudius the God was toppled by the coalition forces; in 1907 its head was found in the river Alde. The Ninth Legion, rushing across country too late to crush the revolt, was ambushed and utterly destroyed. Tacitus heaped the blame on Catus Decianus, who, 'alarmed by this disaster and by the fury of the province which he had goaded into war by his rapacity', fled across the Channel into Gaul.

Meanwhile, Suetonius Paulinus, at the head of the legions, force-marched his men back through hostile territory to London. However, he quickly realized he would never be able to hold the town against the forces heading towards it. So he decided not to try. 'He resolved to save the province at the cost of a single town,' wrote Tacitus. 'Nor did the tears and weeping of the people, as they implored his aid, deter him from giving the signal of departure.'[31] Boudica's army was left free to reduce the place to ashes, and today an 8-inch-thick layer of burnt red clay is the only material evidence of that early Roman trading centre, Londinium. The Roman death toll was now being reckoned at 70,000.

But it wasn't the slaughter that convinced Tacitus that these were true Barbarians he was writing about. It was their complete failure to appreciate the commercial aspects of warfare: 'For it was not on making prisoners and selling them,' he wrote, 'or on any of the barter of war, that the enemy was bent, but on slaughter, on the gibbet, the fire and the cross, like men soon about to pay the penalty, and meanwhile snatching at instant vengeance.'[32]

The great final battle, according to Dio Cassius, began with Boudica addressing her warriors from her war-chariot. The speech that he puts into her mouth is unlikely to have been what she actually said, but it gives an interesting taste of a Roman perception of the occupation of Britain:

> You have learned by actual experience how different freedom is from slavery. Hence, although some among you may previously, through ignorance of which was better, have been deceived by the alluring promises of the Romans, yet now that you have tried both, you have learned how great a mistake you made in preferring an imported despotism to your ancestral mode of life, and you have come to realize how much better is poverty with no master than wealth with slavery.[33]

Boudica also encouraged her troops by pointing out that the Romans were clearly inferior fighters since they hid behind palisades and wore heavy armour. This indicated that they were scared, she asserted, and also gave them less manoeuvrability. 'Let us show them that they are hares and foxes trying to rule over dogs and wolves.'

But in the event, the Roman soldiers just weren't scared enough and didn't seem to be at all weighed down by their armour. The truth is that, when it came to a pitched battle between farmers and professional soldiers, righteous anger was never going to win the day. Tacitus recorded: 'Some indeed say that there fell little less than eighty thousand of the Britons, with a loss to our soldiers of about four hundred, and only as many wounded. Boudica put an end to her life by poison.'[34]

With the failure of the revolt, much of what was left of the Iceni was obliterated by Roman vengeance – so much more justified than the Barbarian variety. Take that treasure buried in Snettisham – everyone who knew where it was must have been killed, so it lay there forgotten until Charles Hodder found it with his metal detector. Seneca never got his money, and the treasure is now on display in the British Museum after 2000 years in the ground.

THE TROOPS REBEL

The cost to Rome of the destruction of the Druids was huge because it undermined the loyalty of the Barbarian auxiliaries used to carry it out. The forces deployed to attack Anglesey included 4000 Batavians (Germans from the Rhine estuary) and they were not happy with their work. We know the Batavian auxiliaries in Britain were involved because they were famed for crossing rivers fully armed, with several foot soldiers swimming alongside a single cavalry soldier and clinging to his horse, and this tactic is described by Tacitus in the attack on Anglesey.[35]

The Batavians were bound to be uncomfortable with the attack on Druid women because prophetic, Druid-like women were highly respected figures in their own culture.[36] And then these men were required to crush Boudica and destroy the Iceni, which would also have been problematic for them. The Batavians and the Iceni knew each other well – the links between East Anglia and southern Holland have always been strong.

The Batavians had migrated into Roman-controlled territory for protection from their neighbours, and the deal was that their men had to serve in the army. It seems that every single Batavian family must have had at least one son in uniform. They were celebrated for their loyalty to their commander – the personal mounted guard of the emperor had consisted of Batavians for some 70 years, since the very first emperor, Augustus. The auxiliaries would obey Suetonius Paulinus no matter what he demanded. But six years later these men were sent out of Britain, and after that their loyalty could not be so readily taken for granted. In AD 67, Nero arrested two leading Batavian nobles on suspicion of treason. In AD 68, his successor, Galba, dishonourably dismissed his Batavian bodyguard.

The following year the Roman commanders on the Rhine rebelled against Galba, and there was a bitterly resented attempt to conscript forcibly even more Batavian troops. That was when a female seer, whom Tacitus calls Veleda (the Celtic word for a female Druid or seer was 'Veleta'), prophesied that Batavians would throw off Roman rule completely. She came from the Bructeri people, neighbours of the Batavians. Both communities were Germanic rather than Celtic, but the distinction was not nearly as crisp as Roman writers suggest. Like a Druid, the virgin Veleda acted as arbitrator in disputes between communities. Her person was treated as sacred; she lived in a tower and spoke through an intermediary.

The revolt was led by a one-eyed general, Civilis, one of the men who had been arrested by Nero. Tacitus makes a point of saying that it was ritually declared in a sacred grove. This Druidic touch was either a Roman fiction or a symbolic artifice, as pollen research shows the area was hardly wooded. The link between the authority of Germano-Celtic 'sorceresses' and opposition to Rome was real enough. The Batavian soldiers who had been forced to overcome their reluctance and kill Druids for Rome[37] became Civilis' army.[38] Their rebellion spread rapidly, and it seemed certain that Rome would recognize the whole region of the Low Countries as independent. By AD 70 two Roman legions had been destroyed and two more were controlled by Civilis, whose authority extended to Cologne. The Roman commander was sent to Veleda as her slave, and she was presented with the flagship of the Roman navy as her barge.

Civilis, however, pressed on with his war, forcing the new emperor, Vespasian, to make the huge military effort needed to crush him and bring the region to heel. But Veleda was still in business as an arbitrator many years later, and Druids remained a focus for disaffection in Celtic regions.[39] Romanizing these people was not as easy as the Romans would have liked.

THE UNRULY BRITS

Instead of being the milch-cow Seneca had hoped for, Britain turned out to be a pain in the neck. It was a trouble spot. In Gaul, after the defeat of Vercingetorix, the natives settled to life under Roman control for a while, but their fellow Celts the British did not submit to Roman rule so easily. In fact, many of them never submitted at all, and Britain stayed less Romanized than Gaul. The fact that English is not a Romance language tells its own story. The Germanic people who eventually occupied France and Spain learnt to speak Latin; the Angles, Jutes and Saxons did not.

The island was never fully conquered, and it is a striking fact that in the second century all Britain's towns were given serious defensive walls, something that did not happen in Gaul. The tiny population created a permanent headache for the Roman super-power. In fact, to keep Britain Roman it took three full legions – a huge undertaking. By contrast, Spain was held by one legion, North Africa by two. Most of the inhabitants of Gaul would hardly ever have seen a legionary unless they lived near the Rhine, where there were four legions holding the frontier against the Germans. But to keep Britain Roman required a force of around 50,000 troops.

This was a huge standing army. No medieval king of England could afford more than a tenth of that number, and it became an ongoing drain on the Roman economy. The population of Britain was less than 5 per cent of that of the entire Empire, yet it took 10 per cent of the Empire's military strength to hold the island down. Most of the troops were concerned not with manning the northern wall, but with facing down the natives in occupied territory.[40]

Strabo had doubted that the financial benefit from occupying Britain could outweigh the cost, and even then he was only reckoning on one legion, not three. On top of their pay and their personal kit, the army needed huge quantities of food – especially wheat, which had to be imported for decades because Britain's original staple crop was barley (which makes a mash for beer and porridge, but was regarded by Romans as animal fodder). The army also needed vast numbers of animals. It has been calculated that each year the occupying forces in northern Britain alone needed 10,000 horses and 4000 mules, plus their fodder, as well as 12,000 calves to provide leather for tents and 2000 animals for sacrifices.[41]

It was all costing Rome an awful lot of money, and the only real financial beneficiaries seem to have been the 'barbarians' themselves – those leaders who were supplying and victualling this enormous force.[42] For Rome it was a pretty poor bargain. According to Appian of Alexandria, writing about AD 150, the Romans 'have occupied the better and greater part of it [Britain] but they do not care for the rest. For even the part they do occupy is not very profitable to them.'[43] So why *did* the Romans bother with this troublesome island?

One reason was silver: the Romans were getting a lot of it out of Britain. Within six years of the invasion of AD 43, the silver mines in the Mendip Hills near Bath were in full production, and by AD 70 Britain was the biggest supplier of silver to the Empire. Without British silver, the currency of Rome would have been dross. The lead from which the silver was extracted was also important. Lead ingots have been found, again in the area of the Mendips, which were inscribed for the Emperor and for individual legions. The Romans used huge quantities of lead both for glazing pottery and for making glass. They also managed to ingest quite a lot of it. Even though they knew that lead was dangerous, they still used lead vessels to prepare a syrup to sweeten their wine, and for sweet delicacies and sauces. In fact, the Romans used so much lead that they produced widespread pollution. Samples from the Greenland icecap and the bogs and lakes of Sweden, Switzerland and Spain reveal a huge increase in lead pollution during the Roman period.[44]

Rome did not bring prosperity or much comfort to most of the peoples it conquered. It has been estimated that between Caesar's arrival in Gaul and the death of Augustus in AD 14 the population of the Empire fell by between five million and 15 million – despite the acquisition of new provinces, including Gaul. In Gaul, perhaps two million fell victim to the conquest, either killed or enslaved, and the population began a steady decline. Things were probably pretty similar in Britain. It has also been estimated that no more than one million out of the Empire's possible second-century population of 65 million lived above subsistence level.

Tacitus put a savage condemnation of the conquest into the mouth of one British leader. His words echo with a chill that transcends the centuries and reverberates today:

> Robbers of the world; having exhausted the land by their
> universal plunder, they rifle the deep. If their enemy is rich,
> they are rapacious; if he is poor, they lust for power; neither
> the east nor the west has been able to satisfy them. Alone
> among men they covet with equal eagerness poverty and
> riches. Robbery, slaughter and plunder they misname
> 'empire'; they make a wilderness and call it peace.[45]

IV
ROMANS ON TOP

The defeat of Boudica left the Romans in the driving seat. But they didn't take over the whole world – it just felt like that. In the second century AD the Emperor Hadrian realized that there would have to be limits to the Empire, and built his famous wall to mark one of the northern boundaries. Nor did the Celts disappear from history, even if that had been Rome's intention.

THE CELTS GO UNDERGROUND

Of course, Celtic culture was soon buried under the stones of new Roman cities – stone building was something that few of the Celts of northern Europe had bothered with. Roman colonists came and settled on Celtic lands, and set about converting into Romans those Celts who had survived the invasions. The Romans got them to dress properly. Druidic education was replaced with a Latin one. The newcomers instilled in them a respect for Roman laws, Roman culture and Roman art. Above all, the occupiers took full advantage of the enthusiasm with which the Celts turned themselves into willing consumers and taxpayers.[1]

If you had toured Gaul and southern Britain at the time of Hadrian, in the early second century AD, you would have formed the impression of a thoroughly Romanized world. The cities, run and developed by wealthy locals, contained streets on a rectangular grid pattern and imposing stone buildings, such as forums, baths and amphitheatres. Celts were offered Roman citizenship, so long as they had enough money and an urban residence – and who would refuse such an offer? It was as important for getting on in the world as a Party card was in the old Soviet Union. In the countryside the large farms of the old Celtic nobility were replaced by the villa farmhouses of the new men who had become rich serving Rome, in the expanding economy that was constantly stimulated by the purchasing power of the Roman army.

But in many ways it was all a veneer. It used to be argued that the Celts eagerly embraced Romanization and that the old Celtic identity more or less disappeared. Archaeologists pointed to the proliferation of Roman-type pottery and luxury goods. Given the chance, the Celts would have taken to McDonald's like ducks to water. Good heavens, the Celts even abandoned their old gods and started to worship Roman deities! That's how things used to be interpreted. Nowadays, however, historians are more cautious.[2]

For a start, the pottery tended to be dated by style, so it was assumed that 'native' pottery was earlier. Then, by circular argument, it was mooted that this demonstrated changes in native ways.[3] Besides, what was called 'Roman' pottery wasn't necessarily Roman at all – it was simply imported from neighbouring peoples who were under Roman control. European and American historians seem to have been disposed to believe in the success of Romanization because of an innate belief in the 'civilizing' effect of their own countries' conquests. So they asserted that the natives joined up to Roman religion once the Romans identified Celtic gods with Roman ones. According to Caesar they worshipped Mercury, Apollo, Mars, Jupiter and Minerva[4] – he just thought that they had the names wrong. But what actually happened was that the old gods lived on in disguise.

The Celtic deity Belenos, for example, masqueraded under the Latin title of Apollo Belenus, but his festivals were still celebrated by priests who claimed to be descended from the Druids. And the Druids continued to practise well into the second century AD, judging from a burial discovered outside the town of Brough in eastern England. Brough was a Roman town, its military fort had been turned into civilian buildings and it had a new theatre. Yet the burial was that of a Celtic priest, a Druid, with an iron-bound bucket and two sceptres, bent and broken as part of the burial ritual. 'Druid priestesses' were apparently around in third-century Gaul to issue a warning prophecy to Emperor Alexander Severus,[5] to be consulted by the Emperor Aurelian,[6] and to tell Diocletian that he would become emperor when he killed a boar.[7] The old Celtic gods still survived; they just adopted and adapted.

It was the same thing with people's names. One of the priests of Apollo Belenus, for example, went by the name of Attius Patera – a good Latin-sounding name, you might think (*patera* in Latin means 'flat bowl'). However, the poet Ausonius, who happened to know Attius Patera, explained that in Gallic *patera* meant 'an initiate'. So Celts were giving themselves and their children Roman-sounding names that were actually cover names for Celtic ones.[8]

Tacitus' father-in-law, Agricola, was Governor of Britain in AD 78–84. The historian describes how, under his relative's gentle guidance, the British were persuaded to adopt Roman dress, speak Latin and help in the building of Roman temples, public squares and 'good houses'. But he adds condescendingly, 'And so they were gradually led into demoralizing temptations of arcades, baths, and sumptuous banquets. The unsuspecting Britons spoke of these new habits as "civilization" [*humanitas*], when in fact they were only a feature of enslavement.'[9] 'Civilization', however, was something to which only privileged Celts could aspire. The sons of chiefs might hope to adopt the Roman way of life, but most Britons were untouched.

Celtic culture did not vanish from the face of the earth, then. Wherever the Romans had conquered, it just went undercover. It was the same throughout western Europe: Britons, Bretons, Gauls and Spaniards all kept the Celtic world alive and well. It changed, of course, as trade grew, and as Roman citizenship and the use of Latin spread, and the Roman roads began to stride across the countryside. But although Romans may have restructured the pattern of Celtic land routes so that all roads led to Rome, they couldn't restructure the sea. Britannia, Armorica (France north of the Loire) and Galicia in Spain still formed an Atlantic network of Celtic peoples that would keep going down the centuries.

But, for the vast majority, it was to be a rough ride.

THE EMPIRE NEEDS GROWTH

It comes as a bit of a shock to learn that the classical Mediterranean world was not the holiday-makers' paradise that most of us think of today. It was, on the contrary, a world forever on the edge of starvation.[10] Celtic towns were centres of trade and manufacture, part of the same economy as the farmers of the countryside. Roman towns, on the other hand, were centres of administration and home to the political elites who lived off the income of their official positions and their estates. Roman towns ruled the land around them and sucked in the produce of that land, enriching themselves at the expense of the rural population.

The great Greek doctor Galen, who lived in the second century AD, explained why malnutrition was so widespread in rural communities. It was, he said, all the fault of the rapacious townsmen: 'The city-dwellers, as was their practice, collected and stored enough corn for all the coming year immediately after the harvest. They carried off all the wheat, the barley, the beans and the lentils and left what remained to the country-folk.' Few Roman cities could supply their own needs; they had to ransack the countryside in order to keep their larders supplied. In this way, the 10 per cent of Romans who lived in the cities exploited the 90 per cent who lived outside.

The same sort of pattern was found in the expanding Roman Empire. Roman citizens within the borders of Italy could live exempt from much taxation – at the expense of provincials dwelling in the conquered territories. True, in Italy taxes were paid on growing crops in the public fields and raising cattle; there were harbour duties and revenues on mines, a sales tax (abolished by Caligula), a property tax, a tax on doors, and even a tax on being a bachelor. Nero actually went so far as to introduce a tax on urine, but that didn't prove too popular. But by far the largest part of the Empire's income came from the tribute imposed on the provincials. To collect these taxes the Romans employed tax farmers, called *publicani*. The right to collect these taxes was in itself a gold mine for whoever was lucky enough to swing the contract, so it became the habit for Rome to auction the position of tax-collector in each province every few years.

And of course the whole system was rife with corruption. So rife, in fact, that in the first century BC the Emperor Augustus abolished the tax farmers and handed responsibility for tax collecting to urban officials.[11] He also introduced a poll tax (a flat-rate tax on each adult) because in years when harvests were poor, the rich paid less land tax and sales tax, but the army still had to be paid. Since the troops took at least 70 per cent of the budget, there was a considerable shortfall. It was made up by raising the poll tax – bad news for the less well off.

So long as Rome was expanding, there was no great problem. The army paid for itself in captured land, captured booty and captured slaves to act as the cheapest of cheap labour. 'Slaves [*servi*] are so called because commanders generally sell the people they capture and thereby save [*servare*] them instead of killing them. The word for property in slaves [*mancipia*] is derived from the fact that they are captured from the enemy by force of arms [*manu capiuntur*].'[12]

Those slaves also provided a workforce on the land, which is what had released the manpower of Rome to become a permanent army.[13] So long as the Roman Empire kept expanding, it was self-enriching. But in Britain the economics started to go wrong: Strabo had thought that occupation there could not yield more income than it cost, and those costs were far higher than he had anticipated. And once expansion stopped in the third century, with a collapse in the supply of slaves, plunder and new land, the whole Empire became one giant taxation machine.

RUNAWAY INFLATION

That was when the pigeons began coming home to roost. Emperors tried to hold on to power by increasing military pay, then meeting the bill by minting 'silver' coins with less and less silver in them. By AD 250 they were 60 per cent bronze, and by 270 they were simply bronze coins washed in silver. So the coinage lost its value and prices soared. It is reckoned that shopping that cost 1 denarius in the second century cost 27 by the late third century,[14] and then rose to 150.[15]

In the third century, pressure on the frontiers demanded a revolution in Roman military organization: the size of the army was doubled and so were its costs. The Roman army now stood at 600,000 men – the largest single group of people the ancient world had ever witnessed, and a constant drain on the emperor's coffers.

But, of course, the emperor wasn't going to go short – it was the taxpayer who would have to do without. In the time of the Emperor Diocletian (ruled 284–305) the complaint was that 'there were more tax-collectors than taxpayers'.[16] Since money was now worthless, taxes were collected mostly in the form of goods and services.[17] Tax collecting became a system of requisition and forced labour.

Inflation, instead of being cured, became even worse. Diocletian specified that a pound of gold was worth 50,000 denarii, but the market rate deteriorated to 100,000 denarii per pound of gold by 307, 300,000 by 324, and an incredible 2.1 billion denarii to a pound of gold by the middle of the fourth century. And somehow, by that mysterious yet ineluctable law of human society, the rich got richer and the poor got poorer. By the fourth century the senatorial aristocracy was five times richer than that of the first century AD. Wealth seemed to drain out of the countryside and the pockets of the ordinary people working the land, and find its way, by mysterious channels and conduits, into the hands of the rich magnates.

The 'trickle-down effect' of wealth was just as much a myth then as it is now. Wealth inevitably siphoned up the social scale, not down, and it did so most spectacularly in Rome itself. A peasant would be lucky to see an annual income of five gold pieces. A merchant might enjoy 200. One of Diocletian's courtiers, on the other hand, could expect an annual income of around 1000 gold pieces, while a Roman senator might count on as much as 120,000. There was just no comparison.

It was evident that the Roman Empire was a pretty good arrangement for the rich, but for everyone else it stank. In 350 the land tax had tripled within living memory and accounted for one-third of a farmer's gross production. Little wonder that the population of Gaul seems to have fallen steadily, and that cities grew at the expense of the countryside. Fewer people, harder work – and as problems grew, the constraints on the freedom of the lesser folk grew ever more intolerable. It became illegal to leave your farm, or for a son to work at a different trade from his father. The poor got poorer, and were forced to pay taxes they couldn't afford, and looked back to a golden age when things hadn't been like that. The only legal option for an impoverished Gaul or Briton unable to meet his tax bill was to give up his mobility and land and put himself under the protection of some great landowner – to become in effect part of the landowner's property – in return for protection against the taxman.

In the fifth century a strenuous critic of his age, Salvian, pinpointed the tax-gatherers as an evil that foments more evil:

... the many are oppressed by the few, who regard public
exactions as their own peculiar right, who carry on private
traffic under the guise of collecting the taxes. And this is
done not only by nobles but by men of lowest rank; not by
judges only, but by judges' subordinates ... Is there anywhere
... where the substance of widows and orphans, nay even of
the saints, is not devoured by the chief citizens? ... None but
the great is secure from the devastations of these plundering
brigands, except those who are themselves robbers.[18]

When the elite of the old Celtic lands felt that things had become
intolerable, they looked to Britain for a solution. This was precisely
because Britain had never fully settled to Roman rule. The huge military force there was just what they needed.

This was a situation that went back to at least 196 AD, when the
Governor of Britain, Albinus, was acclaimed as emperor there by his
troops. He established himself in Lyons with the support of the large
landowners of Gaul and Spain, who were looking for stability in a
period of imperial breakdown after terrible plagues had killed perhaps
a quarter of the population. His military backing was so great that
Rome had, in effect, to reconquer western Europe.

Over the next century civil wars, a collapsing currency and a
falling population, almost certainly associated with further outbreaks
of plague (which killed Emperor Gothicus II in 270), steadily undermined the economy of Europe. From 235, over a period of 50 years,
49 men were proclaimed emperor by different groups of soldiers. We
know that at least 25 of them were killed, not counting the three who
committed suicide and one who seems to have been struck by lightning. In fact, apart from Gothicus, only one of them is known to have
died a natural death – Valerian, who held on to the job for seven years
and was safely locked away as a prisoner of the Persians when he
expired in 260.

For a few years the Empire effectively vanished from western
Europe. In 260 a Gallic governor, Postumus, backed by the Rhine
troops, established his own 'Gallic Empire', which extended to Britain
and Spain. He made no attempt to attack Rome; he was 'the restorer
of Gaul'. Rome eventually made a comeback and in 273 crushed this

breakaway Celtic empire, restoring its own power and taxes. But for a while it looked as though the Roman Empire was finished, and a confederation of Germans, calling themselves Franks ('Free People'), had crossed the Rhine and moved into the region occupied by modern Belgium. Rome was helpless to prevent them. The Franks were sea-going people, and quickly established effective control of the Channel. They are described as robbers and pirates; it seems likely that they were also supplying home-grown bandits, gangs of desperate people who had fled from, or been dispossessed from, land on which they could no longer afford to pay tax.

THE BREAKDOWN OF LAW

Sometimes these companies of warriors operated as mere brigands and highwaymen, robbing and killing as a way of life. Sometimes they acted as a direct challenge to Roman rule, organizing their own courts and putting entire armies into the field of battle. And, of course, there were lots of shades in between. Despite their various and contradictory natures, these gangs became known by a single name: Bagaudae. The Celtic word *baga* means 'war', and when combined with the suffix *-aud* gives 'warrior' or 'fighter', so it probably means 'fighters' (though there was clearly a strong Bagaudae presence in the Pyrenees, and the Basque word *baugaude* means 'we are ready').

There has been a huge learned debate over the identity and goals of the Bagaudae. At one time, when the fourteenth-century Jacqueries in France and the Peasants' Revolt in England were seen as the natural anarchic violence of ignorant rustics, the Bagaudae were taken as evidence of the local failure of necessary social control. Then Marxist historians claimed them as proto-Communist revolutionaries, ideologically led radicalized workers and peasants hoping to bring about an ideal society. More recent studies, which stress the importance of local elites in running everything, argue that the Bagaudae may often have been under the command of local aristocrats in areas where Roman rule had broken down, and that they were actually fighting to salvage the social order rather than to destroy or transform it.

All of these perspectives contain some element of truth, but none tells the whole story. Guerrilla movements are always complicated –

partly outraged risings by the poor and desperate, partly ideological rebellions by the well-educated radical young, partly tools whipped up by local politicians against more powerful enemies, and eventually (when the guerrillas have suffered military defeat, or their leaders have been co-opted back into the system) sheer murderous banditry.

Salvian was full of sympathy for the Bagaudae:

> ... who were despoiled, oppressed and murdered by evil and cruel judges. After they had lost the right of Roman citizenship, they also lost the honour of bearing the Roman name. We blame their misfortunes on themselves ... We call those outlaws whom we compelled to be criminal. For, by what other ways did they become Bagaudae, except by our wickedness, except by the wicked ways of judges, except by the proscription and pillage of those who have turned the assessments of public taxes into the benefit of their own gain and have made the tax levies their own booty?[19]

The Bagaudae first appear in the historical record in the 280s, when economic hardship and disillusionment with Rome had bitten deep into northern Gaul: 'Inexperienced farmers sought military garb; the ploughman imitated the infantryman, the shepherd the cavalryman, the rustic ravager of his own crops the barbarian enemy.'[20] It was the army's job to deal with this problem, and the local commander was Carausius, a Romanized Celt from a humble family of sailors in what is now the Netherlands. In 286 he successfully suppressed the uprising of the Bagaudae in Gaul.

BRITAIN'S EMPERORS

At this time the Emperor Diocletian divided the Empire into two: he ruled the Eastern Empire from Split (in modern Croatia) while Maximian ruled the Western Empire from Milan. Rome was too far from the action. Maximian then appointed Carausius as commander of the North Sea Fleet, based at Boulogne. His job was to rid the seas of the Frankish pirates who were infesting the Channel and harassing the shores of northern Gaul.

Carausius did his job – and more. Maximian began to suspect that he was allowing the pirates to sail down the Channel and raid in Britain or Gaul before intercepting them on the way home and, having done a deal with them, taking a percentage of the spoils. Carausius knew the Franks well – they lived in his own part of the world – and he may have been in cahoots with them. In the end Maximian ordered the death of his powerful fleet commander in the north. Carausius caught wind of the order, and, whether he had been previously planning a rebellion or not, now proclaimed himself emperor in his own right, and moved his entire operation to the safety of Britain. From there he became the *de facto* ruler of Britain and Gaul north of the Loire. Maximian launched a fleet to teach his upstart commander a lesson, but all the pilots with any knowledge of the Channel were in Carausius' pay, and that fact, combined with bad weather, wrecked Maximian's attempt to reassert control. He had to put up with the usurper for the moment.

Carausius was a Barbarian backed by Barbarians – Celts and Franks – but he wasn't a born-again Boudica. He was smart enough not to challenge the Empire, claiming instead that he was a third partner among the emperors. He even minted coins in London bearing the images of the three emperors and inscribed: 'Carausius and his brothers'. That probably went down like a lead balloon with Diocletian and Maximian, who must also have been pretty niggled by the fact that Carausius' coins were far superior to their own. The reduction of the silver content had made Roman coinage a bit of a joke, and although the Emperor Aurelian (ruled 270–5) had tried to reform the currency, he could only aspire to an alloy of at best 20 parts bronze to one part silver. Carausius started producing coins of gold and silver. The silver content was 90 per cent – a purity unknown since the days of Nero. At last someone was minting real money that you could trust.

Carausius knew a thing or two about propaganda, and he knew that his reputation with the army would be made by the distribution of such coins. Gold coins were not really used for everyday commerce – they were more like valuable tokens, often distributed as rewards to the armies. A high content of precious metal made them as valuable as a pension – not just a 'thanks for the memory' souvenir.

In the Roman world such coins conferred legitimacy on whoever issued them. Carausius had the gold and he used it to best effect. The coins he issued were all part of his inspired publicity drive. They made sure that his image was circulated widely – and so was his propaganda: the reverse of the coins featured slogans such as 'Restorer of the Romans'. The Romans minted coins showing Britannia as a woman; Carausius produced one depicting her welcoming him. It reads: 'Come, awaited one', and below that: 'RSR' – which is probably a reference to a line from the Roman poet Virgil meaning 'Return of Saturn's Rule', the Latin equivalent of the Dawning of the Age of Aquarius, with a couple of bonus connotations. The Roman treasury was kept in the Temple of Saturn, so 'Return of Saturn's Rule' could also mean a Golden Age in a very literal sense: 'We've got the gold.' In addition, the passage from Virgil goes on to say that 'the child will guide a world made peaceful by the virtues of his father', which Christians of course took to be a prophecy of their own religion. So Carausius was also connecting with highly literate and well-educated Christians without overtly challenging the imperial cult. The other common message on his coins is: 'Peace'.

Carausius may have been a Celt, but that didn't mean he wanted to replace Roman culture with Celtic. Far from it. He aspired to Roman-ness. For a start, he assumed a very Roman, non-Barbarian title. There is a milestone at Carlisle with the inscription 'IMP C M AVR MAVS CARAVSIO INVICTO AVG' – 'Emperor Caesar Marcus Aurelius Mausaeus Carausius the Invincible Augustus'. The only bit that he started life with was his Gallic name, Mausaeus – and even that was made to sound Latin.

It's all rather reminiscent of the Czech rebellion of 1968, when, at the height of Flower Power, Alexander Dubček introduced what he called Socialism with a Human Face, and thought that if he was tactful with the language, Moscow would not have any reason to send in the tanks. He was wrong, and Carausius' *Romanitas* with a Human Face was equally doomed, though it did last for more than ten years.

The core of Carausius' power was his control of the sea, based on well-defended harbours. But the Empire had endless resources – it just took time to gather them. In 293 Diocletian and Maximian did indeed expand the number of emperors, but to four rather than three, and Carausius wasn't on the list. It was at this moment that Carausius issued the infamous coins bearing the three emperors … If it was a conciliatory gesture it didn't work.

In the west Maximian was joined by Constantius Chlorus, who was ordered to bring the breakaway empire of Britain to heel. He captured Boulogne, and probably dismantled Carausius' reputation at the same time. At all events, Carausius was soon dead – most probably murdered on the orders of one of his officers, Allectus, who then took over as British Emperor. But not for long. In 297 Constantius landed his army in Britain. Allectus was killed and London seized.

However, the underlying problems had still not been addressed. Only ten years later, in 306, the legions in Britain again proclaimed their own emperor, who was immediately accepted in Gaul as the saviour of social order. He set up a regional government at Trier, close to the modern German border with Luxembourg. And this time when the ruler of Rome tried to crush the British-appointed ruler of the Celtic lands, it didn't work. The man in question, Constantine, captured Rome and ultimately took over the whole Empire.

ANTI-ROMAN ROMANS

Constantine was the first Christian emperor; his revolution took place in a Roman Empire that was now fundamentally changed from the way it was at the time of the conquest of Britain. For a start, it no longer had an army of Romans ruling and taming the 'other'. It looks as though during the reign of the first emperor, Augustus (27 BC–AD 14), 68 per cent of legionaries were of Italian origin, but this proportion fell steadily until, in the second century AD, only 2 per cent of citizen soldiers were of Italian origin. And the Empire's army also included large numbers of auxiliaries from the Goths of eastern Europe. The distinction between Roman and Barbarian at the time when Constantine assumed power was not at all clear.

The conversion of the Empire to Christianity did not alleviate the lot of the lowly farmer – far from it. Diocletian had introduced the policy of tying people to their land to safeguard the labour supply, while allowing landlords to tax the poor on behalf of the central government. Tenants were now *coloni*, and these *coloni* were owned by their landlords along with the land itself. So were their descendants. Like slaves, *coloni* had no right to sue their landlords and were forbidden to sell their own property without his permission. A compilation of the laws of the Christian emperors says: 'It is appropriate that those *coloni* who consider flight be bound by chains in the manner of a slave, so that they are compelled to perform duties which are appropriate to a free man while being punished like a slave.'[21] People with a trade or craft were bound to provide labour on a specified piece of land in perpetuity, and so were their children.

In such harsh conditions, revolt was endemic. In Britain, towns were decaying; the public buildings of Wroxeter, south of Chester, for instance, were used as grain stores, and there was a major breakdown of public order in the 360s. Although usually described as a huge attack by a 'barbarian conspiracy', it was probably more of a walk-out by Roman officers, since it was settled by 'a proclamation promising immunity to deserters who returned to the colours'.[22] Nevertheless, Britain was preferable to Gaul for the mega-rich, since it still possessed a standing army big enough to provide some assurance of safety. Many wealthy people seem to have fled Gaul in the fourth century and built vast villas in the British countryside.

Back in Gaul, which had once exported grain to the army in Britain, grain was now having to be supplied from the island.[23] The rural revolt became quite overtly anti-Roman. According to one writer in 362, people preferred to live under the Barbarians.[24]

Once more, the army in Britain was called on to rescue the rich men of Gaul. In 383 Magnus Maximus followed a very similar path to Constantine's, again coming out of Britain to take over western Europe as a paramilitary warlord and moving on to conquer Italy. Emperor Theodosius and his general Stilicho managed to destroy him, and the troops that Maximus had taken out of Britain never returned. Stilicho visited Britain to try to effect a peace settlement in northern Europe, but he too ended up withdrawing troops from the island.

Early in the fifth century impoverished Germanic migrants were pouring into Gaul in ever larger numbers, and with the countryside largely in the hands of guerrilla forces, it was time for Britain to supply yet another saviour to Gaul's wealthier citizens. Most of the legions were now gone, and local landowners were directly financing their own militias. The situation was similar in some ways to the present state of some Latin American countries, where in the absence of effective central government, right-wing paramilitaries battle left-wing guerrillas for control of parts of provinces.

The British set up a number of local warlords in quick succession before finally deciding on a soldier who may have been chosen partly because of his name – he was another Constantine. In 407 they sent him and what legionary troops they could muster across to Boulogne, where he quickly seized control of the local area and declared himself Emperor Constantine III.

He may have called himself emperor, but these people were no longer playing the Roman game.

> The barbarians above the Rhine, assaulting everything at
> their pleasure, reduced both the inhabitants of Britain and
> some of the Celtic peoples to defecting from Roman rule and
> living their own lives disassociated from the Roman law.
> Accordingly the Britons took up arms and, with no
> consideration of the danger to themselves, freed their own
> cities from barbarian threat; likewise all of Armorica [north-
> west France] and other Gallic provinces followed the Britons'
> lead: they freed themselves, ejected the Roman magistrates,
> and set up home rule at their own discretion.[25]

The Atlantic region broke away completely and became self-governing for good.

One example of the extent of the political and social change is the story of a woman called Melania, a Roman matron born about 383 who took up a life of Christian piety.[26] Around 410 she sold nearly all her property in order to donate the proceeds to monasticism. The exception was her property in Britain – probably because the island was now beyond the reach of the Roman system.[27]

The anti-Roman movement had taken over. In the fifth century we find Salvian holding up the Barbarians as a beacon to illuminate the corruption and inhumanity of Roman society and values: 'Almost all barbarians, at least those who are of one tribe under one king, love one another; almost all Romans persecute each other.'[28] Of course, they were still Barbarians and they still smelt. Even Salvian could not ignore 'the fetid odour of the barbarians' bodies and garments'.[29]

But many Gauls would put up with that, and even with living in communities of non-Catholics, rather than carry on living as Romans.

The state has fallen upon such evil days that a man cannot
be safe unless he is wicked ... the poor are plundered, the
widows sigh, the orphans are oppressed, until many of them,
born into distinguished families, and well educated, flee to
our enemies so that they do not have to endure public
persecution. They seek among the barbarians the dignity of
the Roman because they cannot bear barbarous indignity
among the Romans ... So they migrate to the Goths, or to
the Bagaudes, or to some other tribe of the barbarians who
are ruling everywhere, and do not regret their exile. They
prefer to live as freemen under an outward form of captivity
than as captives under an appearance of liberty. Therefore,
the name of Roman citizens, at one time not only greatly
valued but dearly bought, is now repudiated and fled from,
and it is almost considered not only base but even deserving
of abhorrence.[30]

The rejection of Rome was the basis of the development of a new
western European world, but it was constructed to some extent on the
surviving memories of the world that Rome had tried so hard to
replace, the world of the Celtic 'barbarians'. A view is now emerging
from historians that to consider 'Roman' a synonym of 'normal' for
Gaul at any period is simply wrong, and that the Empire's loss of Gaul
was Gaul's gain because it could return to its normal state.[31]

In Britain the shrugging off of *Romanitas* seems even clearer. In
the sixth century Britain adopted law codes that were not Latin (unlike
the Goth and Vandal codes in southern Gaul and Spain), its urban
system collapsed, the tax system vanished, and while Gaul and Italy
continued with a Christianity based on bishops, in Britain even bishops faded away and Christianity became monastic.

The world of the Druids had been destroyed and would not be
revived. But the power of Rome was so much more brutal, more inhuman, more oppressive that it would not need an invasion to get rid of
it. It withered because it was so hated by the people who had to
endure it. And because most of them saw no point to it any more.

PART II

BARBARIANS FROM THE NORTH

V
THE GERMANS

One of the favourite entertainments among the German Barbarians was the equivalent of the Scottish sword dance – although it seems to have had more of an edge to it, if you'll forgive the pun. The dance involved both swords and lances and was apparently capable of proving fatal. Perhaps the spectators held the swords at different heights, or brandished them as if in battle, while the dancers wove in and out of them? We don't know. All we have is a tantalizing description left to us by Tacitus: 'One and the same kind of spectacle is always exhibited at every gathering. Naked youths who practise the sport bound in the dance amid swords and lances that threaten their lives. Experience gives them skill and skill again gives grace … '

But although the danger to life obviously stuck in his mind, the thing that really impressed Tacitus was the fact that the dancers took part for the sheer fun of it – they didn't expect to be paid! 'Profit or pay are out of the question; however reckless their pastime, its reward is the pleasure of the spectators.'¹ The Germans just had no interest in money, according to Tacitus. They did not practise usury. They obtained amber but placed no value on it themselves, and when they got good money for it they 'receive a price with wonder'. By the time Tacitus was writing, Rome was a thoroughly commercialized society and the profit motive drove many of its wheels. German culture, on the other hand, seemed to him to be still possessed by primitive forces such as honour, fidelity, bravery and sometimes simply *joie de vivre*!

THE PROTO-EUROPEANS

These apparently simple, happy folk are arguably the most important of all the 'barbarian' groups in terms of the eventual emergence of a European civilization that would dominate the globe. They are more important even than Rome. The Goths, a late Roman name for them, ended up taking over the Western Empire (see Chapter VIII), and France (Francia), Germany (Alemannia) and England (Anglia) all trace their heritage to German peoples – the Franks, Alemanni and Anglo-Saxons.

But if the word 'Celtic' has been treated with suspicion by historians, they should be even more wary of 'German'. So far as we know, there were no people in the ancient world who called themselves that – it's a word that comes from Roman and Greek writers. The word appears much later than *Keltoi* (Celts); the first person to use the word *Germani* is Poseidonius, a Greek historian, in 100 BC.[2] It may be a corruption of an early German word, *Gaizamannoz* ('spear-men'), used as a name by one community.

It seems clear that around 500 BC the area of north-west Germany and southern Scandinavia was inhabited by people with a common lifestyle, root language and mythology (a mythology best known to us through the Norse sagas), who were spreading southwards. The Italians first became aware of them in 113 BC, when people called the Cimbri and Teutones moved down into the area of Austria. Ten years later they arrived in Italy asking for somewhere to settle. These huge, half-naked warriors inflicted a massive defeat on the Roman army before being completely crushed themselves.

The first real attempt at describing the Germans comes from Caesar, by which time they were moving into western Gaul in significant numbers. It's clear that Caesar only knew about the Germans living close to the Rhine, and his sources of wider information were distinctly dubious. It's from them that he got the story of the elk with no knees, as well as his account of a unicorn in the German forests – a unicorn whose horn blossoms at the tip into spread antlers. It's like no unicorn you've ever seen.

The only other significant Roman source is the historian Tacitus, whose fascinating little book *Germania* reads as though he had been

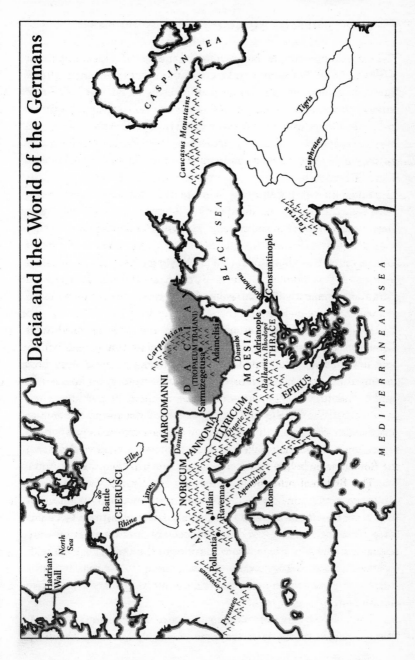

Dacia and the World of the Germans

there. He hadn't: it seems to be based on a work by Pliny – who really did go and do the research – which has been lost. Of course the Germans were much better known by Tacitus' day, a century after Caesar, and he is less interested in showing how savage they are than in holding them up as examples of indigenous natural morality to contrast with sophisticated Roman corruption.

It's quite clear that the people living in north-west Germany were very different from the Celts. The Roman descriptions of them tend to be highly generalized caricatures, but they do contain a kernel of truth. The Germans lived in small, independent settlements that depended on keeping livestock and hunting, rather than on farming. There was not much plunder here for Rome (though the Latin word for money – *pecunia* – comes from *pecus*, cattle).

A DIFFERENT VALUE SYSTEM

The Romans were a little baffled by a society that was so uninterested in wealth, and this lack of interest in profit even extended on to the field of battle. The Roman soldier fought on a salary; his generals displayed their wealth and status by fine living and the exercise of life-and-death power over their troops. Things were completely different among the Germans. A leader displayed his position by his courage, and his wealth by his generosity at feasts and entertainments.

This was a warrior culture in which valour and the esteem of one's peers had more meaning than the accumulation of wealth. Young men, once they reached the age of maturity, did not cut their hair or beards until they had killed their first enemy in battle. And in battle, according to Tacitus, the spur to bravery was the approval or disapproval of one's kinsmen: 'What most stimulates their courage is that their squadrons or battalions, instead of being formed by chance or by a fortuitous gathering, are composed of families and clans.'[3] He explained that this was all about loyalty to the chief: 'To defend, to protect him, to ascribe one's own brave deeds to his renown, is the height of loyalty. The chief fights for victory; his vassals fight for their chief.'

And with loyalty went courage – the courage of peer group pressure. This led the Germans into rather foolhardy habits: ' ... according to their practice, nothing is regarded as more unseemly, or more unmanly, than to use horse armour. Accordingly, no matter how few they may be, they will advance courageously against any number whatever of horse protected by armour.'[4] It was not only their horses that went naked into battle. So did they. When they fought fully protected Romans, their only defence was a wooden or wicker shield.

The German attitude to warfare was chaotic and individualistic compared to the cold professionalism and disciplined planning of the Romans. 'Their view of war seems to have been sporting, in some aspects almost gentlemanly, and the warfare of the time was waged with the spirit and devotion of professionals, but with tactics which did not rise above the amateur.'[5] For the Germans, warfare was dominated by the display of courage rather than the desire for material gain or political advancement.

It's easy to see the link between the German attitude to warfare and the chivalric codes of the Middle Ages. For example, the medieval concept of choosing two heroes from opposing sides to decide the outcome of a battle in single combat has its roots back in the Barbarian wars against Rome. 'Having taken, by whatever means, a prisoner from the tribe with whom they are at war, they pit him against a picked man of their own tribe, each combatant using the weapons of their country. The victory of the one or the other is accepted as an indication of the issue.'[6]

They had no military organization; war was entirely a game of personal heroics. However, they didn't sound particularly dangerous, especially as their weapons were rubbish. 'Even iron is not plentiful with them,' says Tacitus, 'as we infer from the character of their weapons. But few use swords or long lances. They carry a spear (*framea* is their name for it), with a narrow and short head, but so sharp and easy to wield that the same weapon serves, according to circumstances, for close or distant conflict.'[7]

Even when the Germans captured superior equipment from the Romans, they didn't necessarily use it themselves in battle. The archaeological evidence shows that they tended to smash it and then throw it into a bog as an offering to the gods. The Germans 'stood in the same technical relationship to the Roman army as the hosts of Matabele and Zulu to the nineteenth-century armies of Britain'.[8] And even then their lances were often no more than a pointed stick with a sharpened end hardened in fire.

Of course, Tacitus was exaggerating the admirable qualities of the Germans in order to castigate the Roman morals of his own day. But when he describes the structure of Germanic social institutions his account is borne out by other evidence.

GERMAN EGALITARIANISM

Tacitus' picture of a remarkably egalitarian German society is supported by the archaeological evidence. Few German settlements of his day have been uncovered in which a single dwelling dominates – the buildings all seem to be very much the same size. It is only after Tacitus' day, when contact with the Romans had been prolonged, that individuals start accumulating wealth and marking themselves off from the rest of the clan by superior living quarters.

Similarly, there was little private ownership of land. According to Caesar, each year the clan leaders would dole out land among the various families, and then the following year would totally redistribute it to different people. He offers several reasons for this. In the first place, he suggests, it might be to stop families getting too attached to the land and becoming keener on agriculture than on fighting. But the main reason, he feels, is the pursuit of a more equal society. They keep the land moving around amongst the families of the clan in order to stop individuals trying 'to acquire extensive estates'; if they did, the more powerful would 'drive the weaker from their possessions'. Constant reallocation of resources also prevents 'the desire of wealth' from springing up, 'from which cause divisions and discords arise', and in this way they 'keep the common people in a contented state of mind, when each sees his own means placed on an equality with [those of] the most powerful.'[9]

Mark you, Caesar was a fine one to talk about equality in society!

Romans saw society in terms of two kinds of people: free men and slaves. But that is a property-based relationship. Among the Germans, people were not bought and sold, but owed duties, and that was something as baffling to the Romans of those times as wearing trousers.

The master is not distinguished from the slave by being
brought up with greater delicacy. Both live amid the same
flocks and lie on the same ground till the freeborn are
distinguished by age and recognized by merit ... The other
slaves are not employed after our manner with distinct
domestic duties assigned to them, but each one has the
management of a house and home of his own. The master
requires from the slave a certain quantity of grain, of cattle,
and of clothing, as he would from a tenant, and this is the
limit of subjection.[10]

Above all, this egalitarianism was reflected in German political institutions. The basis of political power lay in the folk-moot, at which,
according to Tacitus, minor matters were discussed by the chiefs but
the major decisions were put to the entire assembly. 'Yet even when
the final decision rests with the people, the affair is always thoroughly
discussed by the chiefs.'[11]

He goes on to explain that the independence and freedom of the
people make it very difficult to get everyone to agree to meet at the
same time, so a meeting can take up to three days to get started. Once
it does, however, it is the priests who are in charge. They call for
silence, and then the king or chief is usually the first to speak, but he
is heard 'more because he has influence to persuade than because he
has power to command'. And there is, apparently, no Roman-style
fawning or flattery in a German folk-moot. The hearers are at liberty
to show what they think of a leader's speech: 'If his sentiments
displease them, they reject them with murmurs; if they are satisfied,
they brandish their spears.'[12]

And it is this liberty of the people and the strictly limited powers
available to their leaders that makes the sharpest contrast between
Germanic society and Roman. The performance of kings and leaders
in battle had to be by example, and the powers to coerce were entirely
vested in the priesthood.

These kings have not unlimited or arbitrary power, and the
generals do more by example than by authority. If they are
energetic, if they are conspicuous, if they fight in the front,

they lead because they are admired. But to reprimand, to imprison, even to flog, is permitted to the priests alone, and that not as a punishment, or at the general's bidding, but, as it were, by the mandate of the god whom they believe to inspire the warrior.[13]

THE POVERTY OF THE GERMANS

Caesar was adamant that there was no comparison between the standard of living of the Germans and that of the Gauls: 'Neither must the land of Gaul be compared with the land of the Germans, nor must the habit of living of the latter be put on a level with that of the former'.[14] Of course, he had good reason for distinguishing clearly between Gauls and Germans, and for building up the image of the Rhine as a real dividing line (which it wasn't). That was how he justified his invasion of Gaul. The Gauls were obviously no threat to Rome, but he wanted people to think of the Germans as very different, savage and dangerous. In fact, the Romans had a duty to protect Gaul from them! 'These wild and savage men had become enamoured of the lands and the refinement and the abundance of the Gauls, more were brought over, and there were now as many as 120,000 of them in Gaul.'[15]

Having little in the way of possessions (a fact that is clear from archaeology as well as from the Roman writers), they were highly mobile. It was not hard for Caesar to build up the threat from which he needed to defend Rome by 'protecting' Gaul.

> Caesar saw it would be dangerous to the Roman people if
> the Germans became accustomed to crossing the Rhine, and
> a great body of them should occupy Gaul. He reckoned that if
> such wild and savage people took over the whole of Gaul,
> they would not feel constrained from then invading the
> Province and thence marching into Italy itself (as the Cimbri
> and Teutones had done before).[16]

Tacitus remarked that Germany contained no town-like settlements, but only isolated and scattered habitations, and the buildings tended to be unremarkable. They did keep cattle, but according to Caesar they were 'poor and ill-shaped' and used as draught animals. The children in every household grew up naked and filthy which, claimed Tacitus, endowed them with 'those stout frames and limbs which we so much admire'.

They dressed in cloaks and, if they were well off, trousers – a form of dress that seemed very odd to Tacitus – 'a dress which is not flowing like that of the Sarmatians and Parthians [Easterners who wore baggy pants], but is tight, and exhibits each limb'. He also noticed that the more contact they had with the Romans, the less care they took over their clothing. 'They also wear the skins of wild beasts; the tribes on the Rhine and Danube in a careless fashion, those of the interior with more elegance, as not obtaining other clothing by commerce.'

This sounds rather like indigenous people today, wearing traditional dress until T-shirts and baseball caps start appearing. And, as with modern indigenous people, he describes them learning the value of money for the first time.

> I would not, however, affirm that no vein of German soil
> produces gold or silver, for who has ever made a search?
> They care but little to possess or use them. You may see
> among them vessels of silver, which have been presented to
> their envoys and chieftains, held as cheap as those of clay.
> The border population, however, value gold and silver for
> their commercial utility, and are familiar with, and show
> preference for, some of our coins.[17]

But although there was no money to be made out of them, the Germans had to be taken seriously as the most dangerous of foes. Eventually the words 'barbarian' and 'German' would become synonyms in the West.

HERMANN THE GERMAN

Hermann (whom we shall in future call Arminius) was a young prince of the Cherusci clan, who inhabited an area of Germany around present-day Hanover. For a great national hero he has one major drawback – nobody knows his real name. In the classical sources he is called

Arminius, but that's a Roman name – probably a Latin attempt at his Cheruscan one. The Germans, from the time of Luther on, decided to call him Hermann, but that's based on a mistaken etymology for Arminius. One guess is that he might have been called Erminameraz, but since that's no more than a guess, we'll stick to the name by which he was known to the Romans.

Arminius was adopted as a hero by nineteenth-century German nationalists because he is one of the first identifiable (and likeable) German leaders who scored a military success against the Romans. He is also a prime example of the sort of own goal the Romans started scoring once they relied on training Barbarians to do their fighting for them. Because Arminius was a Roman soldier.

After the Roman conquest of Gaul in the mid-first century BC, the raids and incursions by Germans from across the Rhine became a nuisance, conceivably threatening, and Augustus thought it should not be difficult to civilize them. They were, after all, simple hut-dwelling savages without any organization to speak of. 'Germania' was a huge area – in Roman geography it stretched to the Danube in the south and from the Netherlands to western Russia further north – but the theory was that to create a new Roman province there, to be called Germania Magna, did not really involve a military conquest at all.

The advantages of Roman civilization were so obvious that it could all be done by a little bit of force and a lot of flattery and bribery. In 12 BC an army crossed the Rhine, fought a few skirmishes, did deals with local leaders and three years later was safely on the Elbe. There was obviously no money to be made out of the Germans, but once they had been brought to heel they could certainly provide some useful military manpower. In fact, Augustus recruited his own personal mounted bodyguard from a German community on the lower Rhine, the Batavians, because they were totally fearless and, once they had sworn personal loyalty, they could be trusted more than any Romans.

The Roman army had once been composed of upper-class Romans doing their civic duty, but it was now a fully professional force, a large part of which was no longer Roman at all. Auxiliary troops had always been a necessary supplement to the legions, but hitherto they had mostly been recruited from allied cities within Italy.

Barbarians and Romans – the first encounter (see page 17)
According to the historian Livy, Brennus' Celts entered Rome and found the patricians seated like statues. The simple Barbarians stared at them dumbfounded, until one stroked Marcus Papirius' beard, whereupon the Roman hit him with his staff. Detail from Paul Jamin, *The Sack of Rome by the Gauls in 390 BC*, late nineteenth century.

The 'Corlea trackway' (see page 30)
Built across an Irish bog in 148 BC, it was 1¼ miles long and about 12 feet wide. It is estimated to have involved the cutting of some 500 trees, to make an oak plank road on a birch substructure fastened by some 5000 pegs. The ninth-century Irish saga *The Wooing of Etain* includes an account of the making of just such a road.

Celtic mathematics (see page 34)
This Gallic calendar, made between
AD 50 and 150, is evidently copied
from an original dating to the first
century BC and was probably part of a
temple complex. A fragment of a
similar calendar was found in Jura in
1807, also linked to a temple. It
appears that the calendar was
eventually carefully broken and the
pieces distributed to different people.

Romantic Barbarians (see page 26)
This life-sized marble Dying Gaul,
now in the Capitoline Museum in
Rome, is a Roman copy of a Greek
original, probably bronze, that was
part of a large victory monument
created around 230 BC on the
acropolis at Pergamon in modern
Turkey. Although the figure is
obviously a Gaul wearing a torque, it
was assumed in the nineteenth
century to be a Roman gladiator.

Gallic machinery (see page 36)
This fragment of a tombstone, dating from around AD 240, was found in 1958, embedded in medieval ramparts in the Ardennes in northern France. It provides concrete evidence of the Gallic harvesting machine described by Pliny, although this one seems to be being pushed by a mule rather than by oxen.

France's homage to Vercingetorix (see page 21)
The statue at Alesia, over 20 feet tall, was erected in 1865 at the commission of Napoleon III, and the face appears to be modelled on his own. It is inscribed with Caesar's 'quotation' from Vercingetorix, slightly adapted – 'Gaul united, Forming a single nation, Inspired by a shared spirit, Can defy the world'. In 1870 Napoleon III led France to defeat by Germany.

The Gauls' antique tradition (see page 41)
Four copies of this gold 'stater' have survived; it was struck shortly before Vercingetorix's defeat. One was sold in 1997 for approximately £40,000. In the tradition of Gallic coins, the image is based on the head of the young Apollo on the gold staters of Philip II of Macedon, 300 years earlier. It represents power, wealth and a high level of sophistication.

Britannia's hidden wealth (see page 59)
The Snettisham treasure is a careful deposit of torques, coins, and metal ingots bent to form bracelets. In all there was a total weight of 65 lb, much of it gold and silver. The coins date to about 70 BC, but the enclosure ditch surrounding them contains pottery of the period of Nero – and so of Boudica.

Britannia, the new future (see page 81)
A silver denarius of Carausius showing Britannia (with a trident) clasping his hand saying 'Expectate Veni' – 'Come, awaited one'. This may be from a passage in Virgil's *Aeneid*, where Hector, the slain Trojan hero, returns as a ghost and, in effect, instructs Aeneas to create the new city of Rome. Carausius is evidently now passing that responsibility on to Britannia!

The missing dead (see page 105)
This tombstone, found in Xanten (on the Rhine), shows a centurion with his two freedmen. It says: 'To Marcus Caelius, son of Titus, of the Lemonia district, from Bologna, First Centurion of the 18th Legion, aged 53½. He fell in Varus' war. His bones may be interred here. Set up by his brother Aelius, son of Titus of the Lemonia.' His bones were presumably never identified.

Rome's Barbarian soldiers (see page 97)
A German auxiliary fighting alongside
Roman legionaries, from Trajan's Column.
The Romans wear armour and helmets, apart
from a central figure with a sling and lead shot
– this had a range of 300 yards, so armour was
unnecessary. The German auxiliary (wearing
tight trousers), however, fights half-naked at
close quarters, using a small wooden shield
and a club.

**Germany's homage to Arminius
(see page 96)**
Arminius' monument, the Hermannsdenkmal,
was consecrated by Kaiser Willhelm I in 1875,
shortly after the defeat of France and the
creation of a unified German Empire. It is much
bigger than Vercingetorix's statue (it stands over
175 feet high) and boasts a winged helmet. The
huge sword is engraved 'Germany's Unity is my
Strength – My Strength is Germany's Unity'.

The Roman frontier (see page 127)
Rome's border with the Germans, the *Limes*, was a line of demarcation rather than a fortification, defined by a rampart and ditch, some stone walling, watch-towers and forts. Ignoring the topography of the land, the central sector runs dead straight for 50 miles.

Killing Dacians (see page 126)
Trajan's Column is 125 feet high, and the story of his conquest of Dacia is told in a spiral of story-telling over 656 feet long. This scene, over half-way up, is quite typical – Roman soldiers are industriously killing the natives, whose attempts to defend themselves are hopeless and pose no threat at all. The Romans should be holding metal weapons, but it seems the fixing-points for them were never drilled.

**Looting Dacia
(see page 124)**
This image, almost at the very top of the Column, shows loot being carted off in the form of precious vessels that have been loaded on to a donkey. It hardly does justice to the many tons of treasure that Trajan collected, but it seems he was less interested in celebrating his war as one of plunder than in stressing the splendid slaughter he inflicted.

Trajan's Forum (see page 125)
The modern ruins convey a romantic confusion very different from the original look of the Forum – a complex of libraries, a court and public spaces. Imported coloured marble emphasized imperial power and wealth, and the entire Forum celebrated Trajan's heroic life and his divinity.

Now auxiliaries were raised from the 'barbarian' population of the provinces. What's more, after 25 years of service they could even become Roman citizens.

The ranks of soldiery swelled to perhaps 250,000 or 300,000, which enabled the army to cope with the widening borders of Roman influence. But, at the same time, it meant that the Romans were diligently training, equipping and assimilating the very Barbarians they were trying to keep at bay. It's not surprising that some Barbarians took advantage of their Roman acculturation and tutoring. They included Arminius – Hermann the German.

His family's home must have become part of 'Germania Magna' when he was a small child. His people were induced to send their young warriors into the army, and there he served for five years, along with his brother Flavus, probably from AD 1 to 6. The hand-outs on offer to Rome's new German subjects were huge. As a leader's son, he was a prime candidate for special treatment; we are told he had the rank of *equites*, 'Sir Arminius', which meant that the emperor must have granted him Roman citizenship and property in Italy worth at least 400,000 sesterces – nearly 900 lb of silver. That would yield an annual rent of 20,000 sesterces – 20 times the pay of a legionary. It's amazing what a high-born young Barbarian could do in those days.

And the new Roman province was coming along nicely. Historians used to believe that the province of Germania Magna was little more than a fantasy in Augustus' mind, but in 1997 a Roman town – a real civilian town, that is, not a military camp – was discovered east of the Rhine, about 30 miles north of Frankfurt at Waldgirmes. At its heart were a basilica and a forum with a gold-plated equestrian statue, presumably of Augustus. The finds suggest that very upper-class Romans were living there alongside Germans, which indicates that the new province must have been up and running.[18]

Arminius' brother bought into the Roman system lock, stock and two smoking barrels (if you'll forgive the anachronism). Flavus remained a career officer in the Roman army, but Arminius didn't. He learnt all he needed to know about Roman military techniques, arms and organization, and (perhaps just as importantly) how the army responded to different forms of attack, and then hot-footed it back to his own people. Of course, he remained very polite to the Romans, and spoke Latin and knew all the right things to say, but he never forgot his Cheruscan upbringing.

By a wonderful stroke of good luck another Roman soldier, who fought in a number of campaigns in Germany around this time, later wrote about his experiences. Velleius Paterculus served in Tiberius' army in Pannonia in AD 6 and, since it is likely that Arminius did too, Velleius quite possibly knew him personally. Despite the fact that the man became an enemy – and a successful one at that – Velleius paints him in glowing colours: 'A young man of noble birth, brave in action and alert in mind, possessing an intelligence quite beyond the ordinary barbarian; he ... showed in his countenance and in his eyes the fire of the mind within.'[19] The historian Tacitus, writing some 40 years later, recognized that Arminius had put his Roman training to good use: 'The old German unsystematic battle-order and chaotic charges were things of the past. Their long wars against Rome had taught them to follow the standards, keep troops in reserve, and obey commands.'[20]

Velleius Paterculus also seems to have been well aware of the threat posed by Roman-trained Barbarians such as Arminius. The most dangerous of all the Germanic peoples, he claims, were the Marcomanni in central Germany, led by their charismatic and ambitious king Maroboduus. Maroboduus too had learnt his military craft in Rome, and that was what made him so much to be feared: 'The body of guards protecting the kingdom of Maroboduus, which by constant drill had been brought almost to the Roman standard of discipline, soon placed him in a position of power that was dreaded even by our empire.'[21]

Velleius Paterculus tells us that he had the honour of accompanying the great Tiberius in the military advance that created Germania Magna. The Roman troops swept through Germany, crossed the river Weser, and penetrated an unbelievable 400 miles beyond the Rhine to liaise with the fleet on the river Elbe. The fleet itself had sailed 'from a sea hitherto unheard of and unknown'. Such great deeds!

By AD 8, nothing else was left to conquer except for Maroboduus and his Marcomanni, and they had securely staked out a new territory for themselves in Bohemia. Otherwise Rome was now master of Germany, and all that remained was to impose some good old Roman law and order and to get the natives paying their taxes.

But it wasn't to be like that. Not at all. Terrible things were in store.

GERMANS 3 ROMANS 0

Germany had always held a horrible fascination for Roman writers. They saw it as a dark and treacherous land of bog and forest – a wild and savage place. 'The North Sea is the roughest in the world and the German climate the worst,' wrote Tacitus.[22] And in Roman eyes the people were much the same: 'The Germans ... with their great ferocity combine great craft, to an extent scarcely credible to one who has had no experience with them, and are a race to lying born ... '[23] These were Barbarians for the connoisseur.

Which is how they came to dupe an innocent Roman administrator by the name of Publius Quintilius Varus. Varus had been appointed governor of Germania in AD 7, with the aim of imposing law and order and extracting the usual taxes. Fifteen years of peace had led Augustus to overestimate the extent to which the people of Germania had accepted their new status. Varus was to provide Arminius with his great chance for fame. Not a nice man, Varus 'was born of a noble rather than illustrious family. He was of a mild disposition, of sedate manners, and being somewhat indolent as well, in body as in mind, was more accustomed to ease in a camp than to action in the field.'[24] Varus had been Governor of Syria just after the death of Herod the Great, and there he had apparently lined his own pockets. 'He entered the rich province a poor man, but left it a rich man and the province poor,' says Velleius Paterculus. Tish! An epigram for a soldier-turned-historian to be proud of!

As a patrician and plutocrat, Varus was well aware that the Barbarians of Germany were scarcely human – 'men only in limbs and voice' – but he assumed that they had grasped the idea of licking Roman boots gratefully. He therefore 'entered the heart of Germany as though he were going among a people enjoying the blessings of peace, and sitting on his tribunal he wasted the time of a summer campaign in holding court and observing the proper details of legal procedure'.[25] He also assumed he could treat the Germans as the inferiors they clearly were, and a later historian, writing with hindsight, declared that this arrogance sowed the seeds of his own destruction: 'He not only gave orders to the Germans as if they were actual slaves of the Romans, but also levied money from them as if they were subject nations. These were demands they would not tolerate.'[26]

Another Roman historian of the early second century AD is even tougher on his character, and says that the Germans 'began to detest the licentiousness and pride not less than the cruelty of Quintilius Varus'.[27] That rings true, especially when you consider that this was the man who, in the course of putting down a revolt in Judea, had burnt the town of Emmaus and crucified 2000 Jews.[28] When it came to institutionalized cruelty on an industrial scale, the Romans could teach the Barbarians a thing or two.

But there can be no doubt that the Germans well and truly pulled the wool over Varus' eyes. According to Velleius, they put on a wonderful show for the governor's benefit, entering into fictitious lawsuits in order to keep Varus busy in the courts. And when he diligently sorted out the cases to everyone's apparent satisfaction, they 'expressed their gratitude that Roman justice was settling these disputes, that their own barbarous nature was being softened down by this new and hitherto unknown method, and that quarrels which were usually settled by arms were now being ended by law'.[29]

Whoever was behind this stratagem – and it could have been Arminius himself – it worked a treat. Varus, not in the safe zone of Waldgirmes but further to the east, was being lulled into a false sense of security. He came to look upon himself as a city magistrate 'administering justice in the forum, and not a general in command of an army in the heart of Germany'.

To make matters worse, he had even been tipped off by one of the other Cheruscan chiefs that he was being taken for a ride. The traitor was a man by the name of Segestes, who had long since decided to throw in his lot with the Romans. A remarkably loyal collaborator, he had been rewarded with Roman citizenship by Augustus. Presumably he was on the receiving end of other substantial kick-backs as well because he was adamantly opposed to the whole idea of rebellion against the Romans.

Segestes warned Varus that, no matter how friendly and compliant his fellow Cheruscans appeared, they were actually plotting his downfall. During a feast shortly before the uprising, Segestes even suggested that the Roman governor should arrest Arminius and the other Cheruscan leaders – including himself (presumably to allay suspicion) – 'on the grounds that their removal would immobilize their accomplices and Varus could then take his time in sorting out the guilty from the innocent'.[30] But the man wouldn't listen: 'Fate now dominated the plans of Varus and had blindfolded the eyes of his mind ... And so Quintilius [Varus] refused to believe the story, and insisted upon judging the apparent friendship of the Germans by the standard of his merit,' writes Velleius Paterculus, adding darkly: 'And, after this warning, there was no time left for a second.'[31]

When news of an uprising in the north came to Varus' attention he set out with his three crack legions to teach the rebels a lesson. But the uprising was just a ruse. As the Roman governor proudly marched his men through the dense forests of the upper Weser river basin, Arminius ambushed them. The site of the battle lay hidden from archae-ologists until 1989 because for generations they assumed that it must have been a guerrilla attack in a forest, with wild men leaping out of the trees on to the unsuspecting legion-aries. In fact, this was a planned battle on a large and complex battlefield, with fortified posi-tions that the Germans had prepared in advance.

'Barbarian' didn't mean wild and simple. Arminius had learnt Roman strategy and battle tactics, and persuaded his warriors to act in a planned, coordinated way rather than to rely on the usual individual acts of rash heroism. The result was stunning. Three legions, with their general and all their officers and auxiliary forces, together with the general staff, were massacred almost to a man by Arminius' Barbarians: 'An army unexcelled in bravery, the first of Roman armies in discipline, in energy, and in experience in the field, through the negligence of its general, the perfidy of the enemy, and the unkindness of fortune ... was exterminated almost to a man by the very enemy whom it had always slaughtered like cattle ... '[32]

Of course it was all right for the Romans to slaughter their enemy 'like cattle', but for the Barbarians to do the same to the Romans was unnatural and profoundly shocking. The Romans were being given a taste of their own medicine by a man they had trained and educated. It was a humiliation they would never forget, and for centuries Romans reviled the name of Varus. Overwhelmed by the enormity of the catastrophe for which he was responsible, he did the decent thing (in Roman eyes): he committed suicide. His partially burnt body was 'mangled by the enemy in their barbarity; his head was cut off and taken to Maroboduus' who sent it to Augustus.[33]

Writing some 40 years later, Tacitus had no doubt that the disaster checked Roman ambitions in Germany, and the archaeological evidence supports him. From this year, Waldgirmes and all the forts east of the Rhine disappeared.[34] The Roman historian also makes it quite clear that Rome's objective was the enslavement of the world, and he admires the Germans who resisted: 'It was beyond question that the annihilation of Quintilius Varus had saved Germany from enslavement ... Nature had given even the dumb brutes freedom, and courage was the peculiar excellence of man. Heaven helped the braver side.'[35] The shock waves swept through the Empire, smashed through the gates of the Eternal City and even lapped against the feet of the Emperor Augustus himself.

According to the historian Suetonius, Varus' disgraceful defeat 'nearly wrecked the Empire' – a statement that has acquired new meaning since the discovery of Waldgirmes and the realization that it was not just some soldiers that had been lost, but an entire province. Augustus immediately ordered patrols on to the streets of Rome and put into effect other security measures to make sure there were no uprisings on the back of the catastrophe. He even sent away his Batavian bodyguards. He 'mourned greatly,' wrote Dio Cassius 200 years later, 'not only because of the soldiers who had been lost, but also because of his fear for the German and Gallic provinces, and particularly because he expected that the enemy would march against Italy and against Rome itself'.[36] Suetonius says: 'Indeed, it is said that he took the disaster so deeply to heart that he left his hair and beard untrimmed for months; he would often beat his head on a door, shouting: "Quintilius Varus, give me back my legions!" and always kept the anniversary as a day of deep mourning.'[37]

The shame was so great that the loss of Germania Magna was never referred to. And although the abandoned city at Waldgirmes has finally been discovered, the Romans left no record of what it was actually called – even though it was, presumably, the capital of Germania Magna. No one dared say that Rome had lost more than its legions.

THE QUISLING AND THE FREEDOM FIGHTER

Curiously enough, despite the magnitude of the victory against Varus, it did not immediately establish Arminius as supreme and unrivalled leader of the Cherusci. There were still plenty of Germans who saw their main advantage in collaboration with Rome rather than opposition. And Segestes, the man who had tried to warn Varus of the impending disaster, was one of the leaders of this faction.

He had naturally joined Arminius in the attack on Varus, since not to have done so would have looked suspicious, but his sympathies had always remained where his interests were: with the Romans. Segestes had become Arminius' chief antagonist among the Cherusci, and now the rivalry between the two men grew personal. This was because Segestes had involuntarily become Arminius' father-in-law, and he didn't like it at all. Segestes' daughter, Thusnelda, had been engaged to marry a man whom, one presumes, Segestes approved of. Arminius, however, had come along and stolen not only her affections but her person, and had married her despite her father's protests.[38] Arminius really seems to have been fond of her, and Tacitus tells us that Thusnelda herself 'was temperamentally closer to her husband than to her father'. Segestes and Arminius had always worked for different political ends, but now they thoroughly detested each other.

The Romans were well aware of this dissension. When Augustus died, the new Emperor Tiberius' nephew, Germanicus, returned to Germany to take revenge on the Cherusci. He fully intended to exploit the division. As Tacitus put it: 'These two leaders stood respectively for treachery and goodwill to Rome. Arminius was Germany's troublemaker. Segestes had often warned Publius Quintilius Varus that rebellion was planned.'[39]

Germanicus kicked off his revenge on the Cherusci by exterminating the Chatti people – 'helpless women, children and old people were at once slaughtered or captured' and their capital was destroyed.[40] In the meantime, Arminius had seized power and was besieging Segestes, who appealed to Germanicus for help. Segestes was clearly an important ally of Rome, since Germanicus rescued him and escorted the collaborator back across the Rhine with many relatives and several women of high rank, including his daughter Thusnelda, Arminius' wife. It's not clear how she came to be in Segestes' company, but he must have taken her forcibly from Arminius, presumably at the time when Segestes (as he later claimed) had thrown Arminius in prison. Segestes admitted that Thusnelda was not in his company of her own free will.

In the pages of Tacitus, Thusnelda emerges as a remarkable and strong-minded woman. There she stood, pregnant and separated from her husband, forcibly abducted to the enemy camp by her quisling father – and yet she gave no quarter. 'From her came no appeals, no submissive tears; she stood still, her hands clasped inside her robe, staring down at her pregnant body.'[41] It's easy to imagine that such a woman would have admired her husband, the leader of their country's independence movement, and despised her father, the spy and informer.

Segestes himself steps on to Tacitus' stage as 'a huge figure, fearlessly aware he had been a good ally', who then delivers himself of a self-serving speech of the kind Tacitus imagines he would have made to justify his treachery:

> Ever since the divine Augustus made me a Roman citizen,
> my choice of friends and enemies has been guided by your
> advantage. My motive has not been hatred of my people – for
> traitors are distasteful even to the side they join – but the
> belief that Roman and German interests are the same, and
> that peace is better than war. That is why I denounced to
> your former commander Varus the man who broke the treaty
> with you – Arminius, the robber of my daughter![42]

Germanicus promised Segestes a safe-house in Gaul for himself and his family. Thusnelda bore Arminius a son, who was brought up in Ravenna. Tacitus promises to tell us of 'the ironical fate in store for him', but never does.

ARMINIUS FIGHTS BACK

Arminius was, understandably, a bit hacked off by Segestes' behaviour. In fact, he was more than hacked off. Tacitus says he was 'maddened by his wife's abduction and the prospect of servitude for their unborn child'. So he made a rapid tour of the Cherusci demanding a renewal of war against the Romans. The words that Tacitus puts into Arminius' mouth make stirring reading: 'Germany will never tolerate Roman rods, axes and robes between Rhine and Elbe. Other countries, unacquainted with Roman rule, have not known its impositions or its punishments. We have known them – and got rid of them!'[43]

Whatever it was that Arminius did say, it seemed to do the trick. Germanicus grew alarmed by the size of the rebellion building up against him, and launched attacks on several different fronts to disperse the enemy. One column, while peacefully burning, looting and killing in the lands of the Bructeri, discovered the standard of the 19th Legion, which had been lost with Varus. Eventually they reached the Teutoburgian Forest, where the remains of Varus' legions were still lying unburied. Survivors guided the living to the dead, and, according to Tacitus, 'the scene lived up to its horrible associations … On the open ground were whitening bones, scattered where men had fled, heaped up where they had stood and fought back. Fragments of spears and of horses' limbs lay there – also human heads, fastened to tree-trunks. In groves nearby were the outlandish altars at which the Germans had massacred the Roman colonels and senior company-commanders.'[44]

During the next year's campaign, an extraordinary encounter took place. Tacitus dramatized it, encapsulating the tensions that must have been rife within many Barbarian families as the Empire advanced on them. He describes Arminius coming to a river bank and demanding to speak to his brother Flavus, who was in the Roman camp on the other side. Flavus had lost an eye some years before while fighting under Tiberius. When he came forward Arminius

> asked his brother to explain his face-wound. The place and
> the battle were told him. Then he asked what reward Flavus
> had got. Flavus mentioned his higher pay, chain and wreath
> of honour and other military decorations. 'The wages of
> slavery are low' sneered Arminius.
>
> Then they argued their opposing cases. Flavus spoke of
> Rome's greatness, the emperor's wealth, the terrible
> punishment attending defeat, the mercy earned by

submission – even Arminius' own wife and son [both now living as captives in Ravenna] were not treated like enemies. His brother [Arminius] dwelt on patriotism, long-established freedom, the national gods of Germany – and their mother, who joined him in imploring that Flavus should not choose to be the deserter and betrayer, rather than the liberator, of his relatives and his country.[45]

Tacitus says that the discussion soon became abusive and would have ended in blows (despite the brothers being on opposite banks of the river) if Flavus had not been restrained. Arminius was left 'shouting threats and challenges to fight – a good many of them in Latin'. The next night one of the Cherusci – possibly Arminius himself – rode up to the Roman stockade and taunted the soldiers in Latin, promising every deserter a wife, some land and a hundred sesterces.

The battle, when it came, ran for the Romans. Arminius was wounded, but, having smeared his own blood over his face to avoid being recognized, broke through the ranks of Roman bowmen by sheer physical strength and the impetus of his horse. Germanicus claimed to have defeated Arminius, even though he hadn't killed or captured him. The Romans burnt what they could, killed who they could, got into their boats and went home.

GERMANICUS' TRIUMPH

Tiberius insisted that his commander return to Rome and celebrate a Triumph for his victories over the Germans – quite possibly the Emperor was jealous of his nephew getting too successful and popular with his troops. So even though the war in Germany was not really concluded, Germanicus' Triumph took place on 26 May AD 17. It was quite an occasion.

Arminius must have felt a bit left out, since not only was it *the* big social event of the year, but his wife and the son he had never seen were there ... not as spectators, you understand, but paraded as captives.

The Greek geographer Strabo wrote an account of the Triumph shortly after it took place. Public humiliation was the penalty the Cherusci paid for their guile in destroying Varus' legions: 'They [the

Cherusci] all paid the penalty, and afforded the younger Germanicus a most brilliant triumph – that triumph in which their most famous men and women were led captive, I mean Segimuntus, son of Segestes and chieftain of the Cherusci, and his sister Thusnelda, the wife of Arminius ... and Thusnelda's three-year-old son Thumelicus.' Looking on was the arch-traitor Segestes himself, forced to witness the public disgrace of his own son and daughter: 'But Segestes, the father-in-law of Arminius, who even from the outset had opposed the purpose of Arminius, and, taking advantage of an opportune time, had deserted him, was present as a guest of honour at the Triumph over his loved ones.'[46] Perhaps the Romans were 'rewarding' him for his treachery to his own people.

THE END OF ARMINIUS

It seems that the Germans' opposition to Rome was not simply the expression of love of freedom; it was also linked to their adamant refusal to accept an imperial or even royal structure in place of the traditional tribal social arrangements, with their folk-meetings, law-giving and election of war leaders. Whenever a leader seemed to get too big for his boots and to aim at kingship, he was resented by the rank and file of the Germans. And this is what, in the end, happened to Arminius.

He and the other war leaders had done enough to keep the Romans off their backs, which meant that they could turn to more traditional pursuits, such as fighting each other. As Tacitus put it rather succinctly: 'now that the Romans had gone and there was no external threat, national custom and rivalry had turned the Germans against one another.'[47]

With Segestes out of the way, Arminius' only real rival amongst the other clans was Maroboduus, who was by now leading a group of peoples under the collective name of the Suebi. He seems to have been vain, ambitious and formidable. Velleius Paterculus tells us he was 'a man of noble family, strong in body and courageous in mind, a barbarian by birth but not in intelligence'. He imposed Roman discipline on his own forces, which in his heyday numbered some 70,000 infantry and 4000 cavalry.

What is more, according to Velleius, he had 'in his mind the idea of a definite empire and royal powers'.[48] He actually used the Roman title *rex*. Of course, the Romans prided themselves on their hatred of kings (that was why Caesar had been assassinated when he seemed to want a crown), so a Roman spin may have been put on the surviving accounts of what happened, including that of Tacitus: 'The Suebi did not like the royal title of their leader Maroboduus, whereas Arminius was popular as champion of freedom. So in addition to his old soldiers – the Cherusci and their allies – two Suebian tribes, the Semnones and Langobardi, from the kingdom of Maroboduus also entered the war on Arminius' side.'[49]

Maroboduus ended up sending an SOS to the Emperor Tiberius, requesting his help against the Empire's enemy Arminius. It was the act of a desperate man, and Tiberius quite reasonably pointed out that when Rome had asked Maroboduus for support against the Cherusci he'd turned them down, so why should they help him now? Maroboduus eventually asked for asylum. Tiberius assured him he would be welcome and free to leave whenever he chose, but in the Senate he denounced Maroboduus as one of the greatest threats to Rome. The German spent the next 18 years as a pampered captive in Ravenna, 'growing old, his reputation dimmed by excessive fondness for life'.[50]

After that, Arminius' dislike of monarchy seems to have evaporated, and he now tried to create a German kingdom of his own to face down Rome. He discovered, however, that the Germans were not prepared to knuckle under even to him. And since the Romans had withdrawn from Germania Magna, it seems as though people did not need to surrender their independence even to a home-grown overlord. 'His freedom-loving compatriots,' writes Tacitus, 'forcibly resisted. The fortunes of the fight fluctuated, but finally Arminius succumbed to treachery from his relations.' In other words, they killed him.

Tacitus leaves us with a very generous assessment of Arminius, which shows how much impact his personality and career had upon his enemies: 'He was unmistakably the liberator of Germany. Challenger of Rome – not in its infancy, like kings and commanders before him, but at the height of its power – he had fought undecided battles, and never lost a war. He had ruled for twelve of his thirty-seven years. To this day the tribes sing of him.'[51] A worthy national hero for Germany. If only we knew his name ...

A LESSON LEARNT

Having abandoned Germania Magna, the Emperor Augustus realized that endless expansion of the frontiers was not an option. Accordingly, he advised his successor, Tiberius, to keep the Empire within the natural borders formed by the Rhine, the Danube and the Euphrates.[52] He said ruefully that to strive after a small profit with expensive resources was like fishing 'with a golden hook, the loss of which, if it were carried off, could not be made good by any catch'.[53]

But the Empire needed to keep bringing in new catches. Otherwise the costs of a military system would grow without the profit of new conquests and Rome would be heading for bankruptcy.

Britain, invaded in AD 43, turned out not to be much of a money-spinner. But fortunately for Rome there remained one more land that promised rich pickings for any emperor who could take it. But this time there would be no foolish attempt to civilize its inhabitants. They would be eliminated.

VI
DACIA AND THE
VANISHED WORLD

At the heart of Rome was death. There's an imperial monument right in the middle of Rome that was erected by the Senate in the early second century AD to celebrate the Emperor Trajan. It is a mysterious object; although it has stood in the heart of the city for almost 2000 years, we don't really understand it. But we do know that it commemorates Roman ruthlessness on a grand scale.

Down at ground level, which is all that most people can see in detail of Trajan's Column, the passing stranger is invited to gaze upon the civilized face of Roman society. Dignified statesmen mingle with their wives and children in a peaceful scene of sober celebration. As we look higher, however (which will need some binoculars), we start to glimpse the reality behind the power – the death and destruction of battle depicted in thousands of realistic images. Remember the Emperor Augustus and his distress over Varus' lost legions? That was not sentimentality. Augustus was unmoved by death, as he made plain at the Temple of Augustus in Ankara in Turkey. Today the walls are crumbling and being eaten away by pollution, but here is Augustus' own description of his achievements: 'Three times I gave a gladiatorial show in my own name, and five times in the names of my sons or grandsons, in which shows about 10,000 men fought to the death.'

The German Barbarians never came near this for savagery. The lust for blood, the entertainment of watching men kill each other, was something uniquely Roman. Arminius and his followers had massacred the legions because it was the only chance they stood of defending their lands, their society, their way of life – and it worked.

But the Romans massacred people for the sheer pleasure of watching the blood. They decorated their rooms with expensive mosaics of the gladiatorial slaughters they had sponsored, and they gathered in their thousands to watch criminals being ripped apart by wild animals that were captured and shipped in especially for that purpose.

To enjoy watching people suffer and die was the very essence of Roman identity. In particular, to watch Barbarians suffer and die – Barbarians and other monsters from the savage world beyond the frontier. That's what gladiator costumes were all about. They were stock types: the Thracian Barbarians; the Essedari, kitted out as Celtic charioteers; the Mirmillones, who represented sea monsters; the Andabatae, who were armoured like Persians – and so on. When the Emperor Nero blamed the great fire of Rome on followers of a new religion, Christians, he decided on what he felt was a suitably entertaining punishment. According to Tacitus, some of the Christians were dressed in the skins of wild animals and then thrown to the dogs to be torn to pieces, while others were 'made into torches to be ignited after dark as substitutes for daylight'. Historians suggest that Tacitus was repeating exaggerated stories put about by Nero's enemies, but the fact that such a story was credible is what matters. People associated their emperor with a scale of horror fully comparable with Auschwitz – and perhaps worse. They were prepared to believe that living men and women nailed to posts, soaked in oil and set on fire were used to light a party, because the public enjoyment of torture was part of the fabric of their state. Death screams were part of the fun.

Ruthless brutality, a complete indifference to human suffering, pleasure in watching torture – these were not Barbarian qualities. They were Roman. And the Romans were proud of it. War and the celebration of Triumphs, the slaughter of tens of thousands and the parade of prisoners and loot, the enslavement and public murder of prisoners – all these were important to the dignity of emperors. Augustus was proud of his clemency, but was murderous nonetheless. He states on that temple wall: 'I frequently waged wars by land and by sea, both civil and foreign, throughout the whole world. In the case of foreign peoples whom it was safe to pardon, I preferred conservation to extermination.' Extermination – genocide – was an option, obviously. And sometimes it was the preferred option.

GENOCIDE

Many of the images on Trajan's Column depict Romans slaughtering Dacians. It is ironic that we are left with so many contemporary images of a Barbarian people about whom we otherwise know so little. The Column celebrates Trajan's campaign in AD 101–6, in which he entered the kingdom of Dacia and destroyed the entire Dacian nation. Or at least that's what the Romans liked to think.

Nowadays some historians are reluctant to accord Trajan the honour of achieving total genocide. They point to inscriptions and written documents that indicate sufficient Dacians escaped the Roman holocaust to have ensured some continuity from those days to the present, when what remains of the country of Dacia is known – ironically enough – as Romania. There are records, for example, of at least 12 units of Dacian soldiers being subsequently posted to various parts of the Roman Empire – many of them, according to the archaeological record, to Britain. What's more, the Column itself concludes with an image of Dacians peaceably returning to graze their sheep on the emptied land.

The snag is that in ancient Rome it was common knowledge that Trajan had annihilated the Dacians. The Emperor's doctor, Crito, claimed that Trajan had done the job so well that only 40 Dacians remained – at least that's what the writer Lucian said he said. Crito did write an account of his adventures in Dacia with Trajan, but the book is now lost, and Lucian, who was a satirist and wit, may have been employing comic hyperbole to make a point.

But later writers continued to perpetuate the idea. They included the Emperor Julian (better known as Julian the Apostate) who, in one of his works, imagines Trajan announcing: 'Alone, I have defeated the peoples from beyond the Danube and I have annihilated the people of the Dacians.'[1] The fourth-century historian Eutropius wrote that, when Dacia had been defeated, all that remained was a wasteland that Trajan then repopulated with people from various other parts of the Empire. 'Trajan brought countless masses of people from the whole Roman world to live in the fields and in the cities, since Dacia was exhausted of men after the long war.'[2]

Since this was a widely known story, it could well be that the last images on Trajan's Column depict not the return of Dacians to their native soil, but the repopulation of the empty country by Roman settlers. It has also been suggested, however, that the images may be of Dacians being relocated in the Empire.

As for the deployment of Dacians in the Roman army, that too could be taken as a sign that very few Dacian males were allowed to remain in the country after the campaign. Another writer, who based his information on Crito's account, claims that Trajan pressed half a million Dacians into the Roman army. Although this is probably an exaggeration, it indicates that the Romans were determined to leave very few males on their native soil – a fact confirmed by Eutropius.[3]

One archaeologist, Linda Ellis, describes it as a kind of Year Zero, with the Romans wiping Dacia clean and building a new civilization as though this were *terra nova*, new land. 'There was no continuation of Dacian traditions, either religious tradition or economic or political tradition, so Dacian civilization had been literally wiped from the surface and a new Roman order had been emplaced upon it.' Whether they killed off the entire population or not, the Romans did a thorough job of removing Dacian culture and identity from the world map.

The Dacians, then, have the distinction of being one of the few nations on earth whose destruction has been lovingly recorded in pictures for posterity. So just how barbarous were they?

A LOST CIVILIZATION

It's a bit hard to know who the Dacians were because the Romans did such a good job of extinguishing their society.[4] Trajan's conquest of AD 106 ended with the suicide of their king Decebalus, and the flight of most of the survivors over the Carpathian mountains. The new Roman province, Dacia Traiana (Trajan's Dacia), was a military state run by a general and occupied by Roman troops in new barracks-cities. A new population, mainly of slaves, was imported to work the land and exploit the mines. Even the language disappeared. All that remains of it are a few names and a list of herbs.

So unless you happen to be Romanian, you've probably never even heard of the Dacians. In fact it may come as a bit of a shock to learn that it was one of the great civilizations of the ancient world, following the teachings of a religious leader that one Greek historian compared in importance with Moses. The world of the Dacians, with all their achievements and teachings, has vanished as though it never was. Thanks to Rome.

You would never guess, from those images of Dacian Barbarians on Trajan's Column, that this kingdom was one of the wealthiest in Europe. Before the Romans had relieved them of the chore, the Dacians had been superb metal-workers – a craft they perhaps learnt from the large number of Celts who made up a sizeable proportion of the population.[5] And they had precious metals in profusion to work with.

The only clue given on Trajan's Column is some 'snapshots' of the booty seized. This was a legendary treasure – much more than enough to pay for the whole war. A sixth-century writer,[6] quoting Crito, claimed that the treasure amounted to 1650 tons of gold and 3310 tons of silver, in addition to priceless artefacts. Maybe that's an exaggeration, but even so it was a huge amount. And no wonder, since Dacia was rich in gold, silver and iron. The Dacians had been working the rich seams since long before the Romans invaded, and wooden supports inside one mine have been dated back to the third century BC.

Dacia was not only wealthy, but socially on a par with Rome. It was a highly developed society out of which, at different points in its history, powerful rulers created a confederacy that was able to challenge Rome.

From our modern perspective, it's easy to imagine a Roman army that was vastly technologically superior to the armies of the backward Barbarians who surrounded them. But this wasn't how it was at all. Apart from the artillery, perhaps, these Barbarians' equipment was equal to that of the Romans, and in one area in particular – metallurgy – sometimes better.

They had also been involved in trade with the Romans since the second century BC, and their links with Greece went even further back. They were by no means a backward, isolated bunch of savages. Their aristocracy was literate, and, like the Celts, they used the Greek and Roman alphabets for their own language. They had been minting their own coins for 150 years, and produced elegant pottery that would have graced any sophisticated home.

Their country provided them with rich farmland, and they felt secure enough to build cities that were not totally surrounded by protective walls. Dacian settlements had a smaller fortified citadel at the centre, with religious and industrial areas lying outside the walls. Recent excavations have revealed elaborate Dacian constructions in the mountains of Transylvania, built in a way that is similar to Greek building but clearly distinctive, using limestone blocks transported up to 15 miles on well-made roads through this most difficult terrain. Even back in the first century BC, the powerful Dacian ruler, who probably went by the name of Burebista, lived in a palace that boasted piped plumbing and was ringed by fortresses, although it has disappeared so completely that until recently no one was even sure where it was.

Burebista was the first to forge the Dacians into a confederacy and to stamp his authority over the disparate communities of the area. He subordinated the neighbouring peoples and, according to Strabo, 'began to be formidable even to the Romans'.

A LOST RELIGION

Strabo describes Burebista as a charismatic, ruthless leader who was sophisticated enough to realize that political power was greatly enhanced when supported by religion and the priesthood: 'To help him secure the complete obedience of his tribe he had as his coadjutor Decaeneus, a wizard, a man who not only had wandered through Egypt, but also had thoroughly learned certain prognostics through which he would pretend to tell the divine will; and within a short time he was set up as a god.'[7] This religion was as remarkable as it was home-grown.

High in the mountains was the sanctuary of the priests of Zalmoxis (or Zamolxis). According to the Greeks, Zalmoxis had been a pupil of Pythagoras.[8] Strabo says he was Pythagoras' slave. He spent some time in Egypt – obligatory for anyone in the classical world entering on a career inventing religion – and when he returned to his Dacian homeland he was 'eagerly courted by the rulers and the people of the tribe, because he could make predictions from the celestial signs'. To begin with he was simply the priest of the chief Dacian god, but as time went on, Zalmoxis himself began to be venerated as a god. He lived as a hermit in a cave, visited only by the king and his attendants.

Strabo then gives an analysis of the relationship between Zalmoxis and the king that explains how Burebista was able to harness religion and politics to his advantage. The use of religion to boost political power still goes on today, of course; Burebista was clearly expert at it.

> The king cooperated with him, because he saw that the
> people paid much more attention to himself than before, in
> the belief that the decrees which he promulgated were in
> accordance with the counsel of the gods. This custom
> persisted even down to our time, because some man of that
> character was always to be found, who, though in fact only a
> counsellor to the king, was called a god among the Getae
> [Dacians].⁹

Zalmoxis seems to have been regarded in a similar way to the Buddha, who was Pythagoras' exact contemporary (both are believed to have lived from 560 BC to 480 BC). But Buddhism survived and Zalmoxism didn't – the Romans were far from India, and distressingly close to Dacia. There was a sanctuary, but there were no statues of gods, and no altars or sacrifices. One Greek contemporary of Caesar, Diodorus Siculus, lists Zalmoxis as one of the three great non-Greek philosophers (the others being Moses and the Persian Zoroaster), but we know almost nothing of his teachings. We do know that he said the soul was immortal. According to Plato, writing around 380 BC, Zalmoxis taught that all illness flowed from the body being out of balance: 'The part can never be well unless the whole is well. For all good and evil, whether in the body or in human nature, originates in the soul. So if the head and body are to be well, you must begin by curing the soul; that is the first thing. And the cure has to be effected by the use of fair words which plant temperance in the soul.'¹⁰

To give some idea of how much power Burebista gained from this union of religion and politics, Strabo tells us that he was even able to deal with the problem of alcoholism amongst his people by persuading his subjects to cut down their vines and – horror of horrors – 'live without wine'! Teetotal Barbarians? Obviously the word 'barbarian' doesn't mean quite what we assume.

Burebista was also sophisticated enough to realize that the rising star of Julius Caesar was a potential threat, even when Caesar was still struggling for power in Rome. This, of course, was back in the days when 'Caesar' wasn't a title – it was just a man's name, meaning, oddly enough, 'long-haired'. You know, like Barbarians.

At all events, Burebista was sufficiently concerned about Caesar's ambitions to send a message to Caesar's arch-rival, Pompey, offering him military support in return for the recognition of his state. A Barbarian leader offering to intervene in a Roman civil war? Again, the word 'barbarian' seems to have shifted its meaning.

In the event, Burebista's offer came too late and Caesar took over Rome, which must have been a bit of a worry for the Dacian king. Having declared his hand for Pompey against Caesar, he must have known that he would be number one on Caesar's personal list of the Axis of Evil. Caesar had already conquered Gaul and set up client rulers in southern Britain – Dacia and Burebista were the next target.

Caesar, however, was assassinated before he could act, and (perhaps in some sort of divine symmetry) so was Burebista. The Dacian confederacy fell apart, and it would be another 100 years before a powerful ruler could unite the forces of Dacia to confront Rome again. In the meantime, however, political disunity didn't mean a relapse into 'Barbarism' or anything uncivilized like that. It is said that the great Emperor Augustus betrothed his five-year-old daughter to one Dacian chief, and was himself supposed to be interested in marrying the man's daughter.

Whether the story is true or not, it gives some indication of the equality that was then perceived to exist between the societies of Rome and Dacia. Whatever Trajan was doing when he annihilated the Dacians, he was not ridding the world of ignorant savages.

DECEBALUS AND THE DEMENTED DOMITIAN

Dacia's next charismatic leader, a century later, may not actually have been a Dacian. By the second half of the first century AD the Dacians in the area appear to have been in the minority, outnumbered by Celts, Iranians and Bastarnae (an easternmost Germanic people). So whatever ethnicity Decebalus was, it should be no surprise that he sported a non-Dacian name.[11]

A clever war leader, he proved himself capable of bringing all these disparate population elements together and forging them into a single coherent military force. According to Dio Cassius, Decebalus was 'shrewd in his understanding of warfare and shrewd also in the waging of war; he judged well when to attack and chose the right moment to retreat; he was an expert in ambushes and a master in pitched battle; and he knew not only how to follow up a victory well, but how to manage well a defeat.'[12] He also imported a considerable amount of military expertise from the most obvious place: Roman legionaries who felt like changing sides were offered attractive terms, and these deserters became the backbone of his formidable army. He 'had been acquiring the largest and best part of his force by persuading men to come to him from Roman territory'.[13] It has been estimated that he could bring into the field an army of 40,000 soldiers himself, plus another 20,000 from his allies.

Decebalus certainly ran rings around the megalomaniac Emperor Domitian. In AD 85 the Dacians crossed the Danube and killed the local Roman governor. Domitian decided to take reprisals, whereupon Decebalus offered to negotiate. Domitian ignored these overtures and marched against the Dacians. Of course he didn't actually go himself – that wasn't the way Domitian did things. He sent one of his generals, Cornelius Fuscus, with a large army. Meanwhile, Domitian himself 'remained in one of the cities of Moesia [on the Roman side of the Danube], indulging in riotous living, as was his wont. For he was not only indolent of body and timorous of spirit, but also most profligate and lewd towards women and boys alike.'[14] Decebalus, on learning of this, promptly sent another embassy to Domitian with the insulting proposal to make peace with the Emperor on condition that every Roman should pay 'two obols' a year to Decebalus. Otherwise, he said, he would wage war on the Romans and inflict 'great ills'.

Fuscus crossed the Danube in AD 87, and tried to penetrate into the heart of Dacia by crossing the Transylvanian Alps at the pass known as the Iron Gates. Here he was attacked by the Dacians at a place that the chronicles identify as Tapae. Fuscus was killed in the attack and one of his legions wiped out, its banners and war machines being captured by the Dacians. It seems that some of the Romans then joined the Dacian army.

Two years later, Decebalus found himself on the receiving end of emissaries from the Emperor requesting a truce. The Barbarian king was a skilled negotiator and didn't hesitate to use his current advantage over Domitian, who had suffered reverses in his recent campaign against the Suebian Germans. By the terms of the treaty Decebalus extracted large sums of money from Domitian, as well as 'artisans of every trade pertaining to war and peace' and guarantees of future payments. In return, Decebalus was supposed to hand over captives and arms and pay homage to the Emperor. Decebalus, however, was too canny to present himself personally before the demented Domitian; instead he sent a certain Diegis to Rome as his representative – along with a few captives and some arms that he 'pretended were the only ones he had'.[15] In fact, he was treating the Roman Emperor with complete contempt, for the envoys he sent were not Dacian noblemen, who were distinguished by wearing caps, but lesser persons who sported the long hair that, in Dacia, indicated lower rank. Maybe Domitian was unaware of the insult, or maybe it suited his purpose to ignore it. Whatever the truth, the normally thin-skinned Emperor did not take offence and accepted the agreement.

The fact was that Domitian was planning to make this shambolic peace deal look like a great victory. He had already put on a sham Triumph over Germany in AD 83, in which he is supposed to have dressed up slaves to look like German captives. Now he did the same thing as a Triumph over the Dacians. He crowned the emissary, Diegis, as king of Dacia 'just as if he had truly conquered and could give the Dacians anyone he pleased to be their king', handed out honours and money to the soldiery, and displayed objects from the imperial store of furniture, pretending they were the spoils of war. He then put on triumphal games at which, the indubitably biased Dio Cassius informs us, there was 'nothing worthy of historic record except that maidens contended in the foot-race'! However, he also put on a mock naval battle in a new arena, during which 'practically all the combatants and many of the spectators as well perished'. A violent storm with heavy rains engulfed the proceedings, but the Emperor wouldn't allow anyone to leave or change their clothes – though of course he did himself. As a result, 'not a few fell sick and died'. Dio Cassius also adds that dwarves and women often fought each other, although it's not quite clear whether it was dwarf against dwarf and woman against woman, or dwarf versus woman.[16]

Six hundred miles away, back in Dacia, Decebalus found himself confronted by a new Roman commander, Julianus. This general licked the Roman army into shape and secured a victory against the Dacians – once again at Tapae. Decebalus was thrown back on the defensive, and yet once again managed to turn the tables on the Romans – this time by a trick. Fearing that Julianus was about to storm his royal residence, Decebalus cut down all the trees in the area, then stood the trunks up in formation and hung armour on them 'in order that the Romans might take them for soldiers and so be frightened and withdraw,' says Dio Cassius.[17] And that, apparently, is exactly what happened.

This bizarre military confrontation marked the end of Decebalus' contact with Domitian. He was still notionally a vassal of Rome, but Rome was paying him for the privilege. It was an arrangement that must have suited the Dacian king, but it was not one that the next but one Roman emperor was prepared to tolerate. Domitian was assassinated – to everyone's relief – in AD 96. He was followed by the elderly Nerva, who only reigned for two years, but wisely chose as his successor an eminently sensible Spaniard – Trajan.

DECEBALUS AND TRAJAN

Trajan was as sane as Domitian had been demented, and he was determined to show the Dacians who was boss. In fact you could say that the conquest of Dacia was something of an obsession with him. It was said that when he wanted to lay particular emphasis on anything, his oath would be 'as I hope to see Dacia reduced to a province' or 'as I hope to cross the Danube and the Euphrates on bridges'.[18]

Decebalus must have realized he was going to be in for a rough ride as soon as Trajan became commander of the world's largest army. It was a tradition for any new emperor to kick-start his reign with a little military adventure – and Trajan especially wasn't going to be left out. Kicking ass on the frontiers helped an emperor to stamp his authority on the Empire, built his reputation and kept the army busy. Besides, Trajan took 'delight in war'.[19]

Decebalus must also have been aware that the Empire, when Trajan took over, was in economic melt-down. It needed a cash infusion and it needed it soon. And in Dacia Decebalus was sitting on a gold mine – literally. Yet instead of Rome benefiting from all these riches, Decebalus had managed to negotiate large annual payments from Rome as the price of massaging Domitian's crazed ego. This, says Dio Cassius, was a key reason why Trajan marched against the Dacians: he 'was grieved at the amount of money they were receiving annually, and he also observed that their power and their pride were increasing'.[20]

As Trajan advanced, Decebalus became worried. He knew that in the new Emperor he was facing a foe who was at the height of his powers and who – unlike Domitian – commanded some respect among his own soldiers. 'Decebalus ... knew that on the former occasion it was not the Romans he had conquered, but Domitian, whereas now he would be fighting against both Romans and Trajan, the emperor.'[21] The Dacian king must have been watching in dismay as Trajan set about his conquest with competent thoroughness. Decebalus' spies would have reported that the Emperor had built his much-promised bridge over the Danube (possibly two) and was now constructing roads across the Dacian landscape.

But Decebalus was not one to be cowed easily, and still showed his spirit by taunting the Romans. As Trajan reached the Iron Gates, Decebalus sent him a warning inscribed rather surprisingly, according to Dio Cassius, on 'a large mushroom'. This was probably a mushroom-shaped dish used for ritual purposes, and sadly *not* the only instance in history of diplomatic correspondence by fungi. The inscription advised Trajan to turn back and 'keep the peace'.[22]

Decebalus, of course, wasn't expecting Trajan to accept his advice – in fact he would probably have been very surprised if he had – and Roman forces eventually reached the Dacian capital Sarmizegetusa. They seized some mountain forts, as well as discovering a few captured artillery catapults and even the standard that had been lost by Fuscus. And they also captured Decebalus' sister.

The Dacian leader was beaten. He presented himself before Trajan, fell on the ground and did obeisance to the Emperor. An armistice was drawn up by the terms of which he agreed to become a Roman ally, to surrender the territory that Rome had seized, to demolish forts, and to stop recruiting Roman soldiers and engineers and return them to Trajan. He also sent envoys to the Senate in Rome to secure ratification of the armistice. There, in the Senate, these Barbarian statesmen – presumably still wearing their caps – 'laid down their arms, clasped their hands in the attitude of captives, and spoke some words of supplication'.[23] The treaty was ratified, and they were given back their arms.

Decebalus, however, had no intention of abiding by any of the peace terms that he had agreed – perhaps no more than Trajan had any intention of allowing all that gold to remain in Dacia. Decebalus must have known that Trajan's 'delight in war' would not be assuaged until he had totally subjugated Dacia. The Barbarian king could see the Roman fortifications along the Danube being strengthened, and knew they were there in readiness for the total conquest of his country. At this time, Trajan also replaced the wooden bridge across the Danube with a stone one. It was clear that the Romans were in Dacia to stay.

Decebalus did perhaps the only thing he could – he took the initiative and invaded Roman Moesia, taking control of the forts. The Senate declared him an enemy of Rome, and Trajan once more marched against him. This time, however, the outcome must have looked more inevitable, for large numbers of Dacians began deserting to the Roman side.

Decebalus sued for peace, but yet again would not surrender himself in person – he was too busy doing the rounds, desperately trying to raise a Barbarian army against Trajan. He also tried to assassinate the Emperor while he was in Moesia. Some Roman deserters were despatched to see if they could do away with Trajan, who, according to Dio Cassius, made himself far too accessible to all and sundry and, during 'the exigencies of warfare, admitted to a conference absolutely every one who desired it'.[24] But one of the plotters was arrested and – under torture – informed on the others.

However, Decebalus then pulled another of his crafty tricks. He invited the commander of the Roman army in Dacia, Longinus, to meet him, assuring him that he was now prepared to comply with all the Roman demands. Instead, however, Decebalus coolly arrested Longinus and publicly questioned him about Trajan's plans for the conquest of Dacia. Longinus refused to admit anything, so Decebalus took the Roman commander around with him, unfettered but under guard, and sent word to Trajan that he could have his general back in return for all the Dacian land as far as the Danube that was now under Roman rule. Decebalus also demanded to be indemnified for all the money he had spent so far on the war. Well – it's always worth asking!

Trajan returned an ambivalent reply.

Longinus did what he thought was the honourable thing in an intolerable position. He had obtained some poison from a freed-man. Before taking it he promised to win Trajan over, and with Decebalus' blessing gave the freedman a petition to take to Trajan to this effect. By the time Longinus committed suicide, the freedman had got away.

Decebalus must have been furious at losing such a prestigious and important prisoner, and he demanded that Trajan return the freedman in return for Longinus' body and ten captives. But Trajan was, above all, a practical man who wanted to encourage Dacian deserters. He deemed the safety of the brave freedman, who had taken such a great risk in getting hold of the poison for Longinus, to be 'more important for the dignity of the empire than the burial of Longinus', and refused to return the freedman to his death.

Throughout AD 105 Trajan pursued the war 'with safe prudence rather than with haste, and eventually, after a hard struggle, vanquished the Dacians'.[25] When Decebalus realized that the end had come, he committed suicide and his head was taken to Rome.

LOOT

In Gaul and Britain, Rome had expanded by a war of conquest accompanied by a policy of Romanizing the Barbarian inhabitants. But the policy had come badly unstuck in Germany, and in Dacia Trajan had quite different plans. This was an invasion. He wanted the land and resources, and had no intention of Romanizing the existing inhabitants. The land was swept clean. Survivors fled northward, while Trajan imported a new population of legionaries, peasants, merchants, artisans and officials from Gaul, Spain and Syria. A new Roman Dacia was built, with new cities, new fortresses and new roads.

And the Romans set about extracting all the gold and silver they could as fast as they could, and shipping it out of the country on a massive scale. The mines were worked by huge numbers of slaves, whose bodies were heaped in mounds at the end of their short working lives. The Romans stripped Dacia not only of its deposits of precious metals, but also of all the gold and silver objects that they could lay their hands on. And they must have done a thorough job because hardly any gold has since turned up in the archaeological record.

Among the most important treasures that Trajan hauled back from the bloodshed would have been the Dacian crown jewels. Before committing suicide Decebalus had taken care to bury his hoard of treasure, and he had done so in a pretty foolproof location. Dio Cassius takes up the story:

> The treasures of Decebalus were also discovered, though hidden beneath the river Sargetia, which ran past his palace. With the help of some captives Decebalus had diverted the course of the river, made an excavation in its bed, and into the cavity had thrown a large amount of silver and gold and other objects of great value that could stand a certain amount of moisture; then he had heaped stones over them and piled on earth afterwards bringing the river back into its course. He also had caused the same captives to deposit his robes

and other articles of a like nature in caves, and after accomplishing this had made away with them to prevent them from disclosing anything. But Bicilis, a companion of his who knew what had been done, was seized and gave information about these things.[26]

So prodigious was the amount of booty that Trajan brought back from Dacia that the bottom fell out of the gold market and its price plummeted throughout the Empire.

When Trajan had taken over the imperial throne the Roman economy had been in dismal straits, but with his Dacian windfall he was able to start throwing money around – which was not something that this Emperor did lightly. He lavished gifts on his people and financed games in the circus for a record 123 days, during the course of which 11,000 wild and tame animals were slaughtered and 10,000 gladiators fought. Roman ideas of a good time usually involved killing things.

But he didn't just fritter the winnings away in fun – that wasn't Trajan's style at all. He also embarked on a huge programme of building works that would change the face of the Eternal City for ever. In fact today, when you look at the glories of ancient Rome, you are looking at the proceeds of the loot plundered from the Barbarian Kingdom of Dacia in the year 106.

Trajan erected the Forum that took his name and constructed a road of stone through the Pontine marshes. He rebuilt Rome's port at Ostia, created huge new public baths and put up a giant amphitheatre that could be filled with water to mount sea battles as popular shows. What do you mean, there's not enough water to fill it? Money's no object to Trajan – he's got the Dacian treasure. He built an aqueduct for the purpose, bringing water from 60 miles away. We need a canal to link the Mediterranean to the Red Sea? Dig it![27] We need a bridge over the Danube? Build it! We need another legion? Make that two more! Trajan was suddenly the richest man in the world.

The Forum looks impressive enough even now. When Trajan built it, with its brass roof, it expressed all the might and majesty of the greatest power on earth. And, in the Forum that bears his name, Trajan erected his extraordinary Column so that the Roman world could celebrate the elimination of the once-powerful Dacians.

THE MYSTERY OF TRAJAN'S COLUMN

Potentially, the Roman campaigns in Dacia of AD 101–6 could have been one of the best covered of any war in antiquity. Trajan produced his own account, and another was written by his doctor, Crito. Unfortunately, both have been lost. Our main source for the war is the *Roman History* compiled by Dio Cassius more than half a century later. It is ironic that we possess so little written evidence, and yet more images than for any other single event in antiquity. And therein lies the great mystery of Trajan's Column.

The images at the base of the Column can be viewed from ground level. The stairway on the inside of the Column allows you to ascend to the top and obtain a magnificent view of the city, but does not permit you to see the images on the outside of the Column. This means that, since there is no viewpoint from which you can observe them with the naked eye (and as far as we know never has been), for most of the 1900 years that the Column has been standing in the Forum Traiani the majority of the images have effectively been invisible.

So why carve them? Did the designers simply not realize they would be invisible from the ground? Or were temporary viewing platforms erected to enable people to see them on special occasions? Or was there some other reason? Carvings – especially such lifelike ones – were expensive, and not to be undertaken lightly. Could it be that, by paying for them and then putting them out of sight, Trajan was actually making a sacrifice – an offering to the gods who had presented him with such a great gift as the destruction of an entire nation? But the gods, as the Greeks had frequently pointed out, have a cruel sense of irony. Dacia would be the soil from which Rome's nemesis would spring.

THE INVENTION OF THE FRONTIER

Down through the centuries, there are accounts of Barbarian hordes that swept across Europe bringing death and destruction to the civilized world – as well as total confusion to anyone who tries to follow what was going on. Goths, Visigoths, Vandals, Franks, Lombards, Jutes, Suebi, Marcomanni and Saxons – some 80 Germanic 'tribes' – charge through the pages of history and leave the reader with little chance of coming to grips with them. But at least we can comfort ourselves with the thought that, if that's how it appears now, it's also how it appeared to the Romans.

So they drew a line. In an attempt to bring order where there was chaos, they created the Western world's first frontiers. This side of the line was their world – the world of *Romanitas*. Beyond the line lay the 'other' – the world of the Barbarians. The further those frontiers were from Rome, the safer Rome would be ... or at any rate the safer it would feel and the richer it would be. At least that was the theory.

The idea of frontiers between one people and another was very much a Roman one. The rest of the Western world tended to live in national or family groups that observed certain areas of operation, but would not have been familiar with the concept of a line you did not cross. The Germans never regarded the Rhine as a boundary or even a barrier, and regularly crossed it for all kinds of reasons. So did the Romans, but to them it eventually came to represent the frontier between civilization and barbarity.

The story of Brennus and his occupation of Rome around 390 BC had burnt into the Roman psyche the determination never again to allow Barbarians to violate the sacred heart of their world.

Until at least the fourth century the Roman Empire was the city of Rome writ large, and the frontiers of that empire began to be thought of as extensions of the city walls. To cross the frontier was like entering a city. But it was never a frontier that Rome itself felt in any way bounded by. Heaven forbid! Rome's frontier was not a limit, just a trip-wire to alert the authorities to movements of goods and people, and a series of staging-posts to enable incursions to be made into the lands beyond.[28]

Roman efforts turned away from trying to absorb and change the Barbarians, or to eliminate them; instead, they tried to maintain a defensive line to hold them out. Trajan's successor Hadrian built physical limits: a wall of stone in the north of Britain, and a wooden fence and series of watch-towers in Germany. The barrier, physically simple but heavily patrolled and well armed, was called the *Limes*, the Limit.

The German Barbarians had fundamentally changed Rome's view of its Empire. Once it had been a work in progress that would ultimately civilize all mankind to protect the mother-city. Now it had limits, a frontier. The world would remain divided.

But when Trajan pushed Rome over the Danube, he had conquered a land bordered by mountain ranges that had no defensible frontiers at all. Dacia would be the permeable membrane through which untold numbers of Barbarians would seep into the Empire. The province would be abandoned after 165 years, but that was only the beginning. Rome had ceased the Romanization of the Barbarians. Now the reverse process would begin: the Barbarianization of Rome.

VII
THE GOTHS

The Goths sacked Rome in AD 410. It was an event of historic significance, and yet it's probably one of the most misrepresented moments in history.

The Goths didn't destroy Rome, nor did they massacre the population. On the contrary, the Barbarians took particular care to provide safe-houses for civilians and not to harm public buildings. Nor was Alaric the Goth a savage pagan intent on smashing the heart of Christianity – he was, in fact, a Christian who admired Rome and was simply trying to find a place in the Roman system for his people. In fact, far from being an alien invader, Alaric had actually been one of the commanders-in-chief of the Roman army! And only the year before, he had been able to enthrone his own candidate as emperor, with the Senate's blessing, and then dethrone him a few months later!

The reasons why we harbour such misconceptions about the sack of Rome are as interesting as the story of the sack itself. And it all begins back in Dacia.

THE GOTHS IN DACIA

Trajan had conquered Dacia early in the second century AD, and had filled it with Roman settlers. But it was one thing to conquer Dacia and another to hold on to it. The problem was that its northern and eastern borders were so porous ... impossible to defend.

Trajan's successor, Hadrian, seriously considered abandoning the province and making his frontier on the Danube, which would have made good economic and strategic sense. The problem was the huge number of Roman citizens who had already been brought in to colonize

Dacia; Hadrian felt he couldn't simply abandon them. It would not be until AD 272 that the Emperor Aurelian officially gave up the colony, and by then the population was no longer Roman, but Barbarian – among them a sizeable number of Goths.

No one really knows when or how the Goths came to Dacia, but the archaeological evidence shows that even by the time of the Emperor Philip the Arab (ruled 247–8) most of the Romans must have already quit the area. There are no Roman inscriptions after 258 and no large contingents of troops stationed there after 260. Throughout the century there had been increasing numbers of migrants moving into Dacia, and the Romans were unable to deal with them either by diplomatic manoeuvrings or military action.

The Roman Empire inevitably acted as a magnet to the Barbarians who surrounded its borders. Roman wealth, the trading prospects and the possibility of employment all helped to draw Barbarian peoples to the fringes of the Empire. Thus population pressure was often more concentrated in those regions than elsewhere.

A large number of Goths had settled on the northern banks of the Black Sea, but there they found their farms and villages blocking the natural migration routes of the nomadic herdsmen of the steppes. So they began to make incursions into Roman territory in Dacia.

The Romans tried to stop them, and claimed military victories, but Dacia was fundamentally indefensible and there were other more important parts of the Empire that needed controlling, which was why Aurelian finally threw in the sponge and pulled the borders of the Empire back to the Danube. To save face, however, he renamed another province Dacia so that he could claim that it was still Roman territory.

It was in the real Dacia, however, that Alaric was born, around a hundred years later, to a noble Goth family. By this time the Dacian Goths were living in a settled farming society, literate, prosperous and Christian. The Byzantine historian Procopius tells us that the Goths 'all have white bodies and fair hair, and are tall and handsome to look upon, and they use the same laws and practise a common religion.'[1]

Many Goths had converted to Christianity while still outside the Roman Empire. In the fourth century AD their bishop, Ulfila, translated the Bible into Gothic, using an invented alphabet of Greek, Latin and

Runic letters. Ulfila omitted the Book of Kings, however, because he claimed it was too violent. He said the Gothic people were fond enough of war as it was, and since the Book of Kings was simply a narrative of military exploits, it might encourage them in their bellicosity. They 'were in more need of restraints to check their military passions than of spurs to urge them on to deeds of war'.[2]

This may have been a Barbarian approach to Christianity; it certainly wasn't the Roman approach. Roman Christianity was forged in the fire of the Roman Empire and the ideology of that Empire – an ideology of power and world dominance.

THE GOTHS JOIN THE EMPIRE

In Dacia the Goths lived in prosperous villages, and, as usual with the Germanic peoples, some of them allied themselves with Rome. But around the time of Alaric's birth their world fell apart as Hun horsemen began to appear on their farms. A contemporary described the general stupefaction and terror of those days: 'a race of men hitherto unknown had now arisen from a hidden nook of the earth, like a tempest of snows from the high mountain, and was seizing or destroying everything in its way'.[3] No one was quite sure where they came from, although nowadays most authorities think they came from the Asian steppes or possibly southern Siberia. One thing was for sure: nothing would be the same again.

Alaric's parents retreated to an island in the Danube delta, and it was there that he was born. In 375, when he was about six years old, the Huns appeared in greater numbers than ever before. Some Goths resisted, others threw in their lot with the invaders, but the majority of them fled, with one very large group cautiously requesting permission to cross the Danube into the safe haven of the Empire. These are the people we know today as Visigoths – the Western Goths. And their request has become, in folk memory, the invasion of the Barbarian hordes.

The Empire they entered was in the throes of reorganization after a catastrophic defeat in Persia in 363. Valentinian, a soldier who took control in 364, had decided to concentrate on the defence of northern and western Europe and appointed his brother Valens to rule the East from Constantinople. Valens was in no position to try to stop a mass migration on the lower Danube. He agreed to allow the Visigoths entry, and promised that they would be fed – on condition that they disarmed and provided troops for his army, and that the pagans among them became Christians.

Valens even provided transport for the immigrants across the swollen Danube, which was in flood due to heavy rains. The Visigoths were grouped into companies and then over several days and nights were ferried across 'in boats, rafts and in hollowed tree-trunks'. The officials in charge often tried to reckon their number, but gave up the attempt.

> Who wishes to know this would wish to know How many
> grains of sand on Libyan plain ... [4]

Because of the vast crowd some tried to swim, but were swept away in the dangerous current – 'and they were a good many', says Ammianus Marcellinus.[5]

Valens' motives were not, however, humanitarian. He had committed huge resources to fighting Persia, and had been persuaded that the influx of 'so many young recruits from the ends of the earth' would expand his legions into an invincible army. It was hoped that the annual levy of soldiers from each province could be suspended, and that the resulting savings would swell the coffers of the treasury.[6]

What happened next to the Goths was certainly very far from 'humanitarian'. The refugees were put into holding camps where conditions quickly became intolerable – mainly, it was said, as a result of corrupt practices by the officials in charge: Lupicinus, the commanding general in the Balkans, and a certain Maximus. These two took advantage of the starving Goths and 'devised a disgraceful traffic'. They withheld the food supplies that had supposedly been earmarked for them, and forced the refugees to provide slaves in return for dog-meat – one dog for one slave. 'And among these were carried off also sons of the chieftains.'[7]

Whether or not the exploitation was totally the responsibility of these two generals rather than the result of imperial policy, it is clear that the Visigoths were at this point nothing but vulnerable refugees –

'foreign new-comers, who were as yet blameless'. What's more, they were starving. And then an even larger group of Goths was allowed to cross the Danube.

Trouble was bound to break out sooner or later. The vulnerable refugees turned into an avenging horde, which the Romans would find impossible to contain. At this point Ammianus rather endearingly writes: 'I earnestly entreat my readers (if I ever have any) not to demand of me a strictly accurate account of what happened or an exact number of the slain.'[8]

For the next two years, instead of becoming the backbone of the Roman army, as Valens had hoped, the various Gothic groups 'like savage beasts that had broken their cages, poured raging over the wide extent of Thrace'.[9] Ammianus said it was a madness of the times – as if the Furies were stirring up the whole world to rebellion against Roman rule. Valens' nephew Gratian, now ruler of western Europe and 19 years old, successfully put down a revolt in Germany, and in Thrace the general Sebastianus destroyed some predatory bands of Goths and captured an enormous amount of booty.

THE GOTHS TRIUMPH AT HADRIANOPLE, AD 378

Finally, in 378, Valens was stirred into action, though not, naturally, for any noble reasons. He was, reportedly, consumed with envy of his young nephew and desperate to do some glorious deed to equal him. He therefore quit the comfort of the imperial villa outside Constantinople, and marched a huge army west to confront the Visigoths outside the city of Hadrianople. Here he set up a strong rampart of stakes, and impatiently awaited the arrival of his nephew with the Gallic army.

At this point a fatal piece of misinformation sowed the seed of the coming disaster for the Romans. Spies mistakenly reported that the Goths, whose families and warriors were protected by a huge circle of wagons, numbered only 10,000. The emperor, eager to score a point over his nephew, must have seen the chance of winning an easy victory for which he could claim total responsibility. When a message arrived from the young Gratian, urging his uncle to be patient and not to expose himself rashly to more danger than he need, it probably didn't help matters.

In the battle that followed, the Roman legions were routed by the arrival of a huge force of well-equipped Goth cavalry. Ammianus leaves us with a stirring (though doubtless totally concocted) description of a fatally wounded Barbarian fighting to the last gasp: 'Here one might see a barbarian filled with lofty courage, his cheeks contracted in a hiss, hamstrung or with right hand severed, or pierced through the side on the very verge of death threateningly casting about his fierce glance.'[10]

But it was the Romans who suffered by far the worst. The Emperor Valens himself was killed in the rout. One report said that he picked his way through the dead bodies, 'slowly treading over heaps of corpses',[11] and died amongst the common soldiery. His body was never found. The Eastern Empire lost two-thirds of its military force, perhaps 40,000 men – twice as many as Varus had lost in the Teutoburgian Forest – and would never be the same again. The old-fashioned infantry legions had proved useless against Gothic heavy cavalry. The Empire would have to get them on side.

Valens' successor, Theodosius, made peace with the Visigoths, offering them an entirely new status as an independent people inside the Roman Empire living in what is now Bulgaria, with their own laws and their own rulers. They were required to supply what were called federal troops to the Empire in exchange for a cash subsidy. It was a hard deal for Romans to swallow, and an imperial spin doctor proclaimed that although Theodosius could have killed them all if he wanted, it was better to fill Thrace with peasants than corpses – without mentioning that the peasants were Barbarians.[12] But the Goths would eventually discover that it was a lousy deal, putting them into a kind of Barbarian reservation on land that could not support them.

THE RISE OF ALARIC

All this happened while Alaric was in his early teens. He quickly became an officer in the Gothic federal forces under imperial command, and was clearly a very capable commander of men. By 394, while still very young, he had become a general at the head of 20,000 troops.

The army in which he served was no longer recognizably Roman at all. His emperor, Theodosius, was a Spaniard and the Christian ruler of a glittering Christian city, Constantinople. When Alaric marched to war under Theodosius, alongside his own Visigoths there were Hun mercenaries, German Vandals, Iranian Alans and Iberians, all led by the imperial supreme commander, Stilicho, himself the son of a Vandal. This army didn't even look like a Roman army. The legionaries were kitted out in leather trousers and heavy cloaks, while their officers wore huge chest ornaments and sported swords with cloisonné-worked hilts like those of the Goths. And the whole army used the German battle-cry, the *barritus*, which started as a low murmur when their attack began and rose to a great roar like an ocean crashing on to rocks.

Nor was the enemy they marched against some savage Barbarian – their foe was, in fact, the new Western Emperor Eugenius, a former teacher of rhetoric, whom the army commander in the West had placed on the throne after murdering the legitimate emperor, the 19-year-old Valentinian II.

Eugenius was not only a usurper but also a pagan, fighting under the banner of the pagan gods Hercules and Jupiter. Most of the senators of Rome were on his side. They had resisted Christianity, and now hoped to save the Empire from what they saw as the fatal destruction of its most fundamental traditions. Theodosius, on the other hand, was an ardent Christian, who had recently banned all worship of pagan gods – whether in public or in private – and had closed down the temples. His name means 'Gift of God' in Greek, and he was determined to establish the authority of the Greek Christian civilization of 'New Rome', Constantinople, over the Latin Pagan 'Old Rome'. Now, with the aid of Alaric's Goths, he closed down the pagan Emperor in the West.

The Christians hailed the victory as a miracle, but from Alaric's point of view it was a disaster that cost too much Gothic blood – 10,000 of them were said to have been killed in one day. This was probably an exaggeration, but there were suspicions (probably well founded) that Theodosius had deliberately exposed the Goths to danger in order to reduce their numbers. As the contemporary Christian historian Orosius saw it, Theodosius won two victories – one against the usurper and one against the Goths.[13] There was certainly resentment amongst the Goths, and Alaric decided that the time had come to extract much more out of the Empire than they were being offered. This was when Alaric had his troops declare him their king (Alaric seems to mean 'All-king'), and he began a new career as a forceful negotiator and campaigner for Gothic rights.

Alaric must have known his main chance had come when Theodosius died on 17 January 395, and left the Empire divided between his two sons. The East was nominally ruled by the 17-year-old Arcadius, though the government was entrusted to a regent. In the West the Emperor was the ten-year-old Honorius, but the real power was wielded by Stilicho, Theodosius' most trusted general. Stilicho claimed that on his deathbed Theodosius had appointed him as guardian over both sons. There was clearly a power struggle brewing in the Empire, and what better time for the new leader of the Gothic people to assert his command? In the spring of 395 Alaric revolted, first leading his Visigoths towards Constantinople and then storming into Greece.

It would be a mistake to imagine Alaric and his Visigoths as a wandering band of flower-gathering peaceniks, rebelling against the iron heel of Roman rule. The Gothic invasion of Greece was not a Sunday School outing. Having invaded, 'they immediately began to pillage the country and to sack all the towns, killing all the men, both young and old, and carrying off the women and children, together with the money,' wrote the pagan historian Zosimus 100 years later. 'In this incursion, all Boeotia [a region of central Greece], and whatever countries of Greece the Barbarians passed through ... were so ravaged, that the traces are visible to the present day.'[14]

Alaric's rampage through Greece went on into 397. But he wasn't just giving his troops a treat by allowing them to run wild; he was playing a longer game, forcing the Roman Empire to recognize the Goths as players. At the same time he was playing off the Eastern Empire against the West, and doing so with consummate skill.

In the summer of 397, Stilicho left Rome and took his army by sea to drive Alaric out of Greece. Whereupon Alaric started negotiations with the regent of the Eastern Empire, a eunuch by the name of Eutropius. This man was no fool: he knew that if Stilicho defeated

Alaric, the victor's next step would be to take over Constantinople. So
Eutropius struck a deal with Alaric in which it seems that he gave
Alaric the post of *magister militum* – head of the Roman army – in
Illyricum (the region that for much of the twentieth century became
Yugoslavia). It was the kind of thing that Gothic leaders had been
dreaming of since 376.

But there was something different about Alaric.

ALARIC TURNS WEST

The position of *magister militum* made Alaric an *illustris* – a person of
the first rank in both the Senate and the highest assembly of the
Church, the Consistory. He thus became a significant figure in imperial politics, and – whatever personal ambitions he might harbour – he
was thus better able to lobby for Gothic interests in the Empire.

The truth is that Alaric the Goth was never fighting to destroy
Rome. One contemporary described him as 'a Christian and more like
a Roman'.[15] No, Alaric was fighting for the right to join the club. But
he also wanted to change the nature of that club. The Empire was no
longer a melting-pot in which everyone was supposed to be part of
Roman culture and civilization. It now embraced two major cultures:
Latin in the West and Greek in the East. Alaric wanted his Visigoths
to be recognized as a third, with a proper homeland that could support
them. He was quite unscrupulous, however, in playing off the two
powers in the Empire against each other, and he didn't mind which
side gave him room – East or West.

For the moment Alaric had allied himself to the East, but the
political turmoil there, as regents killed and replaced each other in
quick succession, undermined the stability of any deals he might make.
So in the autumn of 401 Alaric and his Goths took a momentous decision. They resolved to pack their bags back in the wagons, leave the
land they had occupied for the last 25 years, and begin a new migration: over the Alps into the unfamiliar political landscape of Italy. It
would mean severing their connections with Constantinople and forcing a deal on the man who until now had been their enemy – Stilicho.

After plundering the countryside, Alaric's Goths marched on
Milan, which had been the seat of government in the West for over

100 years. Stilicho's 17-year-old ward, the Western Emperor Honorius, fled to the safety of marsh-bound Ravenna. The Roman world was genuinely afraid of this unstoppable Gothic army. A few years later, in the Library of the Temple of Apollo in Rome, the poet Claudian recited a poem to celebrate Stilicho's defeat of Alaric in 402. Even allowing for the poet's role as Stilicho's major spin-doctor, he could not have been totally inventing the very real fear of Alaric's army that he describes: 'You and you alone, Stilicho, have dispersed the darkness that enshrouded our empire and restored its glory. Thanks to you, civilization – which had all but vanished – has been freed from its gloomy prison and can again advance ... We no longer gaze from the ramparts, herded together like sheep by our fears, watching our fields ablaze with the enemy's fire.'[16]

There was a real fear that the Empire was on its last legs, and that all the fierce Barbarians who surrounded it were just waiting for their moment to pounce. Before the battle Claudian has his hero, Stilicho, encourage his troops by claiming that all the other Barbarians are wait-ing for the outcome of this fight and that if the imperial forces won it would deter those Barbarians from rebellion in the future: ' ... all the fierce peoples of Britain and the tribes who dwell on Danube's and Rhine's banks are watching ... Win a victory now and so be conquerors in many an unfought war. Restore Rome to her former glory; the frame of empire is tottering; let your shoulders support it.'[17]

Stilicho attacked Alaric's Goths on Easter Sunday 402, while they were at prayer outside the city of Pollentia, just south of modern-day Turin. Although Claudian and others claimed the battle as a great Roman victory, in truth Stilicho allowed Alaric to escape with his forces more or less intact.

Some Romans became convinced that Stilicho was not doing all he could to suppress Alaric and his Goths. There was even a report that Alaric had done a deal with Stilicho to attack Constantinople, and this could well have been the case. It was certainly only two or three years later that Stilicho and Alaric officially became allies. Alaric pledged his forces to help Stilicho wrest the eastern part of Illyricum from the Eastern Emperor, Arcadius. He and his Goths waited in Epirus (the coastal region of north-western Greece and southern Albania) for Stilicho to arrive. His ally, however, never came. He had too many other battles to fight, as the Western Empire suffered one upheaval after another.

Eventually, late in 407, Alaric lost patience and marched his army to the province of Noricum (present-day Austria). From here he demanded 4000 lb of gold – not only as back-pay for the time he'd kept his troops in Epirus (which was reasonable) but also to pay the expenses of his journey to Milan and then on to Noricum. This was tantamount to demanding that Rome pay for the privilege of being invaded.

At the imperial palace in Rome Stilicho persuaded a reluctant Senate to vote Alaric a compromise of 3000 lb of silver. One high-ranking senator by the name of Lampadius was heard to mutter: 'This is not peace, but a bond of servitude.' [18]

Lampadius was not the only one to think the whole thing stank. Doing deals with Barbarians had become politically untenable, and Stilicho began to lose his hold on Honorius. In May 408 the Eastern Emperor Arcadius died. The heir to his throne was his seven-year-old son Theodosius II, but Honorius was by now obsessed with the idea that Stilicho had imperial ambitions. He had Stilicho's associates murdered and gave orders for the general's arrest. Stilicho sought sanctuary in a church. However, the Emperor's soldiers swore to the bishop that they had come not to kill Stilicho but only to put him in custody. Once the general was handed over, though, the sentence of death was read out to him and he was led off to his execution. His remaining supporters tried to prevent it, but Stilicho told them not to fight and went calmly to his death in the finest tradition of old Roman stoicism. He was in origin a Vandal and they called him a Barbarian, but he wanted to show that he was the last of what Rome had once been, and that with his death, Rome died.

From here, that looks about right. The 23-year-old Honorius had just executed the one general who was capable of dealing with the threat posed by Alaric. And the execution of this Vandal general triggered a catastrophic anti-Barbarian pogrom throughout the Eternal City. The victims were the wives and children of the Barbarian auxiliaries in Stilicho's army.

> Having, as by a preconcerted signal, destroyed every
> individual of them, they plundered them of all they

possessed. When this was known to the relations of those who were murdered, they assembled together from all quarters. Being highly incensed against the Romans for so impious a breach of the promises they had made in the presence of the gods, they all resolved to join Alaric, and to assist him in a war against Rome.[19]

It was said that 30,000 Barbarian soldiers deserted the Roman army to join Alaric's forces. In addition, the thousands of fighting men who had been sold into slavery after the defeats of other groups of Goths now took advantage of the general chaos and fled captivity to swell even more the numbers of Alaric's army.

ALARIC BESIEGES ROME, AD 408

The moment seemed ripe for Alaric to extract the sort of agreement with Rome that he had been looking for. To increase the pressure, he now set out on the long march to Rome. He ordered his brother-in-law, Athaulf, to join him with his considerable body of Goths and Huns. The march south was unchallenged, and even had something of a festival atmosphere about it, according to Zosimus.

Honorius' only reaction was to intensify the witch-hunt against anyone and everyone who had had anything to do with Stilicho. He ordered the general's son to be taken to Rome and executed. Then he rewarded the two eunuchs who performed the deed with the positions of imperial chamberlain and vice-chamberlain. Next he murdered the commander of the troops in Libya because he was married to Stilicho's sister, and gave the post to the man who had killed Stilicho.

The Senate joined in the madness. Instead of taking practical measures to counter the approaching Goths, it voted to have Stilicho's wife, Serena, put to death. The noble senators had become convinced that it was she – and she alone – who was bringing the Barbarians against their city. Their argument ran like this: 'Alaric, upon Serena being removed, will retire from the city, because no person will remain by whom he can hope the town to be betrayed into his hands.' She was duly executed.[20] Which only goes to show that political idiocy is not peculiar to the present day.

To the senators' surprise, Serena's death did nothing to check the advance of the Goths. Alaric besieged Rome, took control of the Tiber and cut off supplies from the port of Ostia. The senators prepared to hold out, assuming that forces would be sent by the Emperor in Ravenna to relieve them. They were either too optimistic or else ill informed about the Emperor's sense of priorities. No help came from the imperial headquarters.

The inhabitants of Rome were equally badly informed about who was besieging them. In the paranoid world of Honorius' obsessive witch-hunting, a rumour had sprung up that the Barbarians at the gates were led not by Alaric at all, but by some relative of Stilicho who had come to wreak revenge. Conditions in Rome became desperate, and the citizens 'were in danger of being eaten by each other'.[21] St Jerome recalled hearing a story of one mother eating her newborn child.

Eventually the Romans sent an embassy to Alaric saying that they were prepared to fight but would negotiate peace. Zosimus tells us that the envoys were ashamed at how badly informed they were about who was attacking them. Alaric was contemptuous. He laughed in their faces, and replied to their proposals with 'arrogance and presumption'. He demanded that the Romans hand over all the gold and silver in the city, all the household goods and all the Barbarian slaves. One of the ambassadors asked: 'If you take all these, what will you leave for the citizens?' Alaric replied: 'Their souls.'[22]

They agreed to pay 5000 lb of gold, 30,000 of silver, 3000 scarlet sheepskins (the Goths must have been a very well turned out army) and 3000 lb of pepper (they were already, of course, well seasoned). To pay the ransom, the Romans stripped the temples of all their silver and gold, and even resorted to melting down the gold and silver statues. Amongst these was the statue of Valour or Fortitude – 'This being destroyed, all that remained of the Roman valour and intrepidity was totally extinguished,' says Zosimus.[23]

Once the money was handed over, Alaric allowed the citizens safe passage between the city and the port, and suspended sales taxes and duties for three successive days. When the Goth leader learnt that some of the Barbarians were interfering with the citizens' right of passage 'he used his utmost endeavours to prevent such proceedings, which were without his knowledge or consent'.[24]

Alaric seemed to be on the point of getting what he really wanted. The praetorian prefect of Italy, Jovius, hammered out a peace agreement on Honorius' behalf. Alaric and his Goths would be granted a certain amount of gold every year, a quantity of corn, and be allowed to settle in the Veneto, Austria and Croatia. This was the deal that would create harmony in the new, three-nation Empire of Latins, Greeks and Goths. It was the only way forward, and Jovius sent it to the Emperor with an accompanying letter advising Honorius to appoint Alaric commander of both his armies, as they needed his troops, and without a suitably high position for Alaric, there would be no peace.

The Emperor, however, was more adept at taking bad advice than good. He reprimanded Jovius for his 'forward temerity' and said 'that no dignity or command should ever be conferred on Alaric, or any of his family'.[25] Alaric, baffled, could think of no other form of persuasion than another threat to Rome. Desperate, he sent a deputation of bishops to Honorius 'to advise the emperor not to suffer so noble a city, which for more than a thousand years had ruled over a great part of the world, to be seized and destroyed by the Barbarians, nor such magnificent edifices to be demolished by hostile flames, but to prefer entering into a peace on some reasonable conditions'.[26] They then presented Alaric's peace proposals, which were as reasonable as he could make them: he dropped the demand for special treatment, desired only to be settled in two areas at the extremity of the Danube, which 'are harassed by continual incursions, and yield to the treasury a very small revenue'. In addition 'he only demanded as much corn as the emperor should think proper to grant, and would remit the gold. And that a friendship and alliance should subsist between himself and the Romans, against every one that should rise to oppose the empire.'[27]

It was too good to be true. How could anyone in their right mind turn down such proposals? Was Alaric really so desperate to get his people settled? Or did he realize that Honorius was never going to come to terms, and therefore put the most outrageously reasonable peace offer on the table in order to exonerate himself from whatever happened next? If Rome suffered, it would clearly be the Emperor's fault.

But Honorius had his reputation of obdurate foolishness to maintain, and the proposals were rejected. Alaric once again marched on

Rome and took over the port. Rome was fed on corn shipped from the Empire's vast colonial estates in North Africa, and the citizens, faced with certain starvation, capitulated. He was allowed to enter the city.

ALARIC THE EMPEROR-MAKER

It was an extraordinary – almost unbelievable – situation. A Barbarian chieftain was now master of Rome, able to dispose offices and appointments at his will. With the agreement of the Senate, Alaric even set a new emperor on the imperial throne. His candidate was the prefect of the city, a traditional Roman pagan named Attalus, and for the time being the city celebrated a momentary improvement in its government. Alaric was appointed co-commander of the Roman army, and everything looked promising. Except, of course, for the fact that Honorius had not agreed to any of this. And since he controlled Africa, Rome's source of grain, Attalus' first job had to be to take over Carthage.

But Attalus was to prove a disaster. He was told by some sooth-sayer that he would subdue Carthage and all Africa without fighting, so he simply sent out to the imperial army in Africa his own commander – who was killed when he got there. Then he sent a whole lot of money to Africa with the hope that it might somehow sort things out. At this point Alaric began to realize that he had placed on the imperial throne a man 'who formed his projects with the most foolish temerity, without either reason or prospect of advantage'.[28] And Honorius, whose orders were obeyed in Africa, ensured that no corn or oil left for Rome. Famine in the city was even greater than in the previous year. The common joke in the Hippodrome was to shout out: 'Fix a price on human flesh!'[29]

Eventually Alaric couldn't stand his protégé's nonsense any longer. He marched to Rimini on the Adriatic, where Attalus was currently sunning himself, and there, in public, stripped his chosen emperor of his diadem and purple robe. Alaric, the Gothic chief, could make and unmake a Roman emperor – just like that. It wasn't bad going for a humble Barbarian from the Danube delta. Alaric's attractiveness as a leading player in history is nowhere more evident than in his treatment of the infuriating Attalus. Having stripped him of his office, the Goth leader took him back to Rome and installed the ex-emperor and his son under house arrest in the palace he had requisitioned there. Attalus was to be kept safe until a peace was eventually reached with Honorius.[30]

Perhaps he had already reached an agreement with Honorius to remove the rival emperor in return for peace. At all events, Alaric sent Attalus' diadem and robe to Honorius, and started out for Ravenna to confirm a treaty between them. However, as he was approaching the city, he was attacked, evidently with Honorius' blessing.[31] Alaric, finding peace once again removed from the agenda, fell back on the last resort. He returned and sacked Rome. The sack of Rome was not a triumph of Gothic military might – it was the last desperate act of Alaric's diplomacy, and it failed.

ALARIC SACKS ROME, 410

Everything about Alaric's sack of Rome is extraordinary. How the Goths got in, what they did once they were in, how they left … it's all a little beyond belief.

Alaric now found himself for the third time outside the gates of Rome, but on this occasion there was no long siege. The Goths got into the city during the night of 24 August 410. The Romans still remembered tales of the Celts who had captured the city 800 years earlier. Ever since that traumatic occasion, the whole purpose of Rome's conquests had been to prevent such a thing ever happening again – to push its power outwards in all directions, Romanize or kill the Barbarians who surrounded it, and make the city safe. And now the whole of that history had turned to failure.

In Bethlehem, St Jerome wrote that he was speechless with grief: 'The whole world perished in one city.' Pelagius the heretic, who was actually in Rome at the time, could only compare it with the Last Judgement, when all humans will stand equal in their terror:

Rome, the mistress of the world, shivered, crushed with fear,
at the sound of the blaring trumpets and the howling of the
Goths. Where then were the nobility? Where then were the
supposedly unchanging divisions in society? Everyone was

mingled together and shaken with fear. Every household had
its grief and an all-pervading terror gripped us. Slave and noble
were one. The same spectre of death stalked before us all.[32]

Really? Because the odd thing is that, once they got into the city,
Alaric and his Goths seem to have behaved like no other invading army
before or since.

In the first place Alaric had given strict orders to limit bloodshed.
Orosius, writing while the memory of the sack was still fresh, reported
that Alaric 'gave orders that all those who had taken refuge in sacred
places, especially in the basilicas of the holy Apostles Peter and Paul,
should be permitted to remain inviolate and unmolested'.[33] There were
a few fires, but the city was hardly damaged.

Alaric also, of course, allowed his men to plunder and loot, and
yet even here restraint was shown. One of the Goths, who was a
Christian, asked an old woman where he could find gold and silver,
whereupon she brought out the sacred plate of the Apostles Peter and
Paul and gave them to the soldier saying: 'Now you must look after
them since I can't.' When Alaric heard the story he ordered a great
procession to be held through the city, in which the sacred plate was
paraded above everyone's heads and under the guard of 'a double line
of drawn swords; Romans and barbarians in concert raised a hymn to
God in public'.[34]

Gold and silver in houses was left strictly alone if it was used for
religious purposes, and would-be rapists backed off in shame when
they were told off by Roman ladies. Amongst the booty carried off by
the Goths was the Emperor Honorius' sister, Galla Placidia, whom
Alaric treated 'with all the honour and attendance due to a princess'.[35]
It wasn't much of a 'sack', really.

Honorius, in Ravenna, seemed to catch the spirit of the occasion.
When one of the eunuchs, who kept the poultry, burst in to inform
him that Rome had perished, the Emperor cried out: 'But it has just
eaten from my hands!' The eunuch, realizing that the Emperor was
thinking of a large cockerel he had that was called Rome, explained
that it was the city that had gone down. The Emperor sighed with
relief and replied: 'But I, my good fellow, thought that my fowl Rome
had perished.' Which only goes to show that Honorius had no idea

how to produce a good punch-line.[36]

It was, all in all, a pretty weird storming of a city, and the ending was just as extraordinary. After three days of this sedate mayhem, Alaric simply upped sticks and left. The Goths obviously could not live in a starving city, and it seems that his plan now was to ship them all to Africa and settle there. But it was not to be. After a successful march down into Calabria, and a rather less successful attempt to organize a naval expedition across the Straits of Messina, Alaric fell ill and died.

For all his attractive qualities, Alaric had been basically unsuccessful. The Gothic people still had no permanent home, and all Alaric had done was sack the city he was so keen to be a part of.

WHAT THE SACK OF ROME MEANT

There is no doubt that Alaric's sack of Rome came as a profound shock to everyone. 'What will remain if Rome falls?' wailed St Jerome. But the significance of AD 410 to those who lived through it was not as we see it today.

The main topic of conversation amongst Alaric's contemporaries was not what economic or political pressures had brought about this catastrophe, but who was to blame for this terrible event – the pagans or the Christians. In 410 the Empire had been officially Christian for less than 100 years. It was only 86 years since pagan sacrifice had been banned, and a mere 19 years since all worship of pagan gods had been prohibited. When Alaric appeared at the gates of Rome, the pagans in the city 'flocked together, saying ... that the City was forsaken and would soon perish because it had completely abandoned its gods and its sacred rites,' wrote Orosius, 'and the name of Christ was publicly loaded with reproaches as if it were a curse upon the times'.[37]

It was a tough one for the Christians to deal with. The evidence was cut and dried. For 800 years Rome had kept the Barbarians at bay. Then it had abandoned the old gods and embraced a new-fangled religion that just seemed to get the worshippers into trouble. And what happens? The unthinkable happens. The story of Brennus is repeated, and the Barbarian hordes once more strut through the sacred streets of Rome.

The primary significance of the sack of Rome for people at the time was that it appeared to deal a body-blow to the Christian religion. Perhaps that's why Alaric, who was after all a Christian himself, abandoned the glittering prize. He simply couldn't bear being the destroyer not only of the city but of the faith of the Christians who inhabited it.

The Bishop of Hippo in North Africa complained that many of those who laid the blame for the sack of Rome at the door of the Christians had only escaped by pretending to be Christians themselves.[38] The good bishop was later consecrated a saint, and is now known to history as St Augustine. So concerned was he about the damage done to the Christian faith by Alaric's sack of Rome that he wrote 22 books to counteract it, of which the overall title was *The City of God Against the Pagans*.

A central argument of Augustine's work is that, far from proving the inadequacy of Christianity compared to the old pagan rites, the sack of Rome in 410 was a glorious vindication of the newer religion because Alaric – unlike any other invader – showed such mercy to the people. Under the chapter heading 'In no previous wars have the victors spared the vanquished for the sake of their gods', he writes: 'What set a new precedent [was] the aspect, novel in history and so gentle, that barbarian cruelty displayed, in that basilicas of the most generous capacity were selected and set apart by decree to be occupied as asylums of mercy for the people, where no one should be smitten, whence no one should be ravished.'[39] Of course, Augustine adds, God forbid that anyone should attribute this forbearance to the Barbarians themselves – of course not! It was Christ who bridled their ferocity and made them act so mercifully – for, of course, Alaric was a Christian.

THE VISIGOTH KINGDOM

Augustine was wrong: he protested too much. In fact the city survived the non-sack perfectly well, and was living its old life again within a few years. But the Western Empire was crumbling with or without the 'sack', and Rome's identity was destroyed by Christians imposing their new civilization on the pagan city. Alaric's Goths had come on to that stage in the service of Theodosius, destroying the pagan Roman army of the Emperor Eugenius.

Augustine and the other Church theologians crusading against paganism and 'heresy' were creating a new political order, which was intended to replace the old Empire. The city of Rome was of sentimental rather than practical importance in this new world; emperors were rarely seen there, most senators stayed away, and by the time Alaric arrived, the city's population had fallen by about two-thirds from its peak of around one million. In the East, the new order became the Christian Empire of Byzantium. In the West, it became a patchwork of Christian kingdoms that identified themselves as Roman but that acknowledged no power in Rome except the Church's. And here the Goths did eventually find their place.

After Alaric's death the Goths moved to southern Gaul under the leadership of his brother-in-law. Athaulf had apparently once taken a different view of Rome from Alaric, wanting to replace it rather than be accepted by it. But now he seemingly despaired of his own people and decided they needed the firm hand of Roman authority. His mature political ambitions were reported in 415 by a citizen of Narbonne to St Jerome, a conversation overheard by the historian Orosius. Apparently Athaulf had said:

> In the full confidence of valour and victory, I once
> aspired to change the face of the universe; to obliterate
> the name of Rome; to erect on its ruins the dominion of
> the Goths; and to acquire, like Augustus, the immortal
> fame of the founder of a new empire. By repeated
> experiments, I was gradually convinced, that laws are
> essentially necessary to maintain and regulate a well-
> constituted state; and that the fierce, untractable
> humour of the Goths was incapable of bearing the
> salutary yoke of laws and civil government. From that
> moment I proposed to myself a different object of glory
> and ambition; and it is now my sincere wish that the
> gratitude of future ages should acknowledge the merit of a
> stranger, who employed the sword of the Goths, not to
> subvert, but to restore and maintain, the prosperity of the
> Roman empire.[40]

One wonders about his repeated experiments.

Athaulf decided to marry Galla Placidia – presenting her with 50 bowls of gold and 50 of jewels – and, just to be on the safe side with his new loyalty to Rome, to install an Augustus of his own choosing. But by 415 he had been murdered. Roman armies drove his Visigoths into Spain and destroyed Athaulf's puppet emperor. But Athaulf's successor Wallia made peace with Honorius, who finally agreed the deal that he had so stubbornly refused Alaric. Wallia returned Honorius' sister Galla Placidia to him, and in 417 was granted Aquitaine as a region where the Visigoths would be based as *foederati* – independent Roman allies who, for the first time, were not part of a frontier. This was what Alaric had struggled so hard to achieve – a negotiated Gothic territory within the Empire, not on its margins. Wallia established his court in Toulouse, which became the capital of a Christian Visigoth kingdom.

It was Christians who finished off the Western Empire. And it was Barbarians who gave us the Europe we live in today.

PART III

BARBARIANS FROM THE EAST

VIII
HELLENES

The Romans were virtually surrounded by Barbarians! There were Barbarians to the west of them, Barbarians to the north of them and Barbarians to the east of them. They dismissed those to the north and west (the Celts, the Goths and the Germans) as primitive and uncivilized. When they did the same to the Barbarians to the east, however, they found they'd bitten off more than they could chew. The east is where the Roman Empire met its match.

And it met its match in two different ways: militarily and intellectually. The empire of the Persians blocked Roman territorial ambitions in the east. The Hellenic world, on the other hand, was politically subsumed into Rome, but then proceeded to transform Roman intellectual life. As the Roman poet Horace put it: 'Greece enslaved, enslaved her savage conqueror'.[1] In both cases, Rome's belief in its own superiority was challenged by what it encountered. But the story we have been left with, a story of the greatness of Rome, has somehow managed to ignore that.

The conquest of Greece led to Rome becoming ever more Greek, until it seemed the most natural thing in the world for the imperial headquarters to relocate to the Greek city of Constantinople. As Rome developed into a predominantly Eastern power, its great conflict with Persia became the biggest item on the imperial agenda – a struggle that lasted for centuries and eventually drove the Empire to suck the West dry to pay for its Eastern defence.

But while the Roman Empire became Greek, Greece was transformed by Rome. Although the Romans came to see it as the home of culture, literature and the arts, Greece had also been the most innovative scientific and engineering civilization on earth; but wherever they ruled, the Romans rejected the new. Nowhere is the dead hand of Roman stasis more clearly demonstrated than in its dealings with the Hellenic world.

THE ANTIKYTHERA MECHANISM

In 1900 a man by the name of Elias Stadiatos was diving for sponges off the Greek island of Antikythera. When he was hauled back on to the deck of the rusty vessel that served as a diving station, he was wild-eyed and babbling about having seen a 'heap of naked women' down on the sea floor.[2] It turned out that the poor fellow was not hallucinating. He had stumbled across the wreck of a vessel that had gone down in ancient times with a priceless cargo of artistic treasures – presumably on their way to Rome.

Over the next few months the divers hauled up an amazing treasure trove: jewellery, tableware, furniture, pottery and dozens of other items, including stone statues as well as smaller bronze ones. Amongst the riches was a lump of marine growth and corrosion surrounding what looked like some kind of gearing. A diver brought it up to the surface because there appeared to be some bronze under the corrosion, but it seemed hardly worth anyone's attention amongst so many wonderful classical works of art. Besides, it broke into several pieces shortly after its exposure to the atmosphere, and what may have been its wooden casing shrivelled up. Many years later, however, it would be realized that this was the most valuable object of all because it would revolutionize our view of the ancient world.

It had astronomical inscriptions etched on it, and for some 50 years it remained a mysterious puzzle that occasionally furrowed the odd academic brow. Some people suggested it was a sort of astrolabe (an early navigational device), but other scholars insisted that this would have been beyond the capacities of the ancient Greeks. And anyway, it was much more complicated than an astrolabe. It obviously wasn't Greek at all, they insisted.

Eventually, however, a British physicist and historian of science, Derek de Solla Price, went to the Athens Museum to carry out a long-term study of this bizarre object. After eight years he announced that it was some form of intricate clockwork.[3] It contained about 30 gear

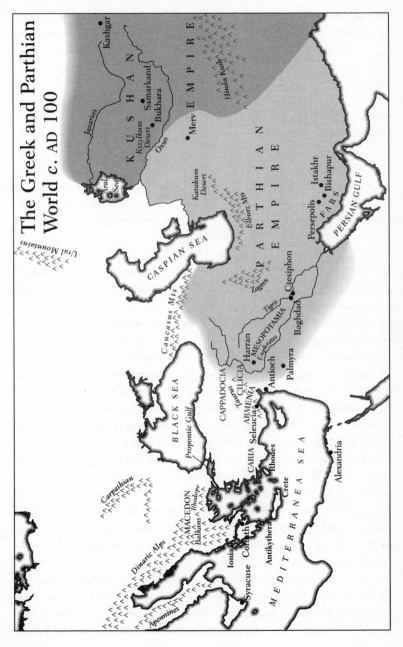

The Greek and Parthian
World c. AD 100

Ural Mountains

Kashgar

KUSHAN EMPIRE

Samarkand
Bukhara

Jaxartes

Kyzylkum Desert

Oxus

Merv

Hindu Kush

Aral Sea

Karakum Desert

Elburz Mts

Istakhr
Bishapur
Persepolis

FARS

PERSIAN GULF

CASPIAN SEA

PARTHIAN EMPIRE

Caucasus Mts

Zagros

Ctesiphon

Tigris

Baghdad

MESOPOTAMIA

Harran

Euphrates

CAPPADOCIA

Taurus

CILICIA

Antioch

Palmyra

ARMENIA

CARIA

Seleucia

Rhodes

Crete

Alexandria

BLACK SEA

Propontic Gulf

Carpathian

MACEDON

Rhodope

Balkans

Dinaric Alps

Ionia

Corinth

Antikythera

MEDITERRANEAN SEA

Syracuse

Apennines

153

wheels, yet had lettering that could only be dated to the first century BC. Such a suggestion was so unthinkable that one professor told him the only way his hypothesis could be true was if someone sailing over the shipwreck more than 1000 years later had dropped the thing over the side.

In 1971, still convinced he must be right, Price persuaded the Greek Atomic Energy Commission to experiment with the new technique of gamma rays to examine the corroded piece of bronze. Photographic plates were produced from which he was able to reconstruct the device and prove when it had been made. Price found himself rebuilding a mechanism that looks like an eighteenth-century instrument – but is actually a clockwork computer created, most probably, on the island of Rhodes off the south-west tip of modern Turkey around 80 BC. It shows the positions of the sun and moon on dials that are marked not for a day or a week but for four years.[4]

And suddenly it was clear that historians had got the non-Roman world very, very wrong. At a time when the Roman calendar was out by over 80 days, so that people were told to celebrate spring festivals in the height of summer, a Greek workshop on Rhodes was designing and making a device to show the exact positions of the heavenly bodies and to provide a simple read-out on dials.

Michael Wright, former curator of mechanical engineering at the Science Museum in London, has built a conjectural reconstruction of the Antikythera mechanism, which has 76 gear wheels and one pointer that completes a rotation every 76 years! It is a sophisticated working model of the solar system. 'The user could dial in any date he or she wanted,' he says, 'and the instrument would show the positions in the sky of the sun, the moon and all of the five planets then known.'

Its use is not at all clear. Perhaps the device was just a way of predicting the phases of the moon or eclipses; or perhaps it was used for astrological predictions. Astrology was a fundamental science of the ancient world. It was the driving force behind the astronomy of Egypt and Babylon, and led to the development of advanced mathematics to compute the apparent movement of the stars and planets. (In fact, the link between astrology, astronomy and mathematics remained strong until after the age of Newton in the seventeenth century.) But perhaps it was simply a tool for exploring the mysteries of the cosmos – the Greeks were fascinated by abstract scientific and philosophical speculation.

Whatever it was used for, its design and construction were certainly well beyond the capabilities of the Romans. Despite what most people think, other cultures could and did make extremely complex machines – until the Romans took over.

ROME THE DESTROYER

Rome established its Empire by destroying other civilizations. Carthage, one of the great cities of the ancient world, was levelled by the Romans in 146 BC.[5] There were once great libraries containing books in that culture's language: Punic. Not a line of Punic remains. The Temple in Jerusalem was obliterated and its contents removed to Rome, so we can only speculate about the way it functioned during the life of Jesus. We know that the Druids had teachings, but virtually all their writings were destroyed. The Dacians had a religious philosophy compared by the Greeks to that of Moses and Pythagoras, but its content has been utterly erased.

How much damage did the Romans do to the history of civilization? We shall probably never know. But the most astonishing and unremarked destruction of all was that of the technological world of the Hellenes. Contrary to everything we have been led to believe, the Hellenic world was one of metal gear-trains and accurate clocks, of pistons and steam-power – a world of advanced engineering. An ancient society might have described fabulous machines, but without the precision nuts and bolts, such things could only be fantasies. It used to be thought that inventions such as the screw-cutting lathe and the universal joint appeared for the first time in the seventeenth and eighteenth centuries, explaining the basis of our industrial revolution. We now know that both of these inventions were in use in the Hellenic world before the first century AD. So what were the Greeks doing with them?

There is a second-century BC Greek papyrus from Alexandria that lists the greatest achievers in history: law-makers, painters, sculptors, architects and – amazingly – mechanical engineers.[6] One of them is a fellow by the name of Abdaraxus, 'who built the machines in

Alexandria'. That is the only record of his name. There is no clue anywhere as to what these machines were, or why they were so famous. His fame has been expunged along with his achievements. How many other Abdaraxuses are there of whom we have no record at all?

Mechanics, unless they were useful for killing people, did not interest the Romans. The first-century BC Roman engineer Vitruvius lists the 12 authors who had written on mechanics.[7] All of them are Hellenes: 'I observe that on this branch the Greeks have published much, and our own countrymen very little.' We know writings from only three of them, and this is the sole record we have of eight of these people. Abdaraxus, of course, is a name that wouldn't impress the Romans. It's not a Latin name. It's Barbarian.

GREEK BARBARIANS

But why do the Greeks, of all people, qualify to be called 'barbarian'? After all, if you look around the Greek world you see the remains of a classical civilization. Wasn't it the Greeks themselves who originally coined the word, to describe outlandish gibbering savages?

'Barbarian' did not necessarily mean a hairy-chested warrior from the north. As early as the fifth century BC it signified simply 'different from us'. In 431 BC the Greek historian Thucydides, trying to understand why Homer did not use the word, concluded that it was 'probably because the Hellenes had not yet been marked off from the rest of the world'.[8]

Hellenes, at that time, meant the inhabitants of what is now southern Greece and its colonies on the Mediterranean and Aegean coasts and islands. A significant part of the Greek-speaking world, however, was excluded, including most of northern Greece. Alexander the Great, for example, spoke Greek but hailed from Macedon in the north, so the Greeks considered him a Barbarian. In 476 BC his ancestor Alexander I of Macedon had turned up at the Olympic Games and demanded to take part. There were outraged protests from the other competitors, who said they would not compete against a Barbarian.[9] He was ultimately allowed to take part after producing an invented genealogy that showed he was of Hellenic descent from Argos.

The issue was not what language he spoke but whether he was

'one of us'. And many of the people of the Greek city-states remained unconvinced. Over 100 years later, when another Macedonian king, Archelaus, attacked a Greek city, a rousing oration was delivered that demanded Greeks to stand together against him: 'Shall we be slaves to Archelaus, we, being Greeks, to a barbarian?'[10] Demosthenes, the great Athenian statesman and orator, declared that Alexander the Great's father, Philip, was 'not even a barbarian from any place that can be named with honour, but a pestilent knave from Macedon, where it has never yet been possible to buy a decent slave'.[11] You get the picture.

So far as the Hellenes were concerned, the Romans were Barbarians too. Although they were prepared to regard them as honorary Greeks when they behaved well, and let them compete in their games from the late third century BC, the Hellenes would refer to them as *barbaroi* when they got upset with them.[12] According to Cato the Elder, a third-century BC Roman statesman, the Greeks 'commonly call us barbarians'.[13]

The Romans, at a very fundamental level, returned the compliment.

Cato described the Greeks as 'morally debased and disordered'; these Barbarians had an interesting literature, to be sure, but he warned his son against going into it too deeply.[14] Just like the Greeks, the Romans used the word 'barbarian' to describe almost anyone who wasn't part of their own civilization. And up to the second century BC, the Greeks fitted into that category.

Later, the Roman Republic became thoroughly Hellenized, so that by the time of Augustus the great poetic myth-makers of Roman identity, Ovid and Virgil, were making it seem as though Rome and Greece were a single civilization. Three hundred years after that, the whole Eastern Roman Empire was dominated by the Greek language and a (transformed) Greek culture. In fact the identification of the Roman Empire with Greek-ness went so far that today the Greek word for their own identity is *Romiosini* – Roman-ness. But things were very different in the early days of the Roman Republic.

The Hellenization of the Romans began after they defeated Macedon in 196 BC and took control of Greece. Around that time Romans started sending their children to be educated in schools, and the sons of wealthier families were taught Greek from the age of 12 or 13.

This did not, however, make the Romans less brutal towards the Greeks. When war resumed with Macedonia in 171 BC, they eliminated that kingdom, destroyed much of Epirus and over the next three years put an end to Greek political life. The Roman conquest of Greece was ruthless and largely driven by a hunger for plunder. When, in 146 BC, almost the entire Peloponnese and parts of central Greece (the 'Achaean confederacy') rebelled against Roman control, the city of Corinth was razed and its inhabitants sold into slavery.

But by now the Romans regarded the Greeks as the original source of civilization (*humanitas*), more sophisticated, better educated and with more elaborate manners than themselves. On the other hand, the Greeks were despised for being so much less manly than their hardened neighbours to the west; they were more effete, decadent, devious and luxury-loving. However much he respected Greek culture, no ambitious Roman wanted to be identified as a Greek.[15] A Hellene was not, for a good Roman, 'one of us'.

MISUNDERSTANDING THE GREEKS

Rome's policy of extending its military and political control over the Barbarians of the east had truly dreadful consequences for the history of Europe. The mechanism found on the Antikythera shipwreck is a clue to the scale of the disaster. And that disaster is only now coming to light, because for many centuries afterwards the few texts recording the scientific, mathematical and engineering achievements of antiquity were disregarded.

Upper-crust Romans disdained practical engineering, and since it has been wrongly assumed that classical Greece and Rome were in effect a single cultural enterprise, it has often been asserted that the Greeks thought the same. In the nineteenth century there were growing doubts in some quarters about whether the Greeks had really been so smart. If they were so clever, why hadn't they discovered the mechanical science that led to Europe's industrial revolution?[16] The answer was a magnificent put-down to these philistines: the ancient Greeks, very properly, had left practical and experimental matters to their slaves and servants.

The authority usually cited for this was Plutarch, an entirely Romanized Greek writing in the early second century AD. He pushed the Roman contempt for mere mechanics back on to the ancient Greeks, deducing that Plato's criticism of experiment meant that 'mechanics came to be separated from geometry, and repudiated and neglected by philosophers'.[17] Plutarch projected his own distaste for the subject on to the Greek Archimedes: 'He viewed the work of the engineer and every single art connected with everyday need as ignoble and fit only for an artisan.' Archimedes, having been dead for 300 years, was in no position to argue – a shame, since given the amount of time, energy and pride he invested in making machines, this assertion is obvious nonsense.

When Plutarch's *Lives* was rediscovered at the start of the Renaissance, it stimulated a new respect for the classics. Greek literature, philosophy and theoretical mathematics have been treated ever since with reverent awe. But classically educated scholars imitated what they thought to be a Greek contempt for practical engineering and technology. Surviving Greek texts on these subjects were either totally ignored or dismissed as impossibly fanciful by scholars studiously ignorant of engineering.

But this was a Roman mind-set, not a Greek one. Greek mechanical science was based on very highly developed practical and theoretical scientific investigation. It was killed off by the Romans, who were not interested and needed a society that changed as little as possible. Rome has triumphed over our understanding of the history of technology as thoroughly as it has in other areas. Romans lived behind frontiers, and what lay beyond was dangerous. That applied as much to their mental world as to their geography.

WAR MACHINES

Roman literary sources don't say much about the technological sophistication of the Hellenes. The first revelations about ancient Greek science were made when a German artillery officer of the First World War, Erwin Schramm, began building his own reconstructions of ancient artillery.[18] His work has been taken much further by the British historian Eric Marsden.[19]

The earliest evidence that something amazing was developing with Hellenic war machines dates to 399 BC. Dionysius the Elder, the 'tyrant' (or, as we might now say, the CEO) of Syracuse, a Greek colony in Sicily that was at war with the great North African state of Carthage, set up a military research and development facility. Much of what emerged was along the lines of 'bigger is better' – the best warships were triremes, effective sea-going rams with three banks of oarsmen. It was worth checking whether extra rowers would make them even more powerful. That experiment was a success, and so the quinquireme was born. The first one, fitted out with silver and gold, was sent to collect Dionysius' bride from a city he needed as an ally. The glittering vessel, with its ornamented beak of a prow and the oars of 500 rowers rippling out from its massive wooden sides, was a spectacular image of organization, wealth and technology.

Back in Syracuse he was simultaneously building 200 ships and refitting and repairing 260 more. Arms and armour were being hammered out on an epic scale. But most astonishing of all, his engineers had given birth to an entirely new kind of weapon – artillery. Up to then, the force of a projectile depended on the strength and skill of the arm that threw it or that drew the bow, but now warfare had suddenly become mechanized.

The machine they had built was called a catapult (literally, 'shield-splitter'); we would immediately recognize it as a cross-bow. One of its most curious features was that the bow was not of the normal European design, a piece of wood to be bent and then released; it is believed to have been a composite laminate of wood, horn and sinew, a technology used in the bows of the Mongolian steppe nomads. This bow is a massively powerful spring, which has to be tensioned by bending it the opposite way to its natural curve (it is often referred to as a recurve bow). In the hands of an experienced warrior it has a range of 300 yards, and at 100 yards will pass clean through an ox no matter where it strikes. Mounted on a stock, with a claw to hold the bowstring, a winch to pull it back, a slider and a trigger, it could be used by inexperienced recruits after just a few days' training.

It's also worth noting that Dionysius achieved these results by employing management techniques that were as advanced as his engineers' inventions.[20] He aggressively recruited the leading artificers of the world by offering very generous rates of pay, organized the breakdown of work into manageable units and personally encouraged and rewarded those who were successful – he had a sort of 'employee of the month' scheme.

This technology was rapidly taken up and developed elsewhere. The Barbarians of Macedonia thought it was extremely useful, and Philip of Macedon set up his own research establishment. This seems to have taken the use of mechanical power to a whole new level, with the replacement of a springy bow by the torsion energy of wound-up bundles of sinews or hair. His 20-year-old son Alexander inherited the kingdom and the war machines in 336 BC and took off with the kit to conquer the world, carrying enough catapult artillery to use it for covering fire as his troops advanced. Alexander the Great's personal charisma obviously contributed to his success, but so did the fact that revolutionary mechanical weaponry used on a large scale against simply equipped traditional defences was irresistible. In 12 years he conquered Asia Minor, Persia, Egypt and a substantial part of India.

Alexander's empire fell apart after his death, but he had left an indelible mark upon the world, and his successors in Alexandria and Macedonia continued to develop their military technology. In 305 BC, when Rome was just an aggressive Italian city battling to dominate its neighbours in a series of small-scale battles, the walls of Rhodes in the Eastern Mediterranean were attacked by the Macedonians with their latest weapon. The Helepolis ('city-wrecker'), nine storeys high and covered with iron plates, was moved on eight great wheels by 2000 men. Shutters in the plates opened to allow missiles to be projected – different-sized shutters for different types of projectiles.[21]

But Rhodes had been doing its own inventing. The advance of the tower was met by a ferocious artillery barrage from the biggest and most complex catapults in the world, and the Helepolis had to back off when its iron plates were dislodged and incendiary bolts set the whole vast machine on fire. It had been on the receiving end of more than 1500 catapult bolts and 800 incendiary missiles.

There is a surviving description of one of the weapons used by the men of Rhodes, which was written about 200 BC by a Greek known today as Philo of Byzantium. He described in detail the gears that powered a chain drive and automatically loaded bolt after bolt into the firing slot. The device seems quite astonishingly modern – in fact, it was a form of machine-gun. When Erwin Schramm demonstrated his replica to Kaiser Wilhelm II, the second bolt hit the target at exactly the same spot as the first, splitting it in half. The problem here was that the device would, in effect, kill the same man over and over again unless it could traverse as it was fired – but since the ancient Greeks had invented the universal joint, the machine could indeed do that.[22]

MACHINES AND MATHEMATICS

And this was only the tip of the iceberg. Philo's texts, the 'Mechanical Collection', describe all manner of devices on which he had worked or that he had invented himself: self-propelled wheels, coded communications systems, the chain pump, the air pump, the piston pump and 78 mechanical constructions operated by hot air or steam.[23] One of them was a steam-powered siren for lighthouses, enabling the warning to shipping to be heard even when it could not be seen. Philo was also in the entertainment business, and for the amusement of his patrons specialized in designing robots, such as a horse that drank water and a girl who poured water on demand.

The Antikythera mechanism has profoundly extended our appreciation of what was being achieved, and makes it clear that much that was confidently described as fantasy and exaggeration is in fact a perfectly truthful description of real machines. The gearing of the mechanism is in itself a marvel. But beyond that, its construction required a sophisticated understanding of astronomy, and one book survives from the man who might have built it, Geminus of Rhodes.

Geminus makes it clear that he knows and wants to make available the data collected by the astronomers of Babylon. All this work depended on a serious understanding of theoretical mathematics, and the Greeks were very serious indeed about mathematics – no one more so than Archimedes, who lived in the third century BC. A list of the things he worked on would be as incomprehensible to most of us today as it was to the Romans at the time. Discussing the quadrature of the parabola and exploring the centre of gravity of paraboloid plane sections may not light up many of our lives, but Archimedes was totally enthralled by those questions, and someone's got to do it.

At least, someone's got to do it if you want a world of advanced engineering, sophisticated astronomy, successful navigation across the open sea and the development of machine power. All these things seem entirely pragmatic and practical, but they actually require abstract theoretical science at a high level.

THE DIVINE ARCHIMEDES

Archimedes was as practical as he was theoretical. His genius for uniting mathematics and physics – for analysing the logical rules that control the behaviour of solids and liquids – translated directly into building machines, especially military machines. When the Romans besieged the port of Syracuse in Sicily, where he lived, he designed the missile launchers that held them off: catapults of varying ranges, which he installed in sequence so that the Romans couldn't get under their range. He also organized the defences so that everything was to hand for the defenders. It was Archimedes who invented swing-beams that could be swivelled out over the city walls to drop heavy weights on the attackers. His surprise weapon – and the one that seems to have caused the Romans most alarm – was a system of grappling hooks that could be swung over the ships below the city walls, and could, by a system of levers, lift them up out of the water.

One of the most telling examples of our difficulty in grasping the technological sophistication of the Greeks is the modern refusal to believe in two of his weapons: a system of mirrors that he used to burn up enemy ships, and a steam-powered cannon that could lob heavy missiles much further than any catapult. We were told when researching this subject that 'no one believes' the stories of these weapons. And yet the effectiveness of the burning mirror was demonstrated in about 1646[24] and in 1747[25]. So what? As recently as 1973, a learned article by Ioannis Sakkas 'proved' mathematically that it was impossible to focus the rays of the sun sufficiently to burn wood.[26] That happened to be the year when a large-scale experiment set fire to a boat 160 feet away within two minutes.[27] The mathematical proof that it couldn't happen is as valid as the calculations proving that bumble-bees can't fly.

The evidence for Archimedes' construction of the device seems compelling; we have references to him setting fire to Roman ships by Lucian of Samosata (c. AD 150)[28] and Galen,[29] and to the use of mirrors to do so by Zonaras,[30] Eustathios[31] and Dio Cassius.[32] Anthemius (the sixth-century architect of Hagia Sophia in Constantinople) noted 'that all the authors who mention the burning machine of the divine Archimedes, never speak of it as one compound mirror, but as a combination of many'.[33] Unfortunately, Anthemius' sources have vanished; we have only a twelfth-century précis of one of them.[34] But during Anthemius' lifetime, in AD 514, a version of the burning mirror is said to have saved Constantinople from a Gothic fleet![35] The last librarian at the great library of Alexandria, Theon, refers to a now-lost manuscript on mirrors by Archimedes, and an Arabic copy of a second-century BC manuscript, published in 1976, mentions a Greek mathematician's attempt, about 160 BC, to find out how burning mirrors were made.[36]

And yet we're still being told that Archimedes couldn't have done it. This particular triumph of prejudice began in the Renaissance, with Kepler and Descartes, and has carried on with real determination ever since.[37] One modern historian has even explained that Archimedes wouldn't have done it because he had other effective weapons that were less expensive – it 'would not have been cost effective'.[38] That's how you can prove that America didn't drop an atom bomb on Japan.

We don't know whether he used a burning mirror or not. But the story can no longer be treated as fantasy. He was said to have done it, it could be done, and he knew how to do it.

Archimedes' steam cannon is less well attested. All knowledge of it was forgotten until about 1350, when the Italian poet Petrarch found a description of it in a manuscript of Cicero in a church library. He described the cannon in *De remediis utriusque fortunae* (*How to Cope with Events*). A century or so later Leonardo da Vinci evidently saw the manuscript and was inspired to improve on it to design what he called the Architronito.[39] Sakkas, who tested the burning mirrors so effectively, built a small version of the cannon in 1981 and demonstrated that it works startlingly well.

The Romans were so rattled by Archimedes' inventions that they became convinced he had superhuman powers and was some sort of sorcerer. Even today, the Romans' descendants in Syracuse threaten their children with: 'Look out! Or Archimedes will come and get you!' Quite a way to remember one of the greatest mathematicians who ever lived.

It took nearly three years for the Romans to break Syracuse – their strength lay not in engineering theory but in relentlessness. And that was the end of Archimedes: 'It is recorded that amidst all the uproar and terror created by the soldiers who were rushing about the captured city in search of plunder, he was quietly absorbed in some geometrical figures which he had drawn on the sand, and was killed by a soldier who did not know who he was.'[40]

The Romans understood that they had done something rather terrible, but the real tragedy for the rest of us was that they had no interest in following up the work Archimedes had been doing. They were interested in the mechanical marvels produced by Greek science, but only as curiosities. According to Cicero, Marcellus, the general who captured Syracuse, took home only one piece of loot – a planetarium belonging to Archimedes.[41] Cicero too was fascinated by such things, and this brings us back to the Antikythera mechanism. When it went down on that ill-fated vessel in 80 BC, it may well have been on its way to Cicero himself. He knew Rhodes well, and was governor of a neighbouring province shortly before the ship containing the mechanism was lost. Since the cargo of statues and other fine objects was probably meant for some wealthy collector, it is not beyond belief that Cicero was the intended recipient.

The island of Rhodes held a special place in the Roman scheme of things. This, unfortunately, was to prove its undoing. And the story of the destruction of Rhodes encapsulates the whole sorry tale of Rome's obliteration of the scientific and technological world of the Hellenes.

RHODES

Before Rome came on to the scene, Rhodes was for many years the dominant force in the Eastern Mediterranean. Its port was the greatest market of that region, and its efficient sea machines and weaponry kept the waters reasonably clear of pirates. The island was dominated by the walled city of the same name, built on a grid pattern around 410 BC. It had five harbours, paved streets, parks, temples and gymnasiums, and was lavishly decorated with monuments and statues. It still boasts an acropolis, ruins of temples to Aphrodite and Apollo, and, of course, the memory of the Colossus of Rhodes, one of the seven wonders of the ancient world. The Colossus was built in 282 BC, and stood over 100 feet high at the harbour entrance until it was toppled by an earthquake. One Roman, Pliny the Elder, said that most people couldn't stretch their arms around the fallen thumb.

Rhodes' role in managing maritime commerce also gave rise to a highly developed commercial legal code, known as the 'Rhodian sea law', which has formed the basis of commercial maritime law right up to the present day. Since this code appears to date from between 800 and 600 BC, it probably has a respectable claim to be the first practical system of commercial law, and rather diminishes any claim that the Romans were the great law-givers of the world.

All this came to an end, however, in the second century BC. Rome was determined to establish control over the Eastern Mediterranean, but Rhodes was far too well defended to invite a military assault. So the Romans chose to undermine the island's economy instead. Rhodes relied on its harbour dues and the taxes on the various goods that went in and out of the port; Rome simply took control of the nearby island of Delos and established a free port there. This subsidized competition gradually eroded the entire Rhodian economy. The harbour tax income fell by 85 per cent. Forced to its knees, in 164 BC Rhodes was compelled to sign a treaty obliging it to have the same friends and foes as Rome.

Finding themselves in reduced circumstances, the islanders had to make a living somehow. They were forced to exploit their one other major asset: that of being an important cultural centre. During its glory days, Rhodes had been phenomenal in its output of artistic and cultural masterpieces of every kind. Quite apart from its scientific achievements, it was celebrated for its poets, writers, historians, philosophers, potters, painters, sculptors and, most important of all when it came to making a living out of the Romans, for its teachers of rhetoric.

The Romans may have been intellectually incurious and uninterested in the scientific achievements of a place like Rhodes, but they were certainly interested in power. The route to power in late Republican Rome was through oratory: the art of winning a following and of winning arguments in public. No Roman was likely to achieve high office unless he could develop the skills of rhetoric, and this was something the Rhodians could offer in spades. It became *de rigueur* for ambitious young Romans to spend some time being trained on the island.

Unfortunately, since the Romans didn't bother to keep up the anti-piracy patrols that Rhodes could no longer afford, the voyage became quite dangerous. When the young Julius Caesar tried to get to school there in 76 BC he was actually captured by pirates. He claims to have been rather a jolly captive, and to have got on very well with the pirates, after being insulted by their initial demand for a ransom of 20 talents. He insisted they raise it to 50:

> He made so little of them, that when he had a mind to sleep, he would send to them, and order them to make no noise. For thirty-eight days, with all the freedom in the world, he amused himself with joining in their exercises and games, as if they had not been his keepers, but his guards. He wrote verses and speeches, and made them his auditors, and those who did not admire them, he called to their faces illiterate and barbarous.[42]

He said he would have them crucified, and they all laughed.

Once his ransom was paid and he was freed, he hired a fleet, set out in hot pursuit and captured 'most of them'. After handing them over to the authorities, he personally arranged their crucifixion. Caesar then went on with his planned course of study.

The story he told about what happened shows how effectively he learnt the art of self-presentation. It may be that he had actually cut a deal with one or more of his captors to enable him to seize the rest. The story is designed to enhance his reputation in the very particular moral climate of Rome – showing not just that he was a young man of style and panache, but also that he was utterly without duplicity (therefore not like the Greeks who were teaching him) and completely ruthless.

The irony of the whole situation is that Rhodes' attempt to sell itself as a finishing school for the young brutes of Rome would finally finish off the island. In 44 BC Caesar was assassinated. One of the conspirators was familiar with the island for exactly the same reason as Caesar: Cassius too had gone there to learn rhetoric. After the assassination, he needed loot to strengthen his position as he jockeyed for power. Casting round for some easy way of replenishing his coffers without too much opposition, his eye lighted on his old alma mater. He knew exactly what was there, and that Rhodes had no capacity to resist him. His excuse for launching his attack was that his enemies – who were, of course, enemies of the Republic – might be helped by Rhodes' ships. So, in 42 BC, ignoring the desperate appeals of his old teacher, he simply walked in and ransacked the place.[43] The Romans had always liked the stuff produced on the island, and Cassius sailed away with 3000 of its artistic masterpieces.

Rhodes never recovered.

ROME TURNS OUT THE LIGHTS

We know now that the propaganda of Roman history, that Rome was the great creator of engineering mastery and scientific thought, is the very opposite of the truth. The non-Roman world of the Eastern Mediterranean was making new discoveries and inventions in each generation, and its knowledge and abilities were not recovered until well into the Middle Ages or later.

Of course, there were some products of Greek engineering that the Romans did develop – for example, they added wheels to the artillery machines, and they saw the practicality of relatively simple inventions, such as the chain-drive bucket for lifting water (four of them have been found in London). But anything a little less obviously practical passed them by. And since all scientific advance depends on rather impractical research, that was a disaster.

For example, look at what happened to the steam engine. In the first century AD, a Greek technical writer named Heron, working in Alexandria, described a practical steam engine. Harnessed to an invention attributed to the great earlier inventor and therefore named the Archimedes screw, which was already used to pump water, it could have offered a simple and hugely effective way to increase the irrigation of land, the water supply of cities and the draining of deep mines.

But that did not happen. One very significant story is told by the historian Suetonius, describing an event that took place in 70 AD. A new emperor, Vespasian, had come to power in a civil war in which the legions had burnt and plundered Rome: now he was busy raising 40 billion sesterces to rebuild the city. The work involved quarrying huge columns of stone and carrying them up to the top of the Capitoline Hill, the sacred centre of the city. At which point Heron, or someone very like him, popped up at court with a device that could do it. We don't know what it was, but it was clearly a machine that replaced human power with mechanical power, and was capable of shifting tons at a time, vertically. It could have been a steam-powered funicular. Vespasian bought the machine and scrapped it, saying: 'I have to feed the common people.'[44] If the Roman Empire had allowed technology to advance, it would have put the masses out of work. Heron's steam machine ended up automatically opening the doors of a temple when a fire was lit on an altar outside.

Heron himself is a bit of an enigma. It seems likely that the amazing inventions he described actually date from the third century BC, and relate to a technology that had already begun to be lost by the time he wrote. One careful student of Hellenist science has pointed out that, although he describes instruments that require precision metal screws and the theory of metal gear-chains, both of which had been used 300 years before he was writing, he describes only the manufacture of wooden screws and the use of friction devices where you would expect gears. This looks like evidence of a steep decline in engineering know-how in the Roman world.[45]

Most of Heron's amazing inventions were devoted to amusement, since in his day there was no interest in making practical use of them. He built complex automata, such as a model of Hercules and a dragon (Hercules would hit the dragon on the head and it would spout water on to his face) and even a complete automatic theatre that rolled out by itself and gave a robotic performance of *Nauplius*, a tragic tale set in the period after the Trojan War. Scenes included the repair of Ajax's ship (much hammering), the Greek fleet (with leaping dolphins) and the destruction of Ajax by a bolt of lightning. Then it closed its curtain and rolled away again.

The interest in technology for entertainment may have gone even further. As well as the moving automata of the theatre, he describes static automata, which he says were safer and allowed for a greater variety of scenes. These were apparently so astonishing that 'the Ancients used to call the creators of such things wonder-makers'.[46] The characters were painted on boards, which were displayed in very rapid succession using a shutter – a cord-driven mechanism coordinated the shutter and the succession of images. Heron says that this system can show a character in motion, or appearing or disappearing.

Never mind the steam engine – the ancient Greeks had cinemas with animated movies!

This was an automated world: Heron even described the coin-operated automat, which dispensed a cup full of water when a five-drachma coin was dropped into the slot. We don't know what it was used for, but there may be a clue in the fact that a refinement also delivered a small ball of soap. It only took 1700 years for the idea to be rediscovered.

Remarkable though Heron's inventions were, they belong not to his own time but to the great technological and scientific leaps that had been made by the Greeks in the preceding centuries, before Rome fully took over. It wasn't just that the Romans were incurious and the Greeks more intellectually alert. In the Roman scheme of things, change was a threat. The system was the system, and anyone who wanted change was an enemy.

The first approach the Romans had to the world was to try to make it all Roman; the next was to build a wall behind which *Romanitas* would continue unchanged from generation to generation. When, in AD 295–305, the emperor commissioned a sort of Domesday Book so that he could correctly tax everyone in the Empire, it was ordered that no one could ever leave their farm or change their job.

Science and engineering were stopped in their tracks, and the study of mathematics and astronomy simply ended and was lost. The wonderful books of Greek science and mathematics that survive do not come to us through Rome at all, even though Rome conquered all these lands. These texts stayed in Greek, eventually to be translated into Arabic and to be used as the basis for scientific and mathematical development by Islamic scholars whose heritage had nothing to do with the Latin world. Europe remained ignorant of all this until, still in the name of Rome, Crusaders for the Roman Catholic Church and the Holy Roman Emperor went back to the Eastern Mediterranean in the late eleventh century – the return of the Barbarians.

We have lost so much that it is hard to grasp what is missing. We tend to assume that the scraps of text that have survived are the most important, but that is clearly not so. We are at the mercy of the Byzantine and Arab copyists, who tended to stick to the easier texts and often copied out only the first sections anyway; we don't, for instance, have any of Philo's theoretical works, which explained the principles of what he was doing.

After the Greek scientific world was put out of business, even the memory of what had been achieved disappeared. Although there are surviving descriptions of some of the machines they built, until very recently no one had really believed they existed. This has been a problem in understanding the whole pre-Roman world. Just as the Antikythera mechanism was regarded as an obviously later artefact, so Celtic mines were assumed to be much later. And, of course, reports of ancient navigations have been repeatedly dismissed as mythical and impossible in the face of what would, on a different subject, be regarded as excellent evidence.

There was a powerful cultural reason for this. After all, if they really could do these things, then the Roman Empire, far from advancing technical and engineering civilization, actually put it back about 1500 years. That can't be right – can it?

And what exactly were those machines in Alexandria, that were once so famous that their forgotten creator was one of the greatest men in the history of the world?

IX
PERSIA – THE EARLY DYNASTIES

The mightiest man on earth in 470 BC was the Persian King Xerxes. In what are taken to be the queen's apartments in the ruins of his father's palace-city of Persepolis, a limestone slab has been found with a long inscription. It begins: 'A great god is Ahura Mazda, who created this earth, who created yonder sky, who created man, who created happiness for man, who made Xerxes king.' This is no more than the conventional invocation of Ahura Mazda, Lord of Light and Truth, the god of the early Persian rulers, and yet it says a lot about the regime that they founded. Human happiness is placed there up front, divinely ordained for man. Duty and law, obedience and tribute to Xerxes are all left to later – the ordered universe is about happiness.

AN EMPIRE OF TOLERANCE

The Persian Empire had been created in the sixth century BC, when the Iranian Cyrus rebelled against the Medes, defeated them and took over their empire in Persia and Assyria. He then conquered Croesus, the king of Lydia still remembered for his wealth (he minted the first gold and silver coins), and finally took control of the great Babylonian Empire and the eastern coast of the Mediterranean. By the end of the century his successors, the Achaemenid dynasty, ruled from Libya to India in the south, and from Bulgaria to the Aral Sea in the north. To ride from one end to the other took six months.

When Cyrus took over Babylon, he was at pains to represent himself as a liberator rather than as a conqueror or oppressor.

Accordingly, he had a clay cylinder inscribed with the following account of his conquest:

> Cyrus always endeavoured to treat according to justice the people over whom [the god] Marduk had made him conquer … When I entered Babylon as a friend I established the seat of the government in the palace of the ruler amidst jubilation and rejoicing. Marduk, the great lord, induced the magnanimous inhabitants of Babylon to love me … My numerous troops walked around in Babylon in peace, I did not allow anybody to terrorize the people … I strove for peace in Babylon and in all my other sacred cities. As to the inhabitants of Babylon who were enslaved against the will of the gods, I abolished forced labour, which was against their social standing. I freed all slaves. I brought relief to their dilapidated housing, putting thus an end to their misfortunes and slavery.[1]

Of course, Cyrus was not bringing liberty in any sense that we would understand it, for he exercised absolute power over his vast dominions. But he was properly respectful towards the customs and religion of his new Babylonian subjects, as his successor Darius would be to Egyptian gods and customs when he conquered that land. The Jews, whom Cyrus released from Babylonian captivity and whom he returned to Jerusalem to rebuild their Temple, claimed that God spoke of him as a messiah (*mashyach* – in Greek, *christos,* Christ), 'whose right hand I have held, to subdue nations before him'.[2]

The statues of gods were thought of as royal figures and their temples were palaces. The Babylonians, like the Assyrians before them, seized the gods of peoples whom they conquered and held them as subjects in the temple of their own supreme deity. Cyrus gave them back. Religious tolerance was no problem for him, unless people worshipped what his own religion designated 'the Lie' and its demons, the gods of the savage nomads of the steppes.[3]

His own deity, Ahura Mazda, was not a statue or idol but a transcendent ethical authority, worshipped through sacred fire. This had the incidental advantage that there was no image of a god living in a palace-temple and possessing more authority on earth than Cyrus himself. He embraced the teachings of the prophet Zoroaster, and the cylinder carrying his extraordinary declaration of religious tolerance has been likened to a human rights charter.

No one is sure whether Zoroaster was Cyrus' contemporary, but this was evidently an age of great religious teachers – the time also of Zalmoxis and of Buddha. Zoroaster proclaimed an ethical monotheism that was a teaching for all mankind. The Supreme Deity, Ahura Mazda, was at the centre of a kingdom of justice that promised immortality and bliss. But there was also a force for evil, Ahriman, locked in combat with the Wise Lord, and human beings were declared to be free to choose between Justice and Truth on the one hand, and the Kingdom of the Lie on the other. Zoroaster equated good with the arts of civilization and government, and evil with the thieving nomad, the enemy of orderly agriculture and animal husbandry. This was really a function of the nature of life in the Middle East, which had been city-based for thousands of years. It was a dramatic step for a conqueror to replace the culture of an ancient city. Rome's idea of civilization, on the other hand, was directed towards the essentially rural cultures of northern Europe. It built mini-Romes to teach the natives *Romanitas*. When Rome encountered great cities in other regions (Carthage, Corinth, Jerusalem) its instinctive response was to flatten them.

The Achaemenid Empire was essentially rooted in trade. There are many English words that come from Persian, such as 'bazaar', 'shawl', 'sash', 'turquoise', 'tiara', 'orange' and 'lemon' – and of course 'paradise', from the Persian word for a garden. The vocabulary travelled with the goods. The scale of trade was illustrated by the discovery, in 1949, of a 6-foot-square Persian carpet – by far the oldest carpet ever found – in perfect condition in a frozen tomb in Pazyryk, in southern Siberia. It dates to the fourth or fifth century BC.

The symbolic heart of the empire was the fabulous palace-city of Parsa (the 'city of Persia', Persepolis), which appears to be dedicated to imperial ritual. It was built around 515 BC by Xerxes' father Darius, and the scale of the place is spectacular even today. At that time, with vast timbered ceilings, great doors with golden fittings, sumptuous curtains and wall paintings, fabulous tile-work and vivid carvings, it must have been gobsmacking. The walls and stairways are covered in relief carvings of people from all parts of the empire bringing gifts. Their offerings are largely symbolic – cloth, garments, young animals, the kinds of gifts that could be considered sacrifices to a god.

This empire was not anything like Rome's. Rome wanted to Romanize the world, imposing not just control, but its own culture, language, literature, religion and social structure. The Persian concept of empire was rooted in the notion of a 'King of Kings', who lived god-like in a palace that was virtually a temple, and whose subject kings, like lesser gods, would naturally rule over their own people in their own ways. So there was a diversity of cultures and religions.

In the relief carvings that cover Persepolis it is noticeable that the subject peoples are led into the presence of the Emperor by the hand rather than the wrist – a sign that they are approaching willingly and not as captives. Rome could never have understood these friezes of tribute-bearers wearing their own costumes and visibly presenting themselves as coming from different cultures. For Romans, you either learnt to look like, dress like and be like a Roman – or you were a Barbarian.

The Achaemenid dynasty came to an end in 330 BC when Alexander of Macedon, armed with artillery and an unshakeable confidence in his mission of conquest, took the empire apart with extreme brutality as he tried to become the King of Kings himself. By way of a drunken thank you for Xerxes' burning of Athens 150 years before, he destroyed Persepolis, carting away the contents of the vast treasury with the aid of 20,000 mules and 5000 camels.

After Alexander's death, Greek communities remained among the most prominent in the disparate world that the empire had covered. When a new dynasty, the Parthians, emerged as the new overlords in the second century BC, they called themselves 'Greek-loving', Philhellenes.

Persepolis was now a ruin and the empire it represented had become a fading memory. But the idea of kingship that it symbolized had not been lost, and the Parthians attached themselves to the tradition of tolerance and diversity that had been practised by the Achaemenids. They allowed people to retain their own languages and cultures in their own areas. This was a decentralized empire, in which the ruler was King of Kings over 18 subject kingdoms, with no central administration. To the Romans this kind of arrangement was incomprehensible – they could see only a political wilderness.

CRASSUS AND THE GREAT ROMAN DEBACLE

In 55 BC Rome was controlled by three men, Pompey, Caesar and Crassus. Caesar was busy conquering Gaul. Pompey had annexed Syria, captured Jerusalem and established a peace treaty with the Parthian Empire. But the third and richest member of the triumvirate, Crassus, decided that it was his patriotic duty to conquer the Parthians, seize their gold and bring their vast Barbarian empire under Roman control. Besides, it would set him up as an equal of the other two.

Crassus had made his money out of fires in Rome. He had bought slaves who were builders and architects, and when buildings caught fire in that overcrowded city he rushed round to buy up the burning building and the neighbouring blocks that were about to catch fire. He got them at rock-bottom prices and ended up owning most of the city. But there's a big difference between business strategy and military strategy.

The Parthians discovered they were about to be invaded, without any provocation and in breach of their treaty, by a huge force – about 40,000 men, seven legions plus auxiliaries. Crassus spent a year extracting cash from some cautiously friendly cities in southern Turkey, and then Artavazd, the ruler of Armenia, offered him 6000 cavalrymen and freedom of passage through his own kingdom.

It's generally assumed that Artavazd was being weak and craven, but Crassus thought more in terms of the likelihood of Armenian ambushes and revenge for past humiliations. He decided to go through Mesopotamia instead. He told Artavazd that his job was to block the Parthian advance. Artavazd said that it would be a pleasure.

Not long after that, Artavazd was visited by a guest with a very, very large army. Orodes II, the Parthian King of Kings, had turned up for a spot of strategic feasting and the intention of arranging a marriage between his sister and Artavazd's son. Artavazd was not really in a position to come through with any help for the Romans.

A lost religion (see page 115)
To the east of the Dacian fortress at Sarmizegetusa, a monumental stone stairway led to a sacred area with a number of shrines. This circular stone shrine has wooden columns and a central hearth. We don't even know what the place was called, let alone what it was for – 'Sarmizegetusa' is a Roman name meaning 'Place of the Sarmatians and Getae [Dacians]'.

Make Trajan's day (see page 112)
The murderous scenes on Trajan's Column were not very portable, but he distributed his image as a Dacian-killer on his coins. This one, inscribed 'SPQR OPTIMO PRINCIPI' – 'Supreme Ruler of the Senate and the People of Rome' – shows Trajan happily spearing a Dacian as though he were out hunting.

Return of the Barbarians (see page 129)
This image of Alaric and his Goths sacking Rome in AD 410 echoes Jamin's picture of the amazement of the Celts entering the city over 700 years earlier, and expresses the fantasy of Barbarians as mindless destroyers. It appeared in *National Geographic* magazine in 1962. It is hard to picture this Alaric as having been the supreme commander of Roman armies.

The lost world of the Goths (see page 130)
A page from the only surviving Gothic manuscript in the world – Ulfila's Gothic Bible. This copy, with gold and silver lettering on purple vellum, was made in Ravenna during the reign of the Arian Gothic Emperor Theoderic. Found in the sixteenth century in a German monastery, it was captured by Sweden in 1648 during the Thirty Years' War and is now in Uppsala.

The Antikythera mechanism (see page 152)
This working reconstruction was made by John
Gleave, an orrery-maker, on the basis of Derek de
Solla Price's analysis. The gearing is set between
perspex plates, with perspex dials in place of the
original bronze to make the mechanism visible.
Michael Wright's recent work suggests that the
original was even more complex.

**Philo of Byzantium's pneumatica
(see page 161)**
This Latin manuscript is a late twelfth-century
translation from Arabic. In the ninth century,
many Greek works on science and philosophy
were brought from Byzantium to Baghdad to
be translated for the Caliph by Jews and Nestorian
Christians; the Islamic Caliphate continued the
old Persian tradition of multi-culturalism.

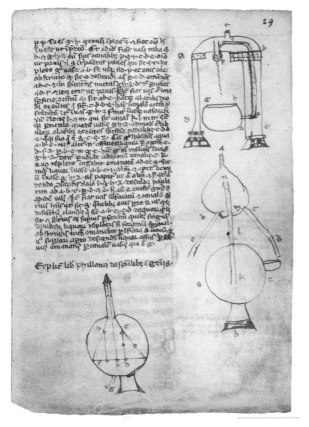

The first steam engine
(see page 168)
This working model is based on
Heron's design for an aeolipile, or
'wind ball'. Water is heated
in the lower boiler. Steam rises
through pipes into the freely
rotating hollow drum and then
escapes from jets, resulting in the
drum spinning. Heron considered
the device an entertaining novelty.

Ancient electricity?
(see page 185)
Replicas of the 'Baghdad batteries'
can produce up to 2 volts, though
amperages may be too low for its
suggested purpose of electroplating.
It has also been pointed out that
similar jars (although without the
outermost clay jar) were used to
store sacred scrolls, and that no
wires were found.

**The first armoured knights
(see page 182)**
This seventh-century relief from
Kermanshah in Iran shows a
cataphract from the final years of
the centuries-long war between
Rome and Persia. The heavily
armoured knight, with helmet,
shield and long lance, and a heavy
horse armoured with what was
probably quilted cloth, looks like a
figure from the high Middle Ages
– except that he has no saddle.

**The 'Parthian shot'
(see page 178)**
Riding light ponies, with long-
range bows, Parthian horse
archers had no need of armour
as they operated out of their
enemies' range. This Etruscan
bronze of a 'Scythian' archer,
c. 500 BC, is a rather earlier
illustration of how it was done.

A Parthian aristocrat (see page 181)
This bronze figure displays the mustachios of the Parthian warrior, and the headband, necklace and belt that show he's completed his seven years of military training. He wears leather trousers, suitable for a man who spends much of his life on horseback. The statue dates to about 250 BC and was found at Shami, in Khuzestan.

The *iwan* (see page 184)
This magnificent seventeenth-century madrassah in Samarkand is an example of the way in which the *iwan* and dome became distinctive features of central Asian public architecture.

The Parthian capital (see page 188)
Ctesiphon, on the site of the ancient city of Opis at the confluence of the Tigris and Diyala,
became the Parthian kings' winter capital in 129 BC and was embellished with the profits of
war against Rome in 41 BC. The city was abandoned after Baghdad was founded nearby in
AD 763. All that remains standing is the ruin of the largest single-span brick arch in the world.

**Emperors at bay
(see page 191)**
This rock carving at
Bishapur shows Shapur
I trampling on Gordian
III, accepting the
submission of Philip
the Arab and holding
Valerian captive. The
winged figure brings
Shapur the ring of
power and a diadem.
One of the standing
figures is possibly the
Zoroastrian High Priest.

Zenobia (see page 204)
This funerary relief in Damascus shows Zenobia, renegade Queen of Palmyra, accompanied by Tyche, goddess of fortune and protector of the city. Optimistically, the Roman Emperor is shown crushed underfoot. Admiration for Zenobia was widespread, but by no means universal – a leading contemporary Jewish Rabbi declared, 'Happy will he be who shall see the downfall of Palmyra'.

Crassus discovered that Artavazd hadn't been much of an ally when, after the Roman forces had endured a long march through barren desert, a messenger arrived from the Armenian ruler saying, in the language of classical diplomacy, 'Oops, sorry.' He added that the Romans had better not go on, as they would be marching into trouble. But Crassus carried on regardless towards the walled town of Harran or Harranu, the city in south-east Turkey where, according to the Bible, Abraham had been born. *Harranu* is Assyrian for 'road'; it was where the road to Damascus crossed the one to Nineveh, and had been the Assyrian capital in the seventh century BC. The Romans called it Carrhae, and had no idea where they were. They had been led by Crassus' confidence and a badly chosen guide, and now they caught their first sight of the Parthians.

THE BATTLE OF HARRAN

As Crassus took his men across the plain of Harran he could see about 10,000 horse archers ahead. They amounted to little more than a quarter of his own force. And Crassus did have some cavalry with him – horsemen from southern Gaul who rode into battle with swords and no armour.

The Parthian commander, Surena – the head of a clan called Suren – was not a man who travelled light. He normally moved around with 1000 baggage camels, 200 chariots for his harem, a bodyguard of 1000 fully armed men and several thousand more lightly armed, as well as a retinue of 10,000 riders. That was just for a peaceful visit. But at Harran, with intentions that were anything but peaceful, Surena kept most of his force hidden. The Romans moved forward confidently.

The Parthian horse archers turned out to be very different from anything the Romans had seen before. Instead of simple wooden bows, they were armed with high-tech double-recurve bows laminated from wood, horn and sinew. These men were more like riflemen than archers. Their maximum range was 300 yards, and at 150 yards they could punch right through the Romans' armour and shields.

And then Surena unleashed his heavy cavalry, who had been camouflaged under cloaks and skins. Now they threw off the coverings, and suddenly men and horses shone with reflected sunlight. The Romans found themselves under attack from a completely new kind of enemy, more like medieval knights than anything in the classical world. Thousands of heavily armoured horsemen, the mounts as well protected as the riders, bore down on the Italian foot-soldiers. They smashed through the infantry legions. Then they pulled back and let the Roman cavalry, led by Crassus' son, chase their archers away.

And that was the next horrible surprise. The pursuing Romans discovered that these archers could shoot backwards with as much power and accuracy as when they were facing their enemies. The 'Parthian shot' would become famous as the apparent retreat that was actually a deadly lure. And then the knights surrounded the Roman pursuers and butchered them all.

Crassus thought that by now the Persians would have run out of arrows; he had no idea. When he tried to advance with his remaining force it was simply shot to pieces. When he ordered his men to charge 'they showed him their hands nailed to their shields, and their feet stuck to the ground' with arrows.[4] And then one of the Parthian knights rode in front of Crassus with his son's head on a spear.

The battle at Harran was something that Rome would not forget. Probably 30,000 legionaries were killed on the battlefield, and the remaining 10,000 were captured and deported to central Asia. The eagles of all seven Roman legions ended up in Parthian temples. Barely 500 Romans ever came home. The shock of this defeat would never be extinguished, and a war had begun that would last for 600 years.

ARMENIAN THEATRICALS

While the Romans were marching towards their doom, and during the battle itself, the Armenian king, Artavazd, and the King of Kings were continuing with their discussion of the wedding that would unite their two houses. It was costing Artavazd a fortune.

It so happened that both of them were aficionados of Greek classical theatre; in fact, Artavazd was known as a dramatist himself, and wrote Greek tragedies as well as histories and orations. When news of the victory over Crassus and his legions was brought to these

Barbarian rulers they were busy listening to a dramatic recitation of Euripides' *Bacchae* given by a Greek theatrical star named Jason.

In the play, the god Dionysius arrives in Thebes from what the playwright calls the barbarian east – the world now of Artavazd and Orodes. Once in the west, with its established classical religion of hearth and home, of male authority and political order, Dionysius draws the Thebans into rapturous disorder. Their rituals are joyous, creative, energized and savage: barbaric in the simplest sense of the word. In the mass hysteria Pentheus, King of Thebes, is torn to pieces by a group of women who believe he is an animal to be eaten in a sacrificial feast. The leader of the cannibal group is his own mother, Agave, who proudly brings what she believes to be the meat of a wild animal to present to her father.

Jason, playing the part of Pentheus, was being applauded after a powerful speech when Surena's lieutenant appeared fresh from the battlefield. He burst into the royal presence carrying the head of Crassus, threw it on to the floor and prostrated himself. Jason immediately grabbed the head, removed his costume and became Agave, Pentheus' crazed and murderous mother, arriving at the palace with her son's dismembered body.

> We bring from the mountain A tendril fresh-cut to the palace, A wonderful prey.

Everyone knew this speech. And everyone knew what came next, from the chorus:

> Who slew him?

That's when one of the newcomers stepped forward, took Crassus' head from Jason's hands, held it up and delivered Agave's denouement. 'I did.' And so he had.[5]

THE TRIUMPH OF CRASSUS

Barbarians were at the very core of Rome's public life because the ritual at the heart of the city was the Triumph. This elaborate celebration of a hero's conquest of yet another group of Barbarians was the only way for a Roman to join the pantheon of immortals and be recognized as having won an eternal place of glory in the city's history. The *triumphator*, as the hero was now called, rode in a gilded chariot behind the prisoners and booty he had brought back to Rome. Pompey had been granted a Triumph, his third, in 61 BC to celebrate his victories in the Middle East: the parade of spoils and prisoners had lasted for two days. Crassus had desperately needed a Triumph to match Pompey's. Surena, with ironic ruthlessness, now gave him one.

He staged it in the seaport of Seleucia, near Antioch. Having taken the prisoner who looked most like the defeated general, he had him dressed as a woman and ordered him to answer to the name of Crassus and the title of Imperator. He was put on a horse and given a procession. In a real Triumph there were trumpeters and officials called lictors, who carried the symbols of Roman authority known as fasces – bundles of rods bound together with an axe in the middle. The mock Crassus had trumpeters too, but his lictors rode camels; their fasces were hung with purses, and severed Roman heads were fastened to the axes. At the back of the procession came prostitutes and musicians 'who sang many scurrilous and ridiculous songs about the effeminacy and cowardice of Crassus'.[6]

But the most expressive statement of contempt for the Romans was made when Surena presented the senate of Seleucia with the collection of pornography found in the baggage of one of Crassus' generals. This 'gave Surena occasion to heap much insulting ridicule upon the Romans, since they could not, even when going to war, let such subjects and writings alone.' In effect, 'What a load of wankers!' It was said in Rome that the Parthians killed Crassus by pouring molten gold into his mouth, as a satisfying tribute to his hunger for wealth.[7]

Ten thousand Roman prisoners vanished into the vastness of the Parthian Empire. Some ended up in what is now Turkmenistan,[8] where they settled and joined the frontier defence force.[9] It looks as though they lost some battle there, too, because they seem to turn up next fighting for a Mongolian warlord in Kazakhstan. A Chinese history records that two generals commanding a substantial expedition there encountered a strange army in a city 500 miles east of Marghiana. They had a fortified position in the form of a double palisade of huge logs, and were drilling with large shields to form a defensive screen in such a way as to appear like the scales of fish. The palisade was a typical Roman fortification – certainly quite unlike anything Mongolian – and the only people in the first century BC who used shields like that, drilled like that and built log defences like that were the Romans.

They lost again, of course. The survivors were brought to China and settled in a frontier post renamed Lijian.[10] Historians have puzzled over whether these people were really Roman soldiers, and have written learned papers suggesting that the Chinese characters represent a word meaning Rome, or maybe Alexandria. Maybe they have been looking at the wrong language. *Lijian* is a Mongolian word. It means 'legion'. It seems pretty obvious who they were. The locals think the same, and proudly point out the number of people in their villages with what they see as Roman physiognomy – high-bridged noses, large deep-set eyes, large-boned figures and – not, you might think, a normal Roman inheritance – curly blond hair. But they're convinced, and in the far north of central China, up on the Wall by the border with Inner Mongolia in the little town of Yongchang (well, little by Chinese standards), are the statues of three people: a Chinese of the ethnic Han majority; a woman of the Muslim Hui minority; and a Roman who lost an awful lot of battles against the Barbarians.

PARTHIAN FEUDALISM

The Romans had known nothing about the Parthians. They could not grasp this society at all, and they wrote about it as a kingdom of 'freemen' and 'slaves' in which almost the whole population, including the armies, comprised bodies of forced labour. Those 'freemen' were actually the Parthian nobility, and the 'slaves' were their feudal tenants whose military service was the rent for their land. This was beyond Roman understanding.

In fact it was a form of society that would not appear in the West until after the collapse of the Western Roman Empire. It is a slight oddity of our modern historical prejudices that we have been brought up to see feudal society as a retrograde step from the centralized structure of the Roman Empire, and the iron-clad knights of medieval

Europe as somehow more primitive than the infantry legions of Rome. In fact, of course, medieval Europe was a natural development from the collapse of the Roman world. It had been presaged centuries earlier in Persia.

The horsemen who had destroyed Crassus' legions were astonishingly similar to Europe's knights 1200 years later. The 18 lesser kings of Persia correspond to Europe's dukes and princes; the satraps who ruled provinces in the name of the king we would recognize as barons, with their own vast estates – Surena was such a figure. The wealthy landowners were heavily armoured cavalrymen, wearing mail and plate armour or breastplates, who galloped into battle with lances which, according to Plutarch, 'had enough impetus to pass through two men at once'.

Like medieval European armies they depended heavily on archers; but whereas European archers were foot-soldiers, Parthian archers were horsemen. The astonishing skill required for the famous 'Parthian shot' that had devastated Crassus' army, the perfectly accurate shot loosed backwards while the horse had all four hooves in the air, came from a lifetime's practice.

Like medieval Europe, this was a chivalric society that understood the ideal heroic knight as a free-living, generous and loyal figure, renowned equally for his physical strength and ability to do unspeakable damage to the bodies of his social equals on the one hand, and his spiritual and religious humility on the other. The similarity of ethos between two societies so far removed in time and space is odd. Perhaps a chivalric mind-set is an inevitable consequence of being very rich, encased in completely protective armour and sharing your life with a horse.

The stories of this chivalric world have not survived, but we have some sense of them from the great Persian epic cycle of the tenth century AD, the *Shahnameh* or Book of Kings. It is a cycle of tales about mythic heroes, and has much in common with the Arthurian legends. Although based on much older material, it is also the product of a master story-teller and poet, Firdowsi, who was commissioned to weave the stories into a 'unified poetical work'; so it is hard to know what was there before. But it is interesting to see the role played by the *Shahnameh* in the Zurkhaneh, the ritual place for the training of warriors, which existed in a slightly different form in Parthian times and still functions in Iran today.

'Zurkhaneh' translates as the 'House of Strength', and it is supposed to provide a form of spiritual and physical preparation for being a heroic knight. Physically, the initiate is drilled in feats of strength. The fully trained strong-man is called a Pehlivan, and he is the chivalric hero.

The Zurkhaneh emerged soon after the Mongol invasion of the thirteenth century as a clandestine meeting-place for warrior-athletes whose activities were being suppressed – their ritualized training had previously been performed in the open. The Parthian tradition was, and is still, preserved. Today the initiates perform their drills in a circular pit about 30 feet across. They are supervised by a master on a platform, who beats a drum and calls out passages from the *Shahnameh* (and, of course, from the Koran). Listening to the deeds of the mythical champion Rustam, who rescued countless kings from peril and who confronted and vanquished evil at every turn, the trainees and champions perform feats of strength with heavy boards, massive Indian clubs and enormous weights, ending with a wrestling match. These Zurkhaneh societies retain a powerful social significance: now they are often places where vigilante groups of deprived men prepare themselves for the use of honourable violence. Chivalry, apparently, is not yet dead in Iran.

PARTHIAN CIVILIZATION

Education was at the heart of this civilization.[11] The peasantry were probably illiterate, but the nobility went to school from about five years old until they were 15. At school children (at least some girls seem to have been educated) would learn to write and would memorize chunks of literature. Astrology was also part of the curriculum. Boys were then trained in riding, archery, polo and the military arts.

A noble education also involved learning to sing, to play musical instruments and games such as chess and backgammon, and general information about wines, flowers, women and riding animals. A pupil further up the social ladder would be taught about social etiquette, ceremonial rites, conduct on festive occasions and the delivery of orations. One piece of evidence suggests that some women were well versed in civil law. For training scribes and secretaries, and for religious studies, there seem to have been specialist schools.

The Parthians' own contributions to the arts of civilization created the 'look and feel' of central Asia. It was they who invented the form of architecture called the *iwan*, the domed hall closed on three sides and open on the fourth, which has given an extraordinary grace to central Asian cities ever since.

The beautiful domes that they introduced to roof their *iwans* could not have been made by the Romans because the structures would have collapsed while being built. Roman domes are shallow and flat-topped, built of ever lighter circles of blocks, like igloos, and were constructed on temporary timber frames, as were their arches. Roman architecture is based on the keystone – the stone in the centre of an arch, against which the sides press, and which actually holds the whole thing together. But until the keystone is in place, the rest of the arch must be held up from below. Roman architecture is actually based on the availability of European forests – the keystone hangs over the ghost of the scaffold that made it possible.

But Mesopotamia and Persia were stripped of their woodland much earlier, so that method of building was no longer an option. When Strabo described the Parthian winter capital, Ctesiphon, around AD 7, he said that instead of having European-type roofs, 'all the houses are vaulted on account of the want of timber'. Such roofs had become possible because they had invented a technology that allowed them to hold blocks in place during construction without a timber scaffold. They put them together with the builder's equivalent of super-glue, an instantly drying cement unknown in the West; it was made out of gypsum. This gave birth to an entirely new architecture, as it became possible to create high paraboloid domes. The construction of such a dome involves a team of men working in synchronized harmony, effectively performing a choreographed dance with their arms as they assemble the dome in a single swift operation while the gypsum is setting.

Even if the Romans had possessed the technology, they couldn't have coped with the engineering. These forms raised interesting mathematical problems for architects. Glazed bricks and tiles were already in use; making curved glazed pieces to fit the paraboloid surface required complex geometric solutions. Quadratic equations and trigonometric curves needed to be resolved in order to keep the roofs over people's heads. The mathematical expertise of the Hellenes, of Babylon and of the ancient Near East was up to the task; Roman mathematics most certainly was not.

The dome was to become the core of Asia's architectural aesthetic. From Persia it spread east to India, and from the blue-tiled *iwans* of Samarkand to the stunning precision of Agra's Taj Mahal eventually gave the world some of the most perfectly beautiful buildings ever constructed. But Rome was a wall blocking this style from the West for centuries. And the science, both mathematical and physical, that lay behind it remained a mystery to the West.

BAGHDAD BATTERIES

The existence of a highly sophisticated and militarily powerful 'barbarian' state was something that Rome could never adjust to. But the Romans had no choice about trading with Persia because the Parthians controlled the gateway between Europe and the Orient. Pepper, perfumes, silk, jewels and pearls all arrived in the Roman Empire from Persia. And it may just be that the good people of Persia helped satisfy the Roman gold-hunger by producing fake golden trinkets using electro-plating.

In 1937 a German archaeologist, William König, director of the Baghdad Museum, was puzzled by a yellow clay pot 6 inches high. Inside it was a 5-inch-long cylinder of sheet copper, 1½ inches in diameter, welded with lead-tin alloy to the bitumen top, and protruding from that was an iron rod that would have been held in place by the bitumen stopper. The bottom of the copper cylinder was capped with a copper disc and was also sealed with bitumen.

It is not clear where König found the jar: some accounts say that it was in the museum basement, others that it came from a grave at Khujut Rabu, a Parthian site near Baghdad. Certainly there are fragments of other jars (or were – since the looting of the museum following the US-led invasion of Iraq in 2004, these artefacts seem to have disappeared). König realized that these might be wet-cell batteries, but the idea was dismissed at that time.

After the Second World War a re-examination of the jar revealed signs of acid corrosion, which inspired Willard F.M. Gray of the General Electric High Voltage Laboratory in Pittsfield, Massachusetts, to try out a reproduction. When filled with an acidic fruit juice, the jar produced a current of 1.5–2 volts.[12] In the late 1970s a German Egyptologist, Dr Arne Eggebrecht, using copies of the batteries with a more efficient electrolyte, claimed to have successfully electroplated a silver statuette with gold.

The idea of the Parthians swindling the Romans with fake gold objects is as entertaining as the idea that they were using electrical wet cells some 1800 years before they were 'invented' by Alessandro Volta. It should be said, though, that we don't actually know what these jars were used for, or even that they were definitely batteries. In this area, as in so many others, we are looking at a lost and forgotten past, trying to understand it by a leap of the imagination.[13]

HOW BARBARIANS NEARLY SAVED THE REPUBLIC

Since the Romans were clearly no match for the Parthians, it is perhaps not too surprising that at least one Roman should try to get them to help him fight his battles against other Romans. The one who thought of that was Cassius, the man who would plunder Rhodes in 42 BC.

He knew exactly how dangerous the Parthian Barbarians were because he had been in charge of one wing of Crassus' army, and had managed to flee with about 500 men. Once he had escaped from the battle, his Arab guides advised him to lie low in a safe place 'until the moon had left the sign of the scorpion', presumably because it was unlucky. He announced that the Archer worried him much more than the Scorpion, and kept moving until he was safely back in Rome.

There he became part of the conspiracy that decided in 44 BC to save the Republic from the royal ambitions of Julius Caesar by murdering him. Rome was now bitterly divided between those who feared the creation of a new form of kingship, in which an emperor ruled everything, and those who thought the old republican constitution had handed Rome to a super-rich oligarchy. In the civil war that followed, the republican Cassius declared himself pro-consul of Syria – Caesar had promised him the governorship and he decided it was safer to grab it than to stay in Rome, where Mark Antony was whipping up a fever of hostility to the plotters.

Once there, and having defeated the incumbent governor who supported Caesar, he found he was in possession of a contingent of Parthian warriors who had joined in this Roman civil war. His bright idea came when he heard that Mark Antony and Octavian (the future Augustus) were on their way to attack him. Cassius sent 'his' Parthians back to Persia with a delegation asking for military support. One of its members, Quintus Labienus, evidently got on very well with the Parthians. When Octavian and Antony defeated the pro-republican army of Brutus and Cassius in 42 BC they counted Parthians among the dead.

Quintus Labienus, though, was not a man to take defeat lying down. As Antony moved southward to take control of Alexandria (and, most famously, of Cleopatra), this Roman general joined the King of Kings in his war against Rome, pursuing his own agenda of trying to bring down Mark Antony and Octavian. He persuaded a number of Roman garrisons to mutiny against the new regime and fight for the old republican constitution. He then led a combined Roman-Parthian army against the men who now controlled Rome. In short order he captured the whole of Asia Minor (today's Asiatic Turkey) and the region of Syria-Palestine. Under the command of this renegade Roman, in just two years the Parthians found their territory restored to almost the extent of the old Achaemenid Empire, including all of Asia Minor except for a few cities. Nothing like this had ever happened before – a Roman general was leading Barbarian forces against Rome itself. This last-ditch effort to use Barbarians to save the Republic from the imperial authority that had taken over Rome is a story that Romans did not like telling, and it has almost been forgotten. But for a while, Labienus and the Persians held the destiny of Rome in their hands.

The Parthians even took control of Judea, with the help of Roman republican rebels. The Tetrarch (governor) of Galilee, Herod, fled to Rome, where Antony and Octavian named him King of the Jews. Meanwhile, the Parthians were profiting from their conquests; money was suddenly pouring in, and it was invested in the development of Ctesiphon, the new winter capital on the river Tigris.

We don't know exactly what Ctesiphon was like – only that it was the most important city in the Parthian Empire and that by the end of the first century AD its walls contained an area three times as large as Rome. But Ctesiphon was not the Persian Barbarian Rome. The Roman Empire was essentially an extension of the city of Rome; first Rome, and later Constantinople, were the very essence of Roman civilization. That is why the 'sack of Rome' would eventually be such a powerful symbolic event. The Parthian Empire was not like that; it had no central control, and no single culture. However large and important Ctesiphon might become, the Persian Empire could manage perfectly well without it.

One feature shared by the two empires was their emphasis on war: successful generals posed a danger to existing rulers. That, after all, was what had brought Julius Caesar to power and plunged Rome into civil war. Parthian rulers did at least have the power and the will to strike at that danger: Orodes had Surena murdered a few months after his great victory, and now Orodes' successor Pacorus was growing worried about his over-successful Roman general. The Parthian ruler became more uneasy the more this became a war of aggression – and eventually he withdrew his support. These Barbarians, unlike the Romans, did not want to conquer the world. Or even Rome.

Fatally undermined, Labienus could not withstand the Roman counter-attack when it came. In 39 BC he was killed and Rome recovered Asia Minor. One year later Pacorus himself was killed in Syria, moving to occupy a Roman camp that he thought was undefended. And Herod personally led another Roman army to retake Jerusalem, capturing the holy city from its Parthian-supported Jewish ruler after a five-month siege.

The Roman Republic was well and truly dead. And the lesson that Rome learnt from Crassus' defeat was not that other people had a right to exist, but that they needed heavy cavalry in their own army.

HAMMERING THE PARTHIANS

The Roman frontier with Persia became an area of unending struggle. War with Persia was now a permanent theme of Roman politics, and through the second century AD it was virtually continuous. Because the Roman army was fully professionalized, and consumed some 80 per cent of the Empire's income from taxes, the Empire became essentially a system for maintaining its armies. It was they who appointed and disposed of emperors. They were originally chosen from a small pool of Romans who were entitled to be considered for the job because of family connections, or who had at least served as consuls, titular high officials. But eventually Roman emperors turned into despotic warlords who were simply creations of the army wherever it could find them. The first of this new breed of ruler was Septimius Severus, a soldier born in North Africa who ruled in military dress. His ruthless authoritarian rule was described as 'oriental despotism', but actually he exercised power that the Parthian kings could only dream of.

Severus doubled the pay of his soldiers, allowed them for the first time to marry in service, and replaced the Praetorian Guard, the elite aristocratic military force that surrounded the Emperor himself, with a new body composed of provincial troops. The Empire was ruled not so much by the Senate or even the Emperor, but by the rule-book and by quartermasters. And, of course, anyone of whom he felt suspicious was dead meat. The security forces in Rome were massively enlarged until the place felt like a police state.

The Empire was, by this time, an economic basket-case. The machine had to keep feeding itself with plunder, and there was no more plunder to be had unless Severus could achieve the kind of victory in Persia that had eluded Rome since the time of Crassus. So that's what he did. Romans liked to think that their campaigns against Barbarians had some greater purpose than loot, and, indeed, they usually arose from a mixture of motives. But Dio Cassius was so struck by Severus' single-mindedness that he wonderingly observed that it was 'just as if the sole purpose of his campaign had been to plunder this place'.[14]

An arch constructed by Severus still stands in Rome today. It was built to illustrate his greatest triumph – when in AD 196 he went into Persia and smacked it very, very hard. This absolutely gigantic monument was the first significant architectural addition to the Forum since the time of Hadrian, 80 years earlier. It celebrated the fact that he had finally got his hands on the money that Crassus had failed to obtain. He captured Ctesiphon and created two new Roman provinces, called Osrhoene and Mesopotamia, out of the western section of the Parthian Empire. And in the process he carried away loot in such quantities that economists reckon it kept the Roman Empire out of the red for 20 or 30 years. The lad from Libya poured some of it into his home town, Leptis Magna, building a magnificent new forum, an elaborate four-way arch at the main cross- roads and a new harbour with a colonnaded avenue going to the city centre. It became a cultural centre rivalling Rome itself, and all done with Persian money.

With Ctesiphon captured, Persia ought, by Roman standards, to have collapsed. It didn't. But it did change, in a way that was not going to be very nice for Rome. Severus' success destabilized the Parthian dynasty, fatally weakening it, and what emerged to take its place would be a mirror image of Rome itself – a ruthless, aggressive, centralized state that would stop at nothing.

> The gods appear in many forms, Carrying with them
> unwelcome things. What people thought would happen,
> never did. What they did not expect, the gods made
> happen.[15]

X
SASSANIANS

Some 60 miles west of the ancient Persian city of Shiraz stands a ruined palace complex that bears the name Bishapur. It was constructed in AD 266, and boasts many of the traditional architectural features that one would expect to find in a palace of such size and splendour ... except that they are not Persian features. They are thoroughly Roman. There are a number of small arches that are quite clearly built in the Roman style, held up by keystones. There were Roman-style mosaics, too, until they were carted off to the Louvre and the National Museum of Iran. Bishapur is in the province of Fars – the heartland of Persia. In fact, since 'F' and 'P' are the same letter in Persian, Fars gives us the word 'Persia'. So what on earth is a Roman-style palace doing there?

Well, one thing is for sure: it doesn't celebrate the triumph of Roman power over the Persians; in fact, quite the contrary. Across the road, carved into a cliff, is a series of large rectangular panels, one of which records the real connection of this place with Rome. The rock relief commemorates the humiliation of not one, not two, but three Roman emperors at the hands of the eponymous founder of Bishapur, Shapur I.

One Roman emperor is being trampled under Shapur's horse. That is Gordian III, whom Shapur defeated in 244 and who was killed by his own troops. Another Roman emperor is shown kneeling in front of the King of Kings begging for his life. That is Philip the Arab, Gordian's successor, who coughed up a king's ransom in return for Shapur allowing him to remain on the imperial throne. A third Roman emperor is shown standing, with Shapur holding him firmly by the wrist – the traditional way of depicting the act of 'capture'. This is

Valerian, who was captured by Shapur and shut up in the palace of Bishapur for the rest of his natural life, with these rock carvings conveniently nearby as a sort of photo-album to bring back happy memories.

The Roman architecture of the palace is due, according to tradition, to the use of forced labour in the form of Roman soldiers (including technicians and builders) captured at the same time as Valerian. But Shapur could have built in any style he liked. He clearly wanted to show that his was a world-empire, and that European style had a place in it alongside what was Asian. Considering how successful Shapur was in his conflict with Rome, it's surprising his name is not better known in the West. But then, in the West it's only the Roman version of events that counts, and that doesn't include successful enemies.

The Sassanian dynasty, to which Shapur belonged, replaced the Parthians with a 'barbarian' colossus, more powerful and better organized than Rome itself, and before which that Empire was humiliated as never before. And in a curious way it was the Romans' own doing. They just couldn't let Persia be, and kept plugging away at it, until they had undermined Parthian rule and opened up the field for a rival dynasty.

Rome's massive assault at the end of the second century accelerated a process that had already begun: the King of Kings' hold over his feudal vassals was weakening, and local overlords were less and less interested in responding to his demands. The Parthian royal house divided and struggled for control of an increasingly chaotic empire.

THE SASSANIAN TAKEOVER

There is a panel carved into another cliff-side, this time at a place called Naqš-i Rustam, near Persepolis, to the north-east of Shiraz. This carving depicts Shapur's father, Ardashir, receiving the ring of power from the spirit of goodness and purity, Ahura Mazda. Both are mounted, and both their horses are shown trampling over the body of a defeated enemy. In the case of Ahura Mazda the prostrate body is that of Ahriman, the evil spirit. Ardashir's horse, however, tramples over his rival, the last Parthian King of Kings, Artabanus.

Ardashir founded the Sassanian dynasty, and his monument really says it all. The Sassanians created nothing less than a revolution in Persian rule and they didn't just trample over the previous dynasty, they set about utterly obliterating it. Ardashir dismantled the crumbling feudal structure of the Parthians, and replaced it with something much more like the Roman model. The Sassanian Empire was to be run from the centre as a military operation. It was split into new regions based on military considerations, designed to be dependent on the King of Kings, free from hereditary interests and feudal rivalries. To weaken any regional authority, his own family domains were scattered across the Empire. The old feudal princes were allowed to remain in positions of authority, but the military services and troops they had to provide were formalized, and alongside the old feudal levies of troops there were now soldiers on salaries. Rome no longer had the only professional army in the world. This 'barbarian' empire was something entirely new.

The past was wiped out, and Ardashir ordered the complete destruction of all record of the Parthians. Can wild, savage Barbarians have an ideological revolution? These people did. Ardashir named his empire Iran, the mythical homeland of the Aryans. This was a myth with a similar force to the Judaic belief in the quasi-mythical kingdom of Solomon – a divinely ordained territory associated with past and future ages of perfect rule. But it had an additional significance because Ardashir divided the world into Iran and non-Iran, a division that was similar to the Roman divide between Roman and Barbarian. Us and not-us.

The Romans called the Persians 'barbarians'. Now they were themselves firmly on the receiving end of the same perception – placed in the land of devils, the Kingdom of the Lie: non-Iran. And nothing of the Lie was to be permitted in Iran.

The determination to wipe out what was unlike themselves was also a mirror of Roman civilization. It was a reflection of the Roman determination to remove Persian identity from the world and Romanize it. Every time the Persians regained control of cities and provinces that Rome had occupied, the Romans denounced them as aggressive Barbarians. One Roman emperor, addressing his troops before battle with the Persians, told them, 'We must wipe out a most troublesome nation.' That particular battle left the emperor in question, Julian, wiped out himself. The two super-powers had their horns locked in a perpetual struggle.

Persia, just like Rome, needed to build an ideology that encouraged people to see their rulers not just as overlords, but as the defenders of civilized values, and Ardashir knew a thing or two about propaganda. He capitalized on the chivalric ethos that had flourished under the Parthians, and took care that his life was publicly presented as that of a chivalric knight in the service of God. After the battles by which he seized the Empire, he is said to have formalized his victory by staging a single-combat joust against the Parthian king Artabanus in AD 224 and striking him down with a club.

Ardashir had himself crowned, naturally enough, in Persepolis. He was consciously linking himself directly to the ancient, and now largely forgotten and mythic, empire of Darius, whose inscriptions declared: 'I am Darius the great King ... A Persian, son of a Persian, an Aryan, having Aryan lineage ... '

The word 'Aryan' has acquired so many unfortunate associations that it is worth tracing its original meaning. It comes from *Arya*, a Sanskrit word indicating 'noble', which really refers to an assembly of skilled or talented people. The word emerged in other Indo-European languages in forms such as the Greek *aristoi* ('most noble' – hence English 'aristocrat') and the Latin *ars*, and from this a whole raft of words connected with skill, art and manufacture. When Darius declared himself an Aryan, he was talking not about his ethnicity but about his aristocratic genealogy.

The Empire that Ardashir had taken over possessed natural frontiers to both north and south. The north was an uninhabitable waste-land stretching east from the Caspian Sea, while in the south the Persian Gulf and the Afghan mountains provided easily defended boundaries. But to the west and east it was vulnerable. In the west the Empire stretched to Mesopotamia – or at least should have done if the Romans had not taken over the territory between the rivers Tigris and Euphrates, along with Syria and Armenia. And in the east the Empire narrowed to a gateway beyond which lay the steppes, the infinite, treeless grasslands of the nomads. This gateway was a key point on what is now known as the Silk Road; it was the portal through which Chinese and Indian goods could move overland to the Mediterranean.

Ardashir set about extending his control over both frontier regions. He sent substantial forces east, establishing his authority over a region

stretching from the Aral Sea into northern India. In the west he challenged the Roman Empire directly, retaking Ctesiphon almost at once,
driving the Romans out of Mesopotamia and moving into Armenia.

THE KINGDOM OF THE LIE

It wasn't too hard to present the Roman Empire as the Kingdom of the
Lie and the home of evil. It had grown pretty bizarre in recent years.
Shortly before Ardashir seized the Persian throne, Rome had been
ruled by one of the weirdest emperors ever to wear the purple.
Elagabalus (also known as Heliogabalus) was the only Roman emperor
who is reported to have dressed as a woman, married a Vestal Virgin
and presented himself for hire naked in brothels.[1]

Septimius Severus had fatally weakened the Parthian regime,
opening the door to the Sassanian revolution, but he had also set up
the events that would cripple Rome by bringing Elagabalus to power.
Severus had tried to strengthen his position in Syria by marrying his
niece, Julia Soaemias, to a Syrian who just happened to be the hereditary high priest of the Syrian sun god El-Gabaal (better known to
most of us as Baal). Their son was manoeuvred by family politicking
on to the imperial throne when he was just 14, and, since his father
was now dead, inherited the priesthood and tried to bring the cult of
Baal into Rome as the imperial religion. 'Elagabalus' was actually the
name of his god. While his mother and grandmother ran the Empire,
he mounted elaborate Syrian religious festivals, largely devoted to
fertility. Elagabalus scandalized Rome.

His mother did nothing to stop his sexual excesses, and in the
end his grandmother decided they both had to go. So she persuaded
Elagabalus to adopt his cousin Alexander, and then bribed the
Praetorian Guard to kill the priest-emperor and his mother. Thus, in
AD 222, another 14-year-old, Alexander Severus, became the new
emperor, and his mother, Julia Soaemias' sister, now began to run the
show. The very un-Roman practices of Elagabalus came to an end.

In AD 231 Alexander and his mother went to Antioch with an
army that was supposed to restore Roman power, and sent envoys to
Ardashir in an attempt to launch negotiations. Antioch was the capital of Syria, and Alexander, as Elagabalus' adopted son, was the new

high priest of El-Gabaal. It's clear that the army they brought from Rome was not very happy about what was going on. According to Herodian, a Syrian who was recording events as they happened, 'The barbarian sent the envoys back to the emperor unsuccessful. Then Ardashir chose four hundred very tall Persians, outfitted them with fine clothes and gold ornaments, and equipped them with horses and bows; he sent these men to Alexander as envoys, thinking that their appearance would dazzle the Romans.'² Ardashir was presenting Alexander and his mother with an image of oriental splendour that they would recognize and be troubled by.

The envoys said that the great king Ardashir ordered the Romans and their emperor to withdraw from all Syria and from that part of Asia opposite Europe; they were to hand back to the Persians the whole Middle East, including most of modern Turkey. The Emperor's mother decided to strip the lot of them, put them under arrest and send in the army. The army had no enthusiasm for any of this, or for her. The result was a stand-off. The Roman army suffered massive losses, and Ardashir lost ground in Mesopotamia. Alexander Severus withdrew, and his mother arranged a triumphal procession for him in Rome in 233. The pair of them were killed two years later by their own troops.

With Rome paralysed, Ardashir established his control over Mesopotamia and Armenia. He then retired to Persia, and his son strode on to the stage as the new King of Kings.

SHAPUR AND THE HUMILIATION OF ROME

The new ruler, Shapur I, who came to power in 241, found himself confronted by a succession of Roman armies over a period of nearly 20 years. Close to Persepolis, by the tomb of Darius, he left a long inscription in Parthian, Middle Persian (his own language) and Greek, recording his humiliation of both Gordian III and his usurper, Philip the Arab, in 244, and his greatest conquest 16 years later when he became the first and only Barbarian ruler actually to capture a Roman emperor alive. Rome had lost legions to the Barbarians before; but now, for the first time, an emperor, Valerian, would live out his days in the custody of an enemy ruler. Worst of all, the Romans realized, the Persian army included women dressed and armed exactly like the men.[3] 'Shameful' hardly begins to describe this defeat.

At Bishapur, next to the ruins of the palace, is a building that has been remembered in folk-history as *zendan-e valerian*: 'Valerian's prison'. Within the palace complex itself, the building that has survived most completely is a half-underground temple to Anahita, the goddess of water and fertility. This recently discovered chamber was designed to be flooded on demand, presumably for ceremonial worship. It seems likely that Valerian was obliged not only to live within easy viewing distance of the rock-cut billboards showing his military defeat, but probably also to take a submissive part in the worship of a fertility-goddess whose cult involved ritual prostitution, and who was also a goddess of war.

After he died, Valerian was apparently stuffed like a hunting trophy and put on display in a temple. This symbol of humiliation was almost certainly shown off to any visiting Roman. Not surprisingly, Roman propaganda went into overdrive. Shapur had captured Valerian by a trick, the story was put about, seizing him under a flag of truce. Shapur's troops had swept like a devouring flame over all Roman Asia. The entire population of Antioch had been butchered. He had filled the ravines of Cappadocia with dead bodies so that his cavalry might ride across. His prisoners had been left to starve, driven to the river once a day to drink like horses. And he had used Valerian as a mounting-block when he went riding.

There is no evidence for any of this – or for the rival theory that Valerian had surrendered to Shapur in order to avoid being one more emperor killed by his own army. There is, however, evidence that even Shapur – this most ruthless of Persian emperors – was a man of culture. He established a scholarly court, commissioned translations of scientific and philosophical works from Greek and Sanskrit, and took a thoughtful interest in religious philosophy. In fact, although under Sassanian rule the Persians may have regrouped into a militaristic society that could rival Rome, they seem to have lost none of their cultural graces.

COURTLY BARBARIANS

The Sassanians appear to have lived lives of elaborate courtliness, about as far removed from any notion of rough Barbarians as anyone could imagine. We don't have much in the way of original sources, but we do have early Arabic and Persian texts derived from Sassanian literature, which describe how things were in what came to be considered a golden age of fine ceremonies and perfect decorum.

Everyday behaviour was entirely dictated by people's status; not only would the lowest-status (or youngest) person be the first to dismount and kiss the ground (the Sassanian equivalent of shaking hands), but that person would also be expected to let anyone of higher status choose what colour to play at chess and backgammon, and make the first move.[4] A man was expected to be properly turned out (a sacred girdle, shoes and a hat, to be politely removed in front of important folk), and to be clean and scented (but not too heavily). On festive occasions men and women walked around holding flowers.

You had to watch your Ps and Qs – never criticize a person for having given bad advice, or guilt-trip anyone for having taken your own excellent advice, and never sit in a more important person's seat or argue about it. You were supposed to be courteous and affable without becoming a crawler. Conversation was a minefield: listen carefully, don't talk too much, never interrupt, speak sedately and eloquently. Enthusiastic agreement suggests that you are claiming to be an authority on the sub- ject, and you must never show off. In fact over-enthusiasm (which can be pretty boring) was not at all the thing. To criticize another country or laugh at a funny name was bad form; whispering, passing on rumours and telling tall stories were all disgraceful. The rule was total and charming politeness.

Table manners were completely ritualized. The host did not sit until he was asked by the guests, and was not supposed to press people to take seconds. He had to make sure that he did not become drunk before the guests and, when they did get a bit tipsy, he had to pretend that he was too. And, of course, prayers were said before and after the meal. Guests had to be careful not to help themselves to food before others and not to look in the direction from which the food was being brought in; they should eat slowly, and make conversation while looking down – it was rude to watch other people eat. No quarrels, then, no insults, and it was really frowned on to behave like a drunk.

Living in Sassanian Persia was a bit like living at Versailles under Louis XIV. The possibilities of seeing your social position slide away from under you were endless.

SASSANIAN RELIGION

Shapur's interest in religious philosophy was doubtless genuine, but it also had extremely useful political spin-offs. His grandfather, Papak, who had launched the Sassanian revolution, had been the high priest of the Zoroastrian fire temple in Istakhr (his predecessor there, Sassek, was his inspiration, and possibly his father – hence the name of the dynasty). The temple was dedicated to Anahita. That goddess was known throughout the ancient Near East under many names: Ishtar, Astarte, Aphrodite. But the sacred fire was uniquely Persian.

It is a manifestation of the divine light of the spirit of goodness and purity, Ahura Mazda, maintained continuously by priests who wear cloths over their mouths to prevent their breath contaminating its purity. Papak himself seems to have been a Zoroastrian revivalist, a determined ethical monotheist opposed to the cultural pluralism of the failing Parthian aristocrats. He was opposed to the Hellenes with their multiplicity of amoral gods, and determined to establish a state religion over the whole Empire as the basis of a new order. He dethroned the governor of Fars and, evidently with the backing of warrior nobles, took over the province.

Papak may have been helped by a Persian reaction against what was, after all, a failing regime, and by a conscious desire to restore old Persian traditions. Much had been forgotten, but the idea that Ahura Mazda stood for settled order, and the Dark Lord Ahriman for chaos, had not. In the days of the Achaeminids, the fire of Ahura Mazda had been identified with the life of the ruler; when he died, the old fire was extinguished and a new one began. Now the Persian ruler was once more fully identified with Ahura Mazda and the sacred fire.

The worship of a single centralized god is also, of course, a useful way of centralizing political power, and Papak's son, Ardashir, seems to have made good use of the power that religion provided. The old religious tolerance of the Achaeminids and Parthians was no longer on the agenda. This new state was a centralized theocracy. Ardashir put the fire-altar on his coins, and declared that religion and kingship were brothers. His deathbed advice to his son was reputed to be 'Consider the Fire Altar and the Throne as inseparable as to sustain each other.' His rule was the will of God. That made disagreement with the King of Kings an offence against morality itself. Non-Zoroastrians could expect a difficult time.

An official religion needs to be properly defined; there is a core text to Zoroastrianism, the Avesta. This is a collection of 17 enigmatic hymns, the Gathas, along with prayers, prescriptions for rituals, and formulas for cleansing one's body and soul. Ardashir had the Avesta put into some sort of order, and used it as the basis of his legal code. The hereditary priesthood, called Magi, ran the courts. They also controlled the schools, as well as performing religious rituals – ceremonies at the births of children, weddings, deaths and so on. They earned fees, and also levied fines on self-confessed sinners – a better option than having your sin laid on you in a trial, when you could be subject to corporal punishment. Besides, the priests warned, sinners and those who did not participate fully in the rituals and prayers would end up in the hands of Ahriman, the devil, instead of enjoying paradise.

There was an obvious philosophical problem with all this: how can there be one God, who is all-powerful, when there is a force for evil which he cannot overwhelm? The official Zoroastrian solution was to say that Infinite Time, Zurvan, was the original godhead and father of everything, both of the good force, Ahura Mazda, and the negative force, Ahriman. This meant that Ahura Mazda was not responsible for the existence of evil.

The logic was that religion provided justice, the basis of an ordered society that could sustain military expenditure. The mantra was 'There can be no power without an army, no army without money, no money without agriculture and no agriculture without justice.' So with religion properly ordered, Ardashir was able to set up a system of justice and taxation that would pay for an army.

SHAPUR AND THE MESSIAH

Religious philosophy was the big issue in both Persia and Rome. The continuous military hammering between Rome and Parthia had not only brought about a crisis in Persia; it was also a major cause of the crisis that afflicted the Roman Empire in the third century. As soon as he took power, Ardashir had closed down the caravan routes to the Mediterranean. Trade between Rome and the Far East broke down, the renewal of war meant that the cost of the Roman army sky-rocketed, and sections of the Western Empire began to break free of central authority and try to organize their own affairs as agriculture faltered and taxes rose. This was the atmosphere in which Christianity began to take hold in the Roman world, and in the buzzing atmosphere of the Zoroastrian revolution in Persia, Christian spin-off cults were attracting serious interest.

In Fars, a cult called the Practitioners of Ablutions believed in the washing away of sins in baptisms. A messianic Jewish-Christian group called Elkesaites, who celebrated the Jewish Sabbath, practised vegetarianism and circumcision and had their own version of the teachings of Christ and of Moses. In this rather fevered atmosphere a religious teacher appeared called Mani, who claimed that he was the final prophet in a line that stretched from Zarathustra through Buddha to Jesus. His emphasis was on the universality of truth, and in a conscious imitation of Paul, he set out on missionary journeys.

Mani brought a messianic message into the Zoroastrian world; now the battle between the forces of good and evil became not just a moral basis for human society but an urgent crisis. Mani taught that the forces of evil were winning, and that redemption – the triumph of good – would come only after a determined struggle by a select group of devotees. According to Mani, the original sin committed by Adam and Eve, from which humans needed to be redeemed, was not, as Christians had decided, the act of sex, but the eating of flesh. Mani did have a core group, the Elect, who lived a life of eye-watering asceticism based on fruit juice and sexual abstinence, but for the rest of his followers, known as Manicheans, he preached occasional vegetarianism and fasting – or, if that was too hard, just believing. This was in preparation for an apocalypse in which the earth would be destroyed, the damned would collect into a cosmic clod of dirty matter and the kingdom of goodness and light would separate from the kingdom of evil and darkness.

Shapur, who had invited Mani to his coronation, placed him under his protection and encouraged him to accompany his campaigns, along with the Zoroastrian priests who came to perform fire-rituals and cleanse the conquered land of evil and demons. Basically, for all his firm devotion to Ahura Mazda, Shapur inclined to traditional Persian multi-culturalism. He enjoyed conversation with Greek philosophers and persuaded the Zoroastrian priesthood to include in the Avesta works on metaphysics, astronomy and medicine borrowed from the Greeks and Indians. Unlike his father, he proclaimed freedom of worship for Manicheans, Jews and Christians in their own communities, so long as they lived under Sassanian law and paid taxes. Following his invasion of Syria, Shapur deported the populations of Damascus and other non-Iranian cities, sending large groups of Greek-speaking Christians from Syria to the provinces of Persis, Parthia, Susiana and the city of Babylon, where they were allowed to organize their own communities and follow their own leaders. There now even appeared a Christian bishop of Ctesiphon.

The fact was that, once he had broken the military power of Rome, Shapur had nothing much to fear. The border became quite porous again, traders moved backwards and forwards, people married across the frontier. This was, after all, the world of the bazaar, of trade, of making deals. Rome may have been built for war; Persia had better things in mind.

PALMYRA

But although he was secure, Shapur failed to hold on to Mesopotamia. He lost it, not to Rome, but to Persia's old trading partner Palmyra, the Levantine link between Persia and the Mediterranean. Palmyra was a rather surprising place, and about to become even more so.

When Shapur came to power, Palmyra was the main city of a Roman province called Syria Phoenice. People in the east found it hard to come to terms with Roman power: the great problem was that the Romans were such upstarts – by the standards of the region, they had a very short history and virtually no culture. There had been a temple at Palmyra, for instance, for 2000 years before the Romans even saw it. Its form, a large stone-walled chamber with columns outside, is much closer to the sort of thing attributed to Solomon than to any Roman. And so it should be. It is mentioned in the Bible as part of Solomon's kingdom. In fact, it says he built it.[5]

Palmyra is its Greek and Roman name, meaning Place of Palms. The locals called it Tadmor, which means the same. The temple was the Temple of Baal. It was rebuilt after the Romans had moved in – a clear statement that these people were not Romanized.

Palmyra's whole ethos was trade. Some people were interested in gods, some in conquest and world domination; Palmyrans devoted their lives and energies to import-export businesses. Most of the trade between the Mediterranean and Persia, India and China was handled by Palmyrans – Arabs, Jews and Persians. As the quintessential middle-men between east and west, they played a long game of trying to be friends with Rome and friends with Persia.

And for a long time they managed it very neatly. They said they were under Roman suzerainty, to avoid getting walloped, but persuaded Rome to designate them a free city – free, that is, of Roman taxes, which is what really mattered. Palmyran chiefs secured safe-conducts for passing caravans from desert sheiks; guides led those caravans through the barren region; mounted archers protected them against Bedouin raids; and the city imposed heavy duties on each arti-cle of merchandise as it passed through its gates. The commodities comprised some of the necessities and many of the luxuries of the contemporary world: wool, purple dye, silk, glassware, perfumes, aromatics, olive oil, dried figs, nuts, cheese and wine.

Palmyra was a desert city, but its merchants owned ships in Italian waters, controlled the Indian silk trade and brought in gold and gemstones to be worked into luxury objects by the guild of fine metal smiths. Agriculture was well organized, and the crops irrigated from a lake created by building a quarter-mile-long dam. Palmyra became one of the richest cities of the Near East. And its population (some of whom accepted Roman citizenship and tacked Roman names on to their Semitic ones) replaced their traditional mud-brick houses with modern limestone. Their houses were richer, larger and more sumptuously decorated than any outside Rome.

New wide streets lined with colonnades were laid out, and the city began to look like a particularly prosperous Greco-Roman town with a lavish Greek-style marketplace and a theatre. But there was no amphitheatre. And there were no gladiatorial contests. When spectators watched imitation Barbarians and real wild animals, and learnt to enjoy the spectacle of death as an entertainment, it was designed to imbue Roman values in them. They didn't go in for that in Palmyra.

The Palmyrans had really pulled off a great trick: they were the only people who managed to live alongside Rome without being Romanized. They simply pretended to be Romans. Of course, they took precautions to protect their money. They trained a splendid army of mounted archers. Their soldiers were at the service of Rome – indeed, Rome rather insisted on that – so some were drafted into the Roman army, and some even served on the Roman wall in Britain.

But as the war between Rome and Persia dragged on, this neat arrangement began to break down. Trade diminished as western Persia became a war-zone, and Ardashir's revolutionary takeover made it impossible to carry on steering a course between Rome and Persia. When the ruler of Palmyra in the 250s offered to be Shapur's ally, he was firmly told that the King of Kings had no allies – only subjects. The Romans made him a better offer, and he took it. The Emperor Valerian made him consul and governor of Syria Phoenice.

When he went on and attacked Persia after Valerian's capture, the new Emperor, Gallienus, assumed that this was a campaign on behalf of Rome and named him *corrector totius orientis*, supervisor of the whole east. The governor of Palmyra, however, was calling himself King of Kings and going nose to nose with Shapur on his own account.

QUEEN ZENOBIA

After the governor's assassination in 267, his wife claimed that title in the name of her son Vallabathus. And so began the wholly amazing reign of that wholly amazing woman, Zenobia. Well, that's what the Romans called her. Her real name was Bat Zabbai, daughter of Zabbai, but this is one case where the Romans got it right. Who's ever heard of Mr Zabbai? Zenobia was a woman in her own right – and there haven't been many like her.

Everyone said she was a striking beauty. Descriptions of her mention pearly-white teeth and large, black, sparkling eyes. On state occasions she wore the purple of the ruling class, the robe fringed with precious gems and with golden waist ornaments. One arm was left bare to the shoulder, and while riding in her gem-encrusted carriage she wore a helmet.

Zenobia ruled as an oriental queen, greeted with prostration as in the Persian court, where the ruler appeared as a living deity. She claimed an aristocratic lineage that seemed especially impressive in a society of traders, saying that she was descended from Cleopatra. This queen had received a very good education, and spoke Greek (and, it has been claimed, Egyptian), as well as Latin, Aramaic and Persian.[6] She is said to have written the first complete history of her country, but was certainly no bluestocking. An accomplished huntress, Zenobia used to go hunting lions and bears with her husband, Odaenathus, while he was alive. She also used to go with him to war, doing full military training, wearing armour and carrying weapons. Instead of riding in a litter, she rode or marched at the head of a column of soldiers, and was given joint credit with Odaenathus for their victories against the Persians.

So it was a mistake for the Roman Senate, led by the Emperor Gallienus, to announce that her authority would be limited, she would not be *corrector totius orientis*, and Palmyra would be reduced to the status of a client-state. Her response was direct and determined. It seems as though Zenobia had decided that the Roman Empire was taking a new form, as a decentralized federation of empires. In Europe, Britain, Gaul and Iberia had broken away under their own Emperor. Roman power in the east had been broken by the capture of Valerian. Her own armies were in control of the Mesopotamian part of Persia. Why should there not be an independent part of the Imperium based on Palmyra, reasserting the ancient traditions of the Middle East?

So she took over Egypt and Syria. As one emperor followed another in Rome, she had a more or less free hand. She was hugely popular, and went so far as to wear the imperial diadem and term herself 'Queen of the East'. Her coins were marked 'Augusta', mother of the Emperor, while her sons received Latin educations and were paraded before the Syrian troops wearing the imperial purple.

But it didn't last. Eventually Rome restructured its army and set about bringing the dissident provinces back under its military command. The Emperor Aurelian confronted Zenobia's opportunistic empire and fought two decisive battles against her. Zenobia was present at both of them, taking an active role, and lost. And seeing how the wind was blowing, her supporters evaporated. She was besieged in Palmyra, escaped, but was eventually caught 60 miles away. Her reign ended in 272, and the following year the city was demolished and its inhabitants slaughtered.

There are different versions of what happened to Zenobia, but the likeliest seems to be that she was taken to Rome to be paraded in Aurelian's Triumph, weighed down with gold chains. Then, having talked her way out of worse trouble, she probably ended up a society hostess in an elegant villa at Tivoli. There is one, rather dubious, source that quotes a letter from Aurelian defending himself for presenting a woman in chains:

> Those persons who find fault with me now would accord me
> praise in abundance, did they but know what manner of
> woman she is, how wise in counsels, how steadfast in plans,
> how firm toward the soldiers, how generous when necessity
> calls, and how stern when discipline demands. I might even
> say that it was her doing that Odaenathus [her husband]
> defeated the Persians and, after putting Shapur to flight,
> advanced all the way to Ctesiphon. I might add thereto that
> such was the fear that this woman inspired in the peoples of
> the East and also the Egyptians that neither Arabs nor
> Saracens nor Armenians ever moved against her.[7]

Even if the letter never existed, it does show how Zenobia was remembered by Romans.

PERSIA AND ROME — THE FIGHT CONTINUES

This affair had kept Rome and Persia apart, and by the time Rome was ready to have another crack at the Persians, Shapur was dead, the Zoroastrian priesthood was back in command and toleration was once more off the agenda. After Shapur's death in 272, Mani had been tried and condemned as a 'bad doctor'. Part of his offence was that he was a pacifist; in the war against the Lie (that is, Rome), pacifism was not to be an option. Mani was imprisoned and killed around 276.

Meanwhile, the new administrative machine had employed its Roman prisoners on a series of irrigation projects that increased the crop yields and settlement of the Fertile Crescent – the region between the rivers Tigris and Euphrates – by 50 per cent.[8] War was resumed in 295, when Rome was repelled from an attack on Ctesiphon but then won a huge victory, capturing the King of King's entire harem. This was not some little matter of half a dozen pretty ladies. The harem was a city of several thousand women and the entire royal family, including the children from whom the successor to the throne would be chosen. The price of their return was loss of control of all Persia's lands in the north-west, including Armenia and northern Mesopotamia.

As a result, at the beginning of the fourth century Rome concluded a peace treaty with Persia, but the pressure of this ever-lasting war was changing the whole nature of the Roman Empire. The sheer cost of the ever-larger army was one thing; another was the fact that defending the border with Persia was a full-time job.

It really looked as though the 'barbarian' empire of Persia was the one that worked, and Rome was the one that didn't. In 309, when the Sassanian Emperor Hormizd II died, his son acceded to the throne. However, there was a general consensus that he was unsuitable for the job, and he was replaced by a foetus still in his mother's womb. Apparently, the coronation of the bump, who was named Shapur II, was a memorable event. Presumably the Magi had already determined by the stars that the bump was a boy.

The Persian Empire could manage in a calm and orderly way with a foetus, and then an infant, on the throne. Rome, on the other hand, was a mess. During Shapur II's infancy it was divided by civil wars that ended in 312 with the thorough-going military conquest of Italy by a Balkan-born military commander, Constantine. There was then a long stand-off between Constantine and the commander of the Eastern Roman forces, which ended with a huge war and some 25,000 dead when Constantine took the Eastern Empire in 324. Having come to power he decided to move the whole focus of the Empire to the East, replacing the palace-city of Byzantium with a great new capital, Constantinople, New Rome, on the very border of Asia.

The old Latin Empire was now doomed to be a peripheral enterprise, concerned with agriculture and the Germans. It was largely left to manage as best it could, with the result that a form of military anarchy often existed on the Rhine as armies promoted their own commanders to power and hired Goths when needed to supplement their own strength. 'Roman' no longer meant 'from the city of Rome', and the heart of the Empire now became Greek. The old distinction between Greeks and Romans, in which each regarded the other with distrust, had become meaningless. Except in the city of Rome, of course, where most leading figures didn't speak any Greek and were very suspicious of what they still saw as duplicitous, decadent and immoral Easterners.

Constantine's Empire was also newly and officially Christian, and that had an impact in Persia. Christianity obviously now belonged to the Kingdom of the Lie, and Christian minorities, especially in the border region of Armenia, were now assumed to be under the influence of the major enemy power. The persecution of Christians had stopped in the Roman Empire, but it was now taken up in Persia.

As Constantine approached his death, it was obvious that the Roman Empire was about to go through another crippling trauma. He had announced a five-way division of the Empire, and it was plain that the inheritors would try to tear each other to pieces. It's hardly surprising that at this point Shapur II, now 26, decided to recover the lands Rome had taken from Persia. From 337 to 350, the two empires fought a war that ebbed and flowed over what were now the Roman fortresses of Mesopotamia.

Rome's assault on Persia had created a 'barbarian' empire at least as well organized, highly centralized and militarily powerful as itself. Now the continuing war was steadily undermining both. For Rome, the concentration on Persia was steadily weakening the Rhine and

Danube frontiers, and leading to ever-larger incursions of Germanic peoples. For Persia, the same struggle was pulling resources away from the eastern frontier in Kushan, the gateway that defended civilization from the horsemen of the steppes.

PERSIA AND THE HUNS

It was impossible for even the longest hand – and it was a motto of the Persian emperor that he needed a long hand – to know what was happening across such a vast territory. It took two months to travel from the war-zone in Armenia to the capital city, Ctesiphon. And Kushan lay as far again to the east. In 350, Shapur II was forced to break off his draining struggle with Rome because it had taken away too many resources from the east – with the devastating result that the Huns had broken through.

East of Kushan lay nearly a quarter of a million square miles of bare steppe-lands, an infinity of open prairie where no trees grew, stretching right across northern China. The tribal peoples who roamed these endless grasslands had a way of life that was simply incompatible with farming and cities. Incompatible, in fact, with what we mean by civilization. For people whose life was spent moving large herds of animals over pastureland, settled farming just got in the way, and cities were simply depots of useful and valuable things to be taken as required. City-dwellers, who were evidently incapable of keeping themselves alive out in the open, were useful if they had helpful trade goods; but, broadly speaking, were probably better off dead.

The settled peoples of Asia had to maintain constant barriers against these nomads, and to man those barriers with capable troops. The Chinese had their Great Wall. The people of Central Asia had a simpler task because their frontier was far smaller, but they must never lose their control there.

The vast Asian steppes run up to the Ural Mountains. Where the Urals peter out in the south, in what is now Kazakhstan, there is an effective barrier to wandering nomads, a desert without pasture. In the middle of the desert is the remnant of a vanished ocean, the Aral Sea. This is the region where the old Soviet Union decided it could most safely place its cosmodrome and nuclear missile-testing site.

The land route west out of Asia passes further south, through a narrow passage north of the Afghan mountains where a string of oases makes the desert passable. The soldiers here were the gatekeepers. Take them away, and Persia was open to the Barbarians of the steppes. The cities of the Near East, and then the Mediterranean, would be vulnerable. Zoroaster, who equated good with the arts of civilization and government, and evil with the thieving nomad, the enemy of orderly agriculture and animal husbandry, seems to have been born in Kushan. And now aggressive nomads had broken through – the Huns.

It's very hard to know who they were. Chinese records refer to a large confederacy of tribal pastoralists, the Hsiung-nu or Xiongnu, which threatened their empire from the north and was broken up by Chinese military action in the first century AD. Some of these people settled inside China. Others moved west to the steppes of eastern Kazakhstan, which they seem to have regarded as a paradise – they called it Nie-Ban, meaning Nirvana, heaven. There are Chinese references to a population of 200,000 people, remarkable for their tidiness. Apparently, they washed and brushed their teeth before eating, three times a day, and trimmed their hair to a fringe.

Perhaps it was these people who were on the move, possibly driven by famine. A journey of 500 miles south-west or so would have brought them to the caravan oases, and once they had broken through that narrow neck into eastern Persia, these presumably starving and desperate people used their skills as horse archers to take what they needed and see off any attempts to remove them. Mongolian ponies have changed little down the centuries. The Hun horses were remarkable for their small size, big heads, lack of finesse and great endurance. Shapur II had to give them his full attention.

It took seven years, and a combination of force and bribery, to persuade some Huns at least to become his allies. By 358 he was able to return to the struggle against the Romans – and this time with considerably more success. That success peaked in 363, when the Emperor Julian, a brilliant but headstrong man in his thirties, marched on Ctesiphon. Julian was the one who told his troops: 'We must wipe out a most troublesome nation.' He not only failed to take the city, but also made insufficient preparation for his army's eventual retreat. Short of supplies and harassed by the enemy, Julian's legions were stopped short when the Emperor was killed in a minor skirmish. His successor, Jovian, was forced to surrender everything that Persia had given up 65 years earlier when the harem was ransomed. That was the only way Jovian could get safely home.

Shapur II's renewed confidence and military success after coming to a deal with the Huns may perhaps have been connected with the fact that Huns appeared just a few years later – in 375 – in Dacia. Is it just coincidence that the Germanic people north of the Black Sea suddenly found themselves under attack from the thundering hooves and high-powered arrows of thousands of strange oriental people, who seemed as welded to their horses as if they were centaurs, and who moved rapidly west? The resulting upheaval wrecked the Roman Empire, provoking a vast Goth migration that destroyed two-thirds of the army that was fighting Persia.

The terrible dominance of Rome was coming to an end.

PART IV

VANDALS AND HUNS

XI
BEHIND THE MYTHS

Of all the Barbarian peoples who swept across Europe in the fifth century AD, none left a more lasting reputation for mindless savagery and destruction than the Vandals and the Huns. And yet, as so often happens with our received history of the Barbarians, nothing is quite as it seems.

Attila came charging out of the east with his horde of blood-crazed Huns right up to the gates of Rome – well, almost – until he was stopped, apparently by the hand of God, represented in the person of Pope Leo I. There are many strange things about this story. For a start, it ignores the fact that Attila claimed he was actually coming to rescue a damsel in distress (really!); but perhaps the strangest thing is that the more one tries to identify the Huns, the more they disappear.

Nobody doubts that Attila existed, but his Hunnic hordes are less easy to pin down. The majority of warriors who followed him were actually Germanic, and it has been reckoned that at any one time there were probably no more than 15,000 Hun warriors in Europe.[1] And when you try to find the traces left by these Huns, a remarkable thing happens: you can't. Not a single portrait of a Hun exists, and not a single dwelling of Attila's has been discovered; there are no more than 200 burials that have any claim to being Hunnic, but even these are now being disputed. On top of this, we have no knowledge of what language they spoke, except that by Attila's time his court was speaking Gothic. Even the names of the Hun leaders of Attila's day are (most probably) Germanic in origin – including Attila himself.

This difficulty in recognizing the identity of the Huns seems to be evidence that they were not, as has been imagined, ruthless killers who annihilated everyone they over-ran. Of course we cannot doubt that there were Huns in eastern Europe, but the lack of evidence of a distinct Hun culture indicates that, rather than wiping out the peoples they subdued, the Huns blended into them. In fact this conclusion has always been pretty obvious from the written sources, if you look at them with an open mind. That is why, as long ago as 1920, H.G. Wells, the novelist, social critic and popular historian, was able to explain that 'Instead of killing, they enlisted and inter-married with the peoples they invaded. They had that necessary gift for all peoples destined to political predominance, tolerant assimilation.'[2]

Ironically, it is this process of assimilation that has wiped the Huns' own identity from the archaeological record, leaving only the identities of those whom they subdued.

We owe the idea of the Huns as merciless killers to European nationalism and the propaganda of the First World War. German romantics traced their history back through old myths that include enthusiastic stories of a heroically violent Hun leader called Etzel (Attila). In 1900 Kaiser Wilhelm II, recalling these stories – and placing them in the wrong period of history – addressed troops going to put down a Chinese rising:

> No quarter will be given, no prisoners will be taken. Let all who fall into your hands be at your mercy. Just as the Huns a thousand years ago, under the leadership of Etzel, gained a reputation in virtue of which they still live in historical tradition, so may the name of Germany become known in such a manner in China that no Chinaman will ever again even dare to look askance at a German.[3]

British newspapers picked up this speech with enthusiastic outrage, and when they reported (fictional) atrocities by German troops in Belgium at the start of the First World War, they used 'Huns' as a generic term for these German savages. Attila the Hun never recovered his good name.

The Vandals have suffered a similar distortion in Europe's imagined past. They have, of course, given us the word for those who deliberately destroy property. And yet the Vandals acted according to

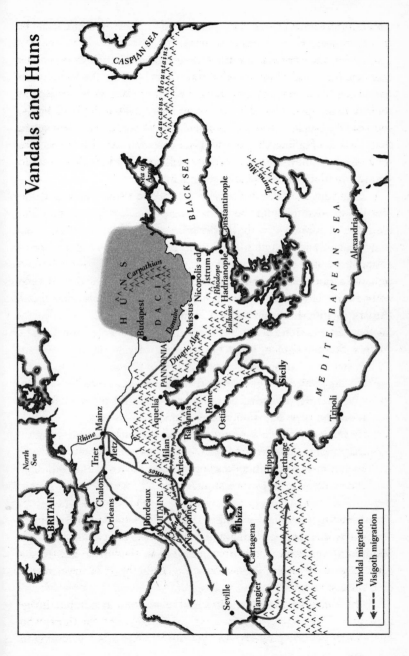

Vandals and Huns

Vandal migration

Visigoth migration

moral principles that we might regard as sterner than our own and wrecked nothing.

The culprit in this case was the (equally myth-based) memory of the Church. After the Gordon Riots in London in 1780, when supporters of Catholic emancipation were attacked, the poet William Cowper called the mob that burnt Lord Mansfield's library 'Vandals'.[4] Cowper had imbibed the Church's depiction of Vandal persecution with his mother's milk; he had spent his entire life in the care of churchmen, and wrote some of England's best-known hymns, including 'Amazing Grace'.

The idea of Vandals as destroyers soon caught on. During the French Revolution, a revolutionary bishop invented the word 'vandalism' to describe the French Republican army's destruction of public monuments and buildings.[5] He described what they were doing as 'Vandalism', and the word caught on.

The basis for this name-calling lies in the way the Romans wrote about their enemies. The written record is not consistently hostile because at different times both the Huns and the Vandals were regarded as allies of the Romans. One Vandal actually supervised the Western Roman Empire for many years. But when they are hostile, the Latin and Greek sources paint an extraordinary and vivid picture of horror. Roman writers did, as we have seen, distort the truth about those whom they regarded as 'barbarians'. But by the fifth century this was being done in a new way because Barbarians were seen in a new way.

Many Barbarian communities had become so much a part of the Roman Empire that the old Roman–Barbarian distinction, so closely tied to the idea of a frontier, was beginning to fall away. But that didn't make the Romans stop seeing Barbarians as 'them'. As the Empire became Christian, 'they' were now the pagans – and when 'they' converted to Christianity, heretics. In a society in which religion infuses every aspect of life, cultural differences are expressed as religious differences, and Christianity's most enduring gift to the world was to demonize those differences as 'heresy'.[6] The real story of the Vandals and the Huns was played out in a world that was changing from its pagan past to Christianity. And it was nothing like the myths.

XII
THE CHRISTIANIZATION
OF THE EMPIRE

According to a Roman poet of the fifth century, Rutilius Claudius Namatianus, all the disasters that were to befall Rome in his lifetime could be traced to a single act that took place around 406. No historian has ever shared his opinion, but maybe that just goes to show how little historians are prepared to share in the world-view of the people they write about. The act in question was a book-burning.[1]

THE SIBYLLINE BOOKS

The books in question had been stored for centuries in the Temple of Apollo Patrous on the Palatine Hill in Rome. They were called the Sibylline Books, and they contained the history of the world – both past and future – as recorded by a Sybil or prophetess. According to legend, in the far-distant days when Rome still had a king, the Sybil appeared before the king and offered to sell the city nine books containing the destiny of the world for 300 pieces of gold. The king declined the offer. She burnt three, and then demanded the same price for the remaining six. Once more she was turned down; once more she burnt three books; once more the price remained unchanged. The king caved in, the Sibyl vanished, and Rome acquired its oracle.

The leaves of the texts (and they probably really were leaves – palm leaves inscribed in Greek) were stored in an underground stone chest in the Temple of Jupiter Capitolinus, possibly around 500 BC. They had special custodians – at first two, eventually 15. These authorities consulted the texts when the Senate ordered it, at times of crisis. If any custodian revealed what they said, he was put to death.

The whole of Roman history was punctuated by consultation of these texts. For instance, when Hannibal was at the gates of Rome in 217 BC, portents filled the sky. According to the Latin sources (and who would doubt them?) the orb of the sun decreased in size, then it appeared to be colliding with the moon, then two moons appeared in the daytime sky. Then, just to ram home the point that something was not quite right, the sky split apart to reveal a brilliant light and then appeared to catch fire.[2] The keepers of the Sibylline Books were put to work, and instructed the now hysterical populace to go out and sit at the crossroads and pray to Hecate, Queen of Heaven. A divine black stone would fall from the sky in Asia, and they should go to fetch it. It did, they did, and Hannibal was unable to make any further headway.[3]

Historians have assumed that was coincidence. They're probably right.

Nearly 500 years later, when the Alemanni threatened Rome in AD 270, the Emperor Aurelian had the Senate decree that the Sibylline Books be consulted.[4] By now they were kept in the Temple of Apollo and were actually different texts, the originals having been destroyed in a fire and new ones bought from mysterious Eastern second-hand prophetic sources. But mysteries are mysteries, and the texts still had their power. This time they demanded 'processions of priests in white robes, attended by a chorus of youths and virgins; ritual purification of the city and adjacent country; and sacrifices, whose powerful influence disabled the barbarians from passing the mystic ground on which they had been celebrated'.[5] And once more, the city was saved.

Again, historians have taken little interest in the ritual except perhaps to giggle at it. But the story does show the extraordinary significance of prophecy and divination to the Romans, who truly believed that their Empire was uniquely protected by the gods. And it shows the profound depth of the revolution that swept through the Empire as Christianity took hold.

The man who ordered the book-burning, the real ruler of the Western Empire at the time, was the great general Stilicho, a determined Christian. He had very deliberately decked his wife in the jewellery worn by the statue of the goddess Victory, who had for centuries presided over the deliberations of the Senate, because he wanted to stamp out paganism from the very soul of Rome. And Stilicho was a Vandal.

ROMAN VANDALS

The process by which a Barbarian became the guardian of the Roman Empire was the ultimate triumph of its policy of Romanizing the world within its frontiers. The Vandals were a not especially war-like nation of Germanic farmers whose history was one of migration under pressure. 'Vandal' (*Wandal*) means 'wanderer'. They moved steadily southwards as slightly more heroic neighbours moved on to their lands, shifting over 300 years or so from what is now central Poland, down into Bohemia and ultimately into the Roman Empire as refugees. They were evidently Scandinavian-looking people, strong on personal morality and rather low on military organization. They were finally settled in the Balkan province of Pannonia by the Emperor Constantine, in AD 330, on terms that made them into peasant farmers and military recruits. And, of course, that made them learn to be imitation Romans.

Many of their young men became auxiliaries in the Roman army, and they settled into their new identity. And then, after 40 years, their world was thrown into chaos by the Huns.

It wasn't the Huns themselves. The area between the Caucasus and the Danube was a kind of geographical billiard table, where the movement of one group of people cannoned into another, who ricocheted off a third. The Huns cannoned into the Goths. The Goths ricocheted off the Vandals. And the Vandals ended up being potted.

THE MYSTERIOUS HUNS

A Goth historian writing nearly 200 years later conveys his people's idea of what real Barbarians looked like. The Huns, he explained, were a race spawned from the miscegenation of Scythian sorceresses with demons of the wilderness, and were originally 'little, foul, emaciated creatures possessing only the shadow of speech'. Now they had grown up into monsters whose faces were 'shapeless black collops of flesh, with little points instead of eyes. No hair on their cheeks or chins but ... deep furrowed scars instead, down the sides of their faces ... they are little but lithe, especially skilful in riding, broad-shouldered, good at the use of bow and arrows ... under the form of man these creatures hide the fierce nature of The Beast.'[6]

They certainly did look startling, and not just because their faces were oriental. Huns modified their skull shapes, binding babies' heads in boards to flatten and elongate them. There is not a single surviving image of a Hun face, but the effect produced can be seen on ancient Mayan paintings and ceramic heads from central America. The Maya were doing exactly the same thing to their own babies, at exactly the same time. The Maya were not, however, scarifying their faces as the Huns were; that is an effect seen on central African faces, where tribal identity is still cut on to men's cheeks today.

There's something odd about the Huns. Very little is known of their identity before they arrived in Dacia, or of what had set them in motion. No one knows where they came from, or how long they had been travelling. Their language is unknown.

The general consensus among historians has been that they had simply come directly west, crossing the entire breadth of Kazakhstan from the east. This seems very unlikely, given the extremely harsh environment around the Aral Sea. There was really no way for herdsmen to move through that territory without losing their herds and starving, or for horsemen to feed their mounts. But in 350 Shapur II had been forced to put his struggle with Rome on hold because Huns had broken through on his eastern frontier. And that breakthrough gave them access to a route from Asia towards the Black Sea, following the river that separates Bukhara from Merv – the Oxus.

Today the Oxus is an unnavigable stream flowing north through the desert towards the Aral Sea – in other words, it leads effectively nowhere. But in Roman times it flowed north-west, not into the Aral Sea, but into the Caspian.[7] Once Shapur regained control of his eastern dominions, in 357, this was their obvious escape route – up to the Caspian, through the Caucasus, then across to the Black Sea and the Carpathian mountains. And as these strange people moved slowly further west, having overcome all the barriers – mountains, deserts, swamps – that divided Asia and Europe, the stories began.

In 1995, Hunnic distorted skulls were discovered in burials of the second to fourth centuries at Pokrovka, north of the Caspian Sea (so west of the Urals).[8] But how did they get there? It's hard to believe they could have done it without passing through the eastern Persian Empire and up through the Caucasus. In later years, the Byzantines would actually subsidize the Persian defence of this gateway because they now understood the perils.[9] If they hadn't thought this was an effective way of blocking the invaders, they wouldn't have wasted their money.

But it may well be that if Rome hadn't fought so long and so hard to weaken Persia, the Huns would never have made it. And an uncomprehending West wouldn't have acquired a stock of nightmares about people who 'roast pregnant women, cut out the foetus, put it in a dish, pour water over it, and dip their weapons into the brew; they eat the flesh of children and drink the blood of women'.[10] The Huns didn't actually do those things, of course, but it does show how scared people were of the most alien-looking humans they had ever seen.

LIFE AS A HUN

It is universally assumed that these Beasts had originally been pastoral nomads on the steppes of Mongolia. Nomads normally have a highly ordered life, which is structured around the survival of their animals: they keep their herds alive, and the herds keep them alive. They do not have permanent homes because they move with their animals twice a year between summer and winter pastures – several weeks a year are spent on the move. They are inevitably a relatively egalitarian society, because during migration everyone depends on everyone else. They are also mobile, and likely to be pretty effective horse warriors, in order to protect the herds.

The Mongolian herds consisted of sheep, goats, cattle, camels and yaks. From these came the Huns' meat and drink (150 different kinds of milk product), their fuel (dung), their clothing and their felted tents. The herds needed constant management – for instance, the sheep and goats had to be taken to pasture after the horses and cattle because they graze closer to the roots. And their encampments were tented cities, with specialized artisans, such as carpenters, weavers and smiths; and, of course, weapon-makers.

The Huns' main weapon was the composite recurve bow, already well known to the people of eastern Europe. It is not an easy weapon to make. Unstrung, it bends in the opposite direction from the strung bow. Horn is spliced and glued into a wooden base to make the inside face of the bow because it resists compression and will therefore spring back forcefully when the bow is bent; sinew is bonded to the outside face because it resists extension and pulls the bent bow back towards its unstrung shape. Every piece of the bow requires complete precision in its selection, its thickness and its taper. It takes a year to make a good bow.

These weapons were powerful, but had an obvious limit. A man on horseback cannot easily use a bow more than about 40 inches long – most bows were some 30 inches. A longer bow would have more power, and be effective at a greater distance, but was plainly impractical. But that, it turns out, was what made the Huns so awesome. A few Hunnic bows have been found in graves, and they are between 50 and 63 inches long – up to twice the size of the 'normal' recurve bow.[11] In fact, 63 inches is as long as many medieval English long-bows, which were the same height as the archers. And the complex construction of the Mongolian bow made it very much more powerful than the weapons that struck through the plate armour of French knights.

It seems unbelievable that horsemen riding little ponies could wield such a weapon. The key was that the bow was asymmetric: the lower section was as short as a normal recurve bow, but there was a huge upper section. The result was a weapon that must have required years of practice to master, but which meant that Huns could kill their enemies while far out of range themselves. It is not what you would expect from people mainly concerned with protecting their herds. It is a first-strike weapon, to be used against an enemy who doesn't yet know he is being attacked.

Nomads normally lived in some relation to settled farming communities because they needed grain, and it was provided as tribute to them. This arrangement, plus the need to move their animals at fixed times to well-known pastures, tended to keep the orbit of nomadic life fairly predictable. But the only information we have about the arrival of the Huns is a Goth myth that suggests they had no animals to pasture. There was an impassable barrier between their world and that of the Goths; the mighty river Don flows from the north into the Sea of Azov, and below that a vast swamp extends to the Black Sea.

How they were living seems to be open to question; were they really nomadic herdsmen? The legend of how they crossed the swamp suggests not. Its oldest-known version comes from a Greek, Eunapius of Sardis (346–420), who evidently did, at first, think they had herds. One day one of their heifers was supposedly stung by a gadfly and fled all the way through the marsh – leading its herdsman to discover a new land inhabited by Goths. But Eunapius decided that the story wasn't quite right – it was simply a reworking of a story in an 800-year-old classic by Aeschylus, *Prometheus Bound* – and revised it. He thought the pursuit through the marsh really described Hunnic huntsmen chasing a stag.[12]

This hunting story was repeated by many other historians, including Priscus, who knew the Huns and met Attila. That suggests these writers did not think of the Huns as having been pastoral nomads. Such people have plenty of meat all around them; they don't waste much time hunting. They might have pursued a luscious fruit or a seductive vegetable into the mysterious swamp, but they wouldn't have been desperate for meat.

We have no idea of the cue for the Huns' movement into Dacia. If they ever had herds, they seem to have lost them and become wide-ranging hunters. And on the western side of the Black Sea they discovered herds of domesticated meat waiting to be eaten. The shock of their coming was astounding. They travelled faster than any warning messenger because each rider galloped with a string of spare horses so that he never rode a tired mount. A cloud of dust, the thunder of hooves – and then the sky turned black with deadly arrows. The Goths ran for their lives.

This is the time when a large part of the Gothic population of Dacia fled across the Danube into the safe haven of the Empire. Now it so happens that Vandals were already occupying the lands into which the Goths fled – which are now Serbia and Bulgaria – and when the Goths became so desperate for land that they turned to robbing and looting, it is little wonder that the Vandals were happy to support the Romans in putting them down (see page 122).

One of the few survivors from the resulting battle of Hadrianople, in which the Emperor Valens was killed, was his loyal Vandal captain, who had married a Roman woman. Their son was destined to become the most powerful man in the Western Empire, despite being a Vandal. His name was Stilicho.

Stilicho did not have much in the way of a career choice. Soldiering, like butchery, baking and peasant farming, was a compulsory hereditary occupation. The Empire was not much into social mobility. This meant that once Barbarians were in the army, so were their descendants. The role of the Roman army as the great Romanizing force of the Empire had disappeared. It really wasn't particularly Roman any more. But then, Rome wasn't exactly Roman any more.

NEW ROME

The Empire had been completely transformed in the fourth century. It's a rather confused story. In 312 a senior military officer, Constantine, captured Rome with an army that he had labelled with Christian symbols. Twelve years later he was the sole ruler of the Empire. He created a hereditary, monarchic rule based on his new Christian city of Constantinople, New Rome, and encouraged conversion to the new faith, over which he presided.

Constantine's Empire had one great enemy, the rival religious Persian Empire. That was a very good reason why the Roman Empire's nerve-centre needed to be so far to the east of Rome. Persia did it a lot of damage. The last emperor of Constantine's dynasty, Julian, was killed by the Persian Emperor Shapur II in 363. As the Persian war swallowed armies, the West was left vulnerable; the legions that had once guarded the frontiers were downgraded to the status of militia and garrison soldiers, with inferior armaments and training, and the safety of Gaul was placed in the hands of a field army of 'barbarian' mercenaries. In fact, the late Latin word for 'soldier' was *barbarus*.

In 364, following Julian's defeat and the swift death of his young successor, the army installed one of its officers as emperor. The Romans refused to call their rulers kings, but it's the word that best fits Valentinian. He took over the Empire as a family operation, with himself ruling the Western Empire from Milan, and his brother Valens

Vandalism (see page 216)
The Vandal sack of Rome in AD 455, as imagined by the German illustrator Heinrich Leutemann in 1865. Gaiseric is shown as a Wagnerian hero, rather than the elderly chap he was. Contemporary accounts stress that there was no killing, no destruction of buildings and no torturing of people to disgorge their wealth – and that the Vandals themselves were quite refined people.

The Vandal who ran the Empire (see page 236)
This ivory portrait of Stilicho appears to be a genuine likeness. It probably dates from AD 395 or shortly afterwards, as it has images of Arcadius and Honorius on the shield, the brothers who inherited the two halves of the Empire after Theodosius' death in that year. He is dressed as an official of the Imperial Court, but his cloak is fastened with a typical Germanic brooch (*fibula*).

Distorted Barbarians (see page 220)
It seems that artificially elongating the skulls of babies was a recipe for beauty among the Huns and their friends; it appears to have been especially popular for girls. Some elongated skulls have been found in Burgundian graves, west of the Rhine, which suggests that Hun influence was quite widespread among Germanic peoples for a while.

Christ the Roman Emperor (see page 233)
The basilica of San Apollinare Nuovo in Ravenna was originally built by the Goth Emperor Theoderic as his palace chapel; the mosaics on the side walls show Christ enthroned as an emperor, wearing imperial purple, and the archangels Michael and Gabriel in court dress.

Jesus the warrior (see page 233)
This mosaic from around AD 500, in the Archiepiscopal Chapel in Ravenna, shows Christ as a man of war. The chapel is a celebration of the Christ of Trinitarian doctrine, an anti-Arian statement by a bishop serving under the Arian Emperor Theoderic. Christ dressed as a Roman soldier tramples on a lion and an adder.

Christ in Rome (see page 233)
The Church of Santa Pudenziana is one of the oldest parish churches in Rome, dating back to about AD 140, and this mosaic, the oldest in the city, was made about AD 390, shortly before the usurper Eugenius was installed by the pagan senators. Here, Christ sits in the same pose as Jupiter in pagan temples (and with the same beard), and the book he carries is not religious, but proclaims him protector of the building.

Death as entertainment (see page 257)
In 1834, five mosaic floors were found at Torre Nuova near Rome. Made in the third century AD, they are a visual record of the gladiatorial fights paid for by the owner. They name the men involved and show them doing each other to death for the entertainment of the crowd, and then for the guests who admired the expensive floors.

Life as a Vandal (see page 256)
This mosaic from Carthage, showing a cheery Vandal leaving his substantial villa around the
year AD 500 on a splendidly decorated horse, indicates that it might not have been easy to see
the Vandals as rough-and-ready barbarian thugs.

Family affairs – Galla Placidia and her children Valentinian III and Honoria (see pages 241–79)
Galla Placidia (above left), daughter of Emperor Theodosius I, was living in Rome when Alaric
took the city. She went with – or was taken by – the Visigoths, and married Athaulf in AD 414.
After his death she married Constantius; when he too died, she fled to Constantinople with their
children, Valentinian (above centre) and Honoria (above right). Her nephew Theodosius II put
Valentinian on the Western throne, and she became Regent. Around AD 449 Honoria got into trouble,
and ended up being virtually imprisoned in Constantinople – with hilarious results, at least if you
were Attila the Hun.

All roads lead to Rome (see page 262)
This section of the Tabula Peutingeriana, a twelfth-century copy of a third-century map, shows Rome, its port of Ostia, and Carthage across the sea. The whole document was a road-map for planning journeys, and shows resting places, towns, thermal baths and recommended hotels (such as The Fig, Hercules' Sandal and The Two Brothers).

Attila the robber chief (see page 265)
A detailed illustration from *National Geographic* magazine in 1962 follows Priscus' account of Attila's banquet quite accurately in form, but the spirit is completely different. Instead of attending a formal court occasion with precise rituals, barbarous Huns are shown feasting in a brigands' hall.

Raphael's painting of the Pope and Attila (see page 264)
This has more to do with 1514 than 451. The Pope shown repelling the Huns with a dismissive wave is Raphael's patron Leo X, Giovanni d'Medici, the son of Lorenzo the Magnificent of Florence. His family had been ejected from Florence, and he himself had been captured by a French army in 1512, but then the French were driven out, the Medicis restored, and he was elected Pope. Any resemblance between the Huns and the Medicis' enemies is probably not coincidental.

The perfect wall (see page 271)
Theodosius' wall around Constantinople
not only resisted Attila's army, it
remained impregnable for nearly 1000
years, only being surmounted (by
Crusaders) in 1204, and finally
breached by Turkish cannon in 1453.

Barbarians destroying (see page 276)
Alphonse de Neuville, a French painter
of military subjects in the mid-
nineteenth century, made his reputation
depicting the sufferings of ordinary
soldiers, especially in the Franco-
Prussian War of 1870. His influential
images of the Hun invasion of Europe
were informed by the horrors of modern
war as the destroyer of civilization.

in a junior role ruling the Eastern provinces from Constantinople. He also created a separate court in Trier, near the modern German border with Luxembourg, to manage the old Celtic lands of Britain, Gaul and Spain, under the symbolic authority of yet another junior emperor, his young son Gratian. Each of these was referred to as emperor.

The Empire was now controlled by the courts of the Emperors, places of impenetrable etiquette and mystery. At the heart of the court was the sacred person of the Emperor, treated as a living god, enthroned behind curtains, and in whose presence all must prostrate themselves on the floor. This was an imitation of the Persian form of kingship.

Government was in the hands of a group of ministries attached to the person of the Emperor. These included the sacred household, with chamberlains, domestic personnel, ushers and guards, as well as senior officials and advisers and the secretariat. There was a legal department; a head of human resources, who supervised appointments and controlled the guard; and a 'count of the sacred largesses' who ran the treasury, including mines, mints, taxes and customs duties, and paid government salaries, as well as directing the imperial weaving factories and organizing the issue of clothing or clothing allowances to the court, the army and the civil service. There was a 'count of the privy purse' dealing with state property, and a praetorian prefect in charge of military logistics, the postal system, roads, bridges and so on. This administrative machine served itself and served the army, which consumed almost all the income of the Empire. The army protected the court; the court protected the army. The Emperor himself was not, strictly speaking, necessary except as a symbol of authority.

So when Valentinian died in 374 (of a stroke brought on by rage while trying to negotiate with Barbarians on the Danube), and Gratian took over in Milan, the army and bureaucracy recognized Gratian's eight-year-old brother as Emperor Valentinian II in Trier.

THE ARIAN CHRISTIAN EMPIRE

Gratian's capital, Milan, was where Constantine had accepted Christianity 60 years earlier, and power there was shared between the court and the cathedral.

When the Goths came over the Danube into this Christian empire in 375, Valens insisted that they convert to Christianity. The advantage that Constantine had seen in Christianity was that its bishops, unlike pagan priests, exercised a unified authority over their flock, and if the Emperor controlled the bishops, that gave him a wholly new kind of power. Of course, it had meant an imperial takeover of theology. The Emperor was associated with the sun, so the Christian Sabbath had moved from Saturday to Sun-day, Christ was portrayed as the sun god, and by 352 the Church was dutifully celebrating the birthday of Jesus on 25 December, the feast of *Sol Invictus* (identified with the Emperor) and the birthday of Mithras, the deity whose cult ran through every level of the army.

And Constantine had been keen that the bishops should agree on whatever it was they believed. That produced a vicious and bewildering debate at a Church council that he called in Nicaea in 325. The philosophical question of how to describe the difference between Jesus and God became savage; there was more than salvation at stake. Constantine had introduced tax-breaks for the clergy, and wealthy citizens vied with each other to contribute to the new official religion in order to keep in the Emperor's good books. So there was plenty of money involved, as well as political power, and all this on top of the spiritual mastery of the Roman world. No wonder different elements within the clergy sought to assert themselves as the only legitimate leaders and, consequently, the only valid claimants of such glittering prizes.

Officially, the winners were bishops who argued that God and his son were made of identical substance, while the losers (called Arians, after their main spokesman, Bishop Arius from Libya) pointed out that Jesus was 'begotten' and must therefore be different and, to some extent, subordinate. In fact, the Arians then out-manoeuvred their opponents, baptized Constantine and won the prize.

With the brief but notable exception of Julian, a pagan who thought 'no wild beasts are so dangerous to man as Christians are to one another',[13] every emperor from Constantine to Valens subscribed to Arius' theology. It was quite a tolerant regime: Christians of other persuasions were allowed to continue their arguments, but just didn't have any official status. The Goths and Vandals had come into an Arian

Christian Empire. That became their new religion. And that would, eventually, be the cause of an awful lot of trouble.

THE ANTI-ARIAN COMEBACK

Given the nature of the new Roman state, an emperor who was not a soldier was hemmed in by the machinery of his court. But he had supreme power in matters of religion, and Christianity offered him an arena of real authority. It is perhaps not surprising that a charismatic Christian teacher would have considerable influence in that situation, and the role was filled to overflowing by Ambrose, a well-educated lawyer who had become bishop of Milan in 374, when Gratian was 15 and moved his court to the city. Ambrose was a vigorous polemicist, lived as exemplary a life as he could, and was hugely popular there.

Ambrose was a new sort of Christian, a Trinitarian. The doctrine of the Trinity as a single unified godhead of Father, Son and Holy Ghost is a development of the anti-Arian argument that had been aired in the Council of Nicaea in 325, that God and his Son are of the same substance. The concept is essentially mystical, not rational. As Thomas Aquinas was later to explain, 'It is impossible to arrive at knowledge of the Trinity of the Divine Persons by natural reason.'[14] In fact, it follows that anyone who offers a coherent interpretation must be a heretic. So the stage was set for a resurrection of that wonderfully baffling debate that was really about something quite different.

What it was about was power, money and that old lingering Latin suspicion of the cunning, untrustworthy Greeks. Trinitarianism was growing in popularity in the west when Ambrose was still pursuing a secular career as governor of the Milan region. When the old bishop of Milan died, there was a dispute over the succession, which got out of hand and Ambrose went to the basilica to calm things down. He was the son of a Roman civil servant and, like most upper-class Romans, was not himself a Christian. But somehow he found himself co-opted to the bishopric by popular acclaim. He made a show of reluctance, but was baptized and took the job. It was the best career move possible.

Up until his ordination Ambrose had been naturally inclined to support the official version of Christianity, Arianism, but that soon changed. He brilliantly manipulated theological arguments to build himself a political platform that would suck power away from Constantinople towards himself. The basis of that argument was that the official form of Christianity, Arianism, which he wildly carica-tured, was evil, and that he could bring God in on the side of an Emperor who supported his beliefs against the Arian Goths.

In the process, he wrote the first Latin treatise on the Holy Spirit, which was based on a Greek work by Didymus: St Jerome complained that Ambrose had turned good Greek into bad Latin.[15] He wrote it as part of his campaign to win over Gratian and persuade him to convert the Empire to Christian Trinitarianism, known as Catholicism.

OLD ROME

Although Rome was the city of St Peter, Constantine's enthusiasm for Christianity had relatively little impact there. By the time of his death Rome had seven churches and the shrine of St Paul, but that shrine and five of the churches were outside the city walls. Only the Lateran Basilica (the residence of the bishop of Rome) and the church of Santa Croce in Gerusalemme were within the city, and they were both tucked away in a relatively remote eastern corner. The centre of Rome was still a place of pagan monuments, and the majority of the Roman senators remained determinedly pagan.

The most fundamental pagan icon of the Roman Empire was Victory. Dio Cassius describes the altar at the far end of the Roman Senate House with her golden statue, a winged goddess.[16] It was placed there in 29 BC by the first Emperor, Augustus, to celebrate Rome's victory over Antony and Cleopatra, and decorated with spoils from Egypt. Senators traditionally burnt incense and offered liba-tions before the altar. And that is where senators took oaths, including the oath of loyalty to an emperor on his accession. The goddess of victory was a symbol of Rome itself and a frequent pres-ence on its coins. No single image so represented Rome, and in the eyes of the Christians no single image so represented the old order that they wanted swept away.

In 378, four years after Ambrose's ordination, he persuaded Gratian to renounce the title of *pontifex maximus* – the head of the imperial priesthood, a position that Constantine and his successors had held with honour. Gratian then withdrew the state subsidies that funded many pagan activities and removed the Altar of Victory from the Forum. When a delegation of senators went to plead with him to put it back, he refused to see them.

That was the year that Valens was killed at Hadrianople, trying to suppress the rebellious Goths (see page 121). Gratian, now 19, replaced him with his most senior military commander, Theodosius, who was a Spaniard and a Catholic. Ambrose's version of Christianity had been installed at the heart of power.

THE TRIUMPH OF CATHOLICISM

The new man in Constantinople immediately began to surround himself with his own people. Two days after arriving he dismissed the Arian bishop of Constantinople and replaced him with the leader of the (small) Catholic community there. And in 380 he issued an imperial decree outlawing Arianism:

> It is our pleasure that all the nations, which are governed by
> our clemency and moderation, should steadfastly adhere to
> the religion which was taught by St Peter to the Romans;
> which faithful tradition has preserved; and which is now
> professed by the pontiff Damasus, and by Peter, bishop of
> Alexandria, a man of apostolic holiness. According to the
> discipline of the apostles, and the doctrine of the gospel, let
> us believe the sole deity of the Father, the Son, and the Holy
> Ghost; under an equal majesty, and a pious Trinity. We
> authorize the followers of this doctrine to assume the title of
> Catholic Christians; and as we judge, that all others are
> extravagant madmen, we brand them with the infamous
> name of Heretics; and declare that their conventicles shall
> no longer usurp the respectable appellation of churches.
> Besides the condemnation of divine justice, they must expect
> to suffer the severe penalties, which our authority, guided by
> heavenly wisdom, shall think proper to inflict upon them.[17]

Catholicism was aggressively intolerant, displaying all the Christian ferocity that had so appalled Julian. Throwing Christians to the lions was almost humane compared with throwing Arians to the Catholics. The inhabitants of Constantinople felt they were living under an alien occupation, as their churches were suddenly declared heretic and their tax privileges withdrawn. Ordinary people there, in defiance of their Emperor, became vigorous enthusiasts for Arianism and for the notion that Christ, having been born human, was less than God. Everyone became a bar-room theologian: 'If you ask for change, the man launches into a theological discussion about begotten and unbegotten. If you enquire about the price of bread, the answer is given that the father is greater and the son subordinate; if you remark that the bath is nice, the attendant announces that the son was created out of nothing.'[18] In Alexandria, Arians marched through the streets chanting songs about their belief.

And although Catholicism had taken over Constantinople from above, and was now the popular creed in the West, the third emperor, Gratian's little brother Valentinian II in Trier, was still an Arian – as was their mother, in Trier with him. Obviously, any usurper interested in taking over from Valentinian II would now use religion as a useful extra weapon. So when Magnus Maximus, a Spaniard remembered in Welsh legend as Macsen Wledig, was proclaimed Emperor in Britain by the island's Roman garrison, he declared himself to be a Catholic and denounced little Valentinian as a heretic.[19] Then, in 383, he invaded Gaul. Valentinian and his mother fled to Milan. The defence of Trier was left to Gratian, whose main forces were African Moors and Iranian Alans; unfortunately, they preferred Maximus. So did the Alemanni, who were now being used as Roman auxiliaries. Maximus was the Barbarians' favourite to be emperor of the old Celtic lands. Gratian was killed by his own troops.

Maximus replaced Gratian and set up his court at Trier. Valentinian II was now even more vulnerable. Ambrose, whose loyalty to the ruling family obviously came before anything else, was sent to negotiate with Maximus as one Catholic to another, and refused to surrender the boy to the usurper. So Maximus put together a force composed mainly of Alemanni to invade Italy. Theodosius had no choice but to recognize Maximus as emperor in Trier, in return for leaving Valentinian II as emperor in Italy. After this agreement, in 384 Maximus named his infant son Victor as emperor and no longer recognized Valentinian II.

THE RISE OF A VANDAL

This was the world in which young Stilicho, the son of a Vandal father and a Roman mother, was making his military career. War was brewing between Maximus and Theodosius. But before going to war in the West, Theodosius needed to ensure that his border with Persia was secure. He didn't want to be caught out with war on two fronts. The Persian government was looking weaker than in the past; perhaps it would be possible to negotiate a peace treaty, and the man he picked for the job was Stilicho.

When Stilicho was sent to Persia in 387 he was probably about 28, and there was a lot riding on how he managed the job. He needed to be convincing about the possibility of renewing the war, but at the same time tactful enough to feel his way through a court protocol even more extreme than that of Constantinople without ever giving offence. He needed to convey the immensely sophisticated urbanity of a courtier barely concealing the confident and ruthless brutality of a Barbarian. Evidently, he was very good at it: Stilicho returned with a peace treaty in which the disputed land of Armenia was divided between the two empires.

Given that Rome and Persia had been at war for over 400 years, the achievement of a long-term peace treaty was a major success. Theodosius was now in a position to turn West and deal with Maximus. Stilicho was made commander-in-chief of Theodosius' army and married to the Emperor's niece.

Maximus decided that he dared not wait any longer. In the late summer of the same year, 387, he launched an invasion of Italy and displaced Valentinian II once and for all. Valentinian fled to Theodosius in the East and requested help. Theodosius apparently told the young man that as an Arian he deserved all he got,[20] but he would destroy the usurper. That's where Stilicho came in.

Theodosius could have accepted Maximus, acknowledged that he had no control over this new Western Emperor, and had a quiet life

– at least until Maximus decided to take over the East as well. Or he could go to war with the object of setting up Valentinian II as his junior partner in the West, under his own supervision. Theodosius was a soldier, and his eastern frontier was secure; it wasn't a hard choice. His price for rescuing Valentinian II was the hand of Valentinian's sister, integrating him into the dynasty that had appointed him. And, of course, all that Arian heresy just had to go.

In 388 Maximus was defeated and executed. Valentinian II was 'restored' as emperor of the West, under the direct supervision of the man whom Theodosius trusted most: Stilicho.

VICTORY OVER PAGANISM

Ambrose now exercised extraordinary power. In 390 he excommunicated Theodosius for having punished a lynch-mob with traditional Roman brutality. The Emperor did penance. This was astonishing evidence of a real revolution within the Empire. And that revolution gathered pace. In 391 Theodosius declared that Catholic Christianity was the only religion now to be permitted. Sacrifices were forbidden, temples were converted into churches, paganism was formally proscribed.

Having organized things in the West to Theodosius' satisfaction, Stilicho went back East and left Valentinian II in Vienne (near Lyons in France) in the care of his general, Arbogastes. Remarkably capable as he was in many ways, Stilicho sometimes made odd mistakes. This was one of them. Arbogastes was a Frank, and the Franks were not Christians.

It was said that Valentinian committed suicide. By strangulation.

Arbogastes then quit Vienne for Rome and set up a pagan emperor in the West, to the delight of the pagan senators. This was Eugenius, who signalled Rome's return to its traditions by rebuilding the temple to Hercules in Ostia, and sponsoring pagan games and festivals. What is more, he agreed to restore the Altar of Victory, the ultimate symbol of Old Rome.

Paganism was on the march – literally, as Eugenius' army went out to confront Stilicho's. Bishop Ambrose in Milan was so afraid of the pagan senators that he fled as they approached. Arbogastes and the new Prefect of Italy promised to stable the army's horses in the basilica of the church of Milan and to enrol the clergy in the military on Eugenius' victorious return. They were fighting under the banner of the pagan gods of Rome, Hercules and Jupiter. Theodosius, on the other hand, invoked the Christian God supported by visions of the apostles as Gothic cavalrymen.

With the aid of Alaric's Visigoths, Theodosius and Stilicho defeated Eugenius (see page 123). The war between paganism and Christianity had been won decisively; there would never be another pagan Roman army. The Altar of Victory was finally disposed of, and the goddess's necklace was placed around Stilicho's wife's neck. Old Rome and paganism were the past; Stilicho, Theodosius and Constantinople were the future. And now there was just one emperor. Theodosius ruled it all, under God.

The Catholic version of Jesus, with the same nature as God himself, was a kind of transcendent emperor. A mosaic in the apse of the church of Santa Pudenziana in Rome from about 390 shows Theodosius' new imperial Christ, haloed, bearded like Jupiter and, like the old Roman god, sitting on a throne facing the onlooker. He has replaced Jupiter as the Empire's protector. The Arch of Constantine in the city shows the Emperor seated on a throne with a halo – which at the time was the symbol not of sanctity, but of imperial authority.[21] The figures around him raise their arms in supplication, just like the disciples in the Church mosaic. As Ambrose put it, Christ was now at the head of the legions.[22]

ARIANS – THE NEW BARBARIANS

But the Goths who made up such a large part of the army of victory would not convert from their Arianism. After having been used as the ancient equivalent of cannon fodder in the war against Eugenius, they were not inclined to see themselves as members of the Roman club. A new line was being drawn between Barbarians and Romans. The old division between the two made no particular sense. 'Roman' had not meant anything to do with the city of Rome for centuries; Rome the city was far less significant than Rome the Empire. Nor was Roman-ness a matter of citizenship; all free men living in the Empire had been entitled to citizenship since 212. Barbarians were no longer outsiders; they lived in every part of the Empire and made up most of the army. Since the Empire was a military machine, that meant there were Barbarians in senior positions – Stilicho being the most prominent. The distinction between Roman and Barbarian had become, in effect, racial; Stilicho's mother was Roman, but his father was a Vandal, so he himself was a Barbarian.

But Alaric and his Goths were not just racially different; they were now heretics to boot. This was actually helpful to Theodosius. It obviously encouraged Greeks to move from Arianism to Catholicism; they didn't want to be identified with Barbarians.

ROME'S WAR ON REASON

The historians of the Empire had once thought the only stories worth telling were the struggles of Emperors and armies. Now salvation replaced power as the story worth telling. For example, Sozimen, a historian writing in Constantinople about 30 years after Alaric's capture of Rome, devotes only four lines to an account of what happened and 54 lines to a story about the 'discovery' of the head of John the Baptist.

Catholic Trinitarianism was profoundly and determinedly irrational, and it became a natural consequence for Catholics to identify rationalism and science with paganism. They pursued their agenda with astonishing violence. One of the most extreme examples of this was the Catholic treatment of Hypatia of Alexandria, the first woman known to have made a substantial contribution to the development of mathematics.

Her father had been the head of the library there, the greatest literary treasure-house of the ancient world. Founded in 283 BC, the library is reckoned at its peak to have held over half a million documents from Assyria, Greece, Persia, Egypt, India and many other cultures. It was associated with a museum that was actually a university, where over 100 scholars lived to research, write, lecture and translate and copy documents. Part of the library was kept in the Temple of Serapis. When Christianity took over in Alexandria all this came to an end, and when Hypatia's father died no successor was appointed. Independence of mind was regarded as in itself heretical by the Patriarch of Alexandria, Theophilus, who set out to destroy all pagan temples in Alexandria, including the Temple of Serapis.

To the formidable weight of Church condemnation he and his associates added the information that God was not necessarily forgiving, and was quite prepared to send people to hell for all eternity if they sinned – and the definition of sin was more or less the same as not obeying Theophilus. God was, apparently, very similar to Theophilus; bad-tempered, authoritarian, ruthless and sufficiently of one nature with Christ to have 'eyes, ears, hands and feet like men'.

Immediately after Theodosius' proclamation of 391 banning pagan worship, he took over a temple and converted it to a church in such an aggressive way that a riot was provoked and Christians killed. Theophilus then demanded that the prefect and military governor in Egypt strictly enforce the new religious laws. The pagans of Alexandria responded by taking refuge in the Serapeum. According to the historian Rufinus, this temple/library stood on an enormous platform, 100 or more steps high. 'In the middle of the entire area rose the sanctuary with priceless columns, the exterior fashioned of marble, spacious and magnificent to behold. In it there was a statue of Serapis so large that its right hand touched one wall and its left the other', suspended in mid-air by hidden magnets.[23]

Emperor Theodosius, having been given what the Patriarch regarded as an objective account of the riot, declared the slain Christians to be martyrs. His judgement was that the defenders of the temple of Serapis should be pardoned but the temple itself destroyed. The Patriarch led a Christian mob and demolished it so that it could be replaced by a martyr's shrine and a church. The books were destroyed as pagan objects.

It was in this kind of atmosphere that Hypatia became head of the Platonist school at Alexandria in about 400, to lecture on mathematics and Neoplatonic philosophy. She was a glamorous woman who famously rode around in a chariot; she is also credited with inventing the astrolabe. Hugely admired by her students, she was hated by the Catholic Church – not surprising if, as has been claimed, she taught that 'All formal dogmatic religions are fallacious and must never be accepted by self-respecting persons as final', 'Reserve your right to think, for even to think wrongly is better than not to think at all' and 'To teach superstitions as truth is a most terrible thing.' [24]

In 412 Theophilus went to find out whether he was right about eternal damnation, and his job passed to his cousin Cyril. Cyril, who had been living as a fanatical fundamentalist Catholic monk in the mountains, arrived in Alexandria with the intention of extirpating any deviation from what he considered orthodox faith. He organized a personal army of enforcers, Christian fundamentalist monks from his mountain retreat whom he called the *parabalani*.

The word was originally used for Christians who dared assist plague victims, and meant extreme gamblers, high-rollers, dare-devils. The similarity to the Afghan Muslim Taliban (meaning 'students') is striking. Eventually the Emperor insisted that the number of *parabalani* be kept down to 500. Cyril led them in person. With this mob, in 415 he attacked the synagogues of Alexandria and ordered the expulsion of the city's large Jewish population. When the Roman prefect Orestes objected to Cyril's order, trying to maintain secular authority, the *parabalani* attacked him. Cyril proclaimed that they were all now saints.

Hypatia was said to be Orestes' adviser, so in a generous spirit of gentle chastisement the *parabalani* seized her, dragged her to a church, stripped her naked and sliced her body to pieces with sharp oyster shells. They then burnt her remains. [25] But what else could you do with a woman who 'was devoted at all times to magic, astrolabes and instruments of music, and beguiled many people through Satanic wiles'? [26]

Cyril is still revered as a saint.

STILICHO TAKES OVER

Theodosius' lone rule of the Roman Empire lasted only two years. He died in Milan in 395, just 49 years old. Stilicho, aged about 35, reported to the world that on his death-bed the Emperor had appointed his two sons, Arcadius and Honorius, to rule respectively in Constantinople and Milan; and that since Honorius was only nine years old, he (Stilicho) had been appointed guardian. Stilicho the Vandal ruled the West. Actually, he claimed that he had also been appointed guardian of Arcadius, but that was firmly resisted by Arcadius' court in Constantinople.

Stilicho, who was as committed to Christianity as Theodosius and his sons, set about stripping away Rome's pagan heritage. Now the Empire had a more proper form of divine protection, in the shape of the Christian God. And, to the horror of unreformed pagans, such as the poet Rutilius, Stilicho was prepared to put this new faith to the test by destroying Rome's link to its past and its future by burning the Sibylline Books.

Around the time of this bold act, two babies were born within a couple of hundred miles of each other, on opposite banks of the Danube. These were the children who would lead the armies whose names would reverberate down the centuries. In the smoke of the burning leaves of the Sibylline Books were the unexamined instructions for propitious acts that Romans would once have performed to protect themselves from those armies. One of the babies would grow up to lead the Huns. The other would become King of the Vandals.

The terrible irony is that the half-remembered, half-understood history that has seeped into the language we use confirms the poet's deepest fears. 'Attila the Hun' is less a name than an epithet for unthinking savagery. 'Vandal' simply means pillager, ravager, plunderer, wrecker, though the Vandals themselves were described as deeply moral. And the Huns, who were pagans, did not destroy the Christian city of Rome but turned away from it when the Pope asked them to, and left the Empire completely.

After the irony comes the paradox. It was the Vandals' morality and the Huns' withdrawal from Italy that finished off the Western Roman Empire, and gave birth to medieval Europe. These two peoples were intimately connected with each other because the Vandals were a nation running away from the Huns.

XIII
Vandals

The Vandals were not propelled into flight directly by the Huns; it was a severe case of the 'knock-on' effect. Huge numbers of Goths had escaped from the Huns by moving across the Danube, on to lands where the Vandals had already settled. With their farms destroyed, and the Huns probably coming any day now, the Vandals decided to move out. They seem to have been rather nervous people, not much in the mould of heroic Barbarian warriors.

THE VANDAL 'INVASION'

In 401 the Vandals seem to have moved with a group of Suebi and Alans into Rhaetia in the Alps. It was an odd grouping: the Suebi were Germanic, the Alans Iranian, but they seem to have decided to pool their efforts and see what they could persuade Stilicho to offer them. He went up to meet them and did some sort of a deal, returning with a number of their young warriors in his service.

He took them to fight the Goths who had driven them out. Under Alaric, the Goths were demanding their own homeland and threatening Constantinople. Stilicho fought them in a rather half-hearted way; he let Alaric escape, and Constantinople was forced to offer the Goth a high-ranking military position. This seemed to suit Stilicho, who had evidently agreed with Alaric that the best place for a Goth homeland should be in Illyria on the eastern Adriatic, territory controlled by Constantinople. Maybe moving the Goths there would even allow the Vandals to go home.

But that was not likely; the Huns were too close, and more Germanic groups, desperate to move away from them, were pushing west. They seem to have been hoping for new homelands too. In 405 a huge gathering of pagan Goths, which some people have suggested might have been 100,000 strong, stormed across the Danube from the Hungarian plain under the leadership of one Radagaisus, and got as far as northern Italy.[1] They must have been horrified to find that the Huns, whom they thought were behind them, were actually there to confront them – thanks to Stilicho again. The huge army he mustered included not only some of Alaric's Christian Goths, but also a contingent of Hun mercenaries under their own commander.[2] The Huns were no longer the raiding nomads of a generation earlier. They were now becoming settled, and willing to do the same kind of deals with the Empire as everyone else. After the battle, 12,000 of Radagaisus' invaders were drafted into Stilicho's army, and so many prisoners were taken that the bottom dropped out of the slave market.

Stilicho was now evidently developing a grand plan, which involved taking Dacia and Macedonia away from Constantinople and settling Alaric and his Goths there. This meant taking military control of the East, and he withdrew most of the Roman garrisons from the Rhine in preparation for this struggle. With the Rhine now undefended, on the last day of the year 406 a huge group of Vandals, Suebi and Alans – some historians think another 100,000 or more – crossed the frozen river at Mainz, into territory controlled by the Franks. This was not a military invasion. Like the Goths who had come across the Danube 30 years earlier, these were migrants, a huge population of families.

Had this been set up? Stilicho's deal with the Vandals in the Alps five years earlier remains a mystery. He was himself a Vandal – had he suggested to his kinsfolk what an opportunity this offered them? There were voices in the Empire that said so, but no evidence.

He was certainly seen as a Barbarian-lover. Rutilius, the pagan poet who was so upset by the destruction of the Sibylline Books, called him 'dire Stilicho', blaming him for destroying the defences of the Alps and Apennines, which the provident gods had interposed between the Barbarians and the Eternal City, and for planting the cruel Goths, his skin-clad minions, in the very sanctuary of the Empire. His cunning was, apparently, wickeder than the cunning of the Trojan horse. He was worse than Nero; Nero killed his own mother, but Stilicho killed the mother of the world!

Deliberately or not, Stilicho had certainly made the Rhine crossing easier for the Vandals and their friends. But if Stilicho was expecting them to cope on their own when they met the Franks, he was sadly mistaken. The result was a disastrous battle in which the not very war-like Vandals were said to have lost 20,000 people, including their king Godegisel. His place was taken by his eldest son, who took the name Guntheric, 'King of the Warriors'. The title implies that he was hoping, like Alaric, to hire out his nation as an army to the Empire. The response from Rome was along the lines of 'Don't call us – we'll call you.' Another survivor was Guntheric's baby brother. He would eventually call himself Gaiseric, 'Caesar-King'.

That was the man who would one day enter Rome as its conqueror.

ANTI-ROMAN ROMANS

Tens of thousands of thieving, desperate migrants who have no way of feeding themselves except plunder can cause a certain level of alarm. Stilicho had failed Gaul, which was now undefended. And Gaul was a region with a long history of social breakdown, anti-Roman guerrilla warfare and independent military authority.

The Vandals, Suebi and Alans who had survived their terrible battle with the Franks were now moving through a land in which many people had simply stopped wanting to be Roman. They were engaged in a long and pathetic march across western Europe, trying to keep themselves alive by living off the land. Which doesn't mean they had turned themselves into innocent hunter-gatherers, living off roots and berries. It actually means that they made their way through Gaul pillaging and looting: a large armed group in a landscape of armed groups. 'All Gaul was filled with the smoke of a single funeral pyre.'[3] It was very bad for business: 'He who once turned the soil with a hundred ploughs now labours to have just a pair of oxen; the man who rode through splendid cities in his carriages is now sick and travels wearily on foot through the deserted countryside.'[4] The large landowners took control of their own destiny, financing their own paramilitary forces led by a British warlord who declared himself Emperor Constantine III, and began running their own private empire (see page 76).

Stilicho obviously felt it was more important to deal with Constantine III than to attack the Vandal refugees, but the army he sent under a Goth general, Sarus, was defeated and had to negotiate a deal with the Bagaudae guerrillas in the Alps to get back to Italy. By 408 Constantine III was based in Arles in southern France, controlled all Gaul and was taking over Spain.

THE END OF STILICHO

When Stilicho had proposed to the Senate in Rome the need to pay a subsidy to Alaric, the Senate had fiercely disputed it with speeches that spoke of Barbarians and Roman honour (see page 127). The right-wing anti-Barbarian, anti-guerrilla backlash had begun, and it led to Stilicho's death on Honorius' orders. Stilicho the Vandal had lived for the Empire, and his murder was a kind of imperial suicide. But for many Romans, what mattered was that the West was no longer ruled by a Barbarian.

Anti-Goth pogroms in Rome followed immediately. Thousands died, tens of thousands fled the city. And then the Goths, led by Alaric, took their revenge on Rome, starving it, demanding huge ransoms from it, and eventually pretending, in a three-day show of force, to sack it. When they left, Alaric took Honorius' sister Galla Placidia as a hostage.

By then the Vandals and their allies had moved through northern Gaul and turned south, through Bordeaux and Narbonne, probably being driven south by Constantine III's backers. In 409 they moved over the Pyrenees, apparently with the blessing of the Bagaudae who gave them an easy passage into Spain. They were moving through territories where Rome had no control, areas where 'Constantine III' was the notional boss. He seems to have been a pretty average kind of paramilitary leader, lazy, self-indulgent and arrogant, and his subordinates in Spain and Britain soon stopped taking orders from him. His troops in Spain apparently did nothing to block the passes. Constantine blustered, fought, negotiated, lost and ended up as a detached head on display in Ravenna in 411. The military power that Stilicho had once wielded was now in the hands of a proper Roman by the name of Constantius. By 413 he had established himself as the sole emperor of the West.

VANDALS IN SPAIN

Constantine III's failed rule in Spain had led to it becoming a break-away province and to the emergence of an independent 'emperor', called Maximus, who was based on the Mediterranean coast. The invasion of migrants into the region has been described with all the lascivious bloodthirstiness that historians can muster:

> The irruption of these nations was followed by the most
> dreadful calamities; as the Barbarians exercised their
> indiscriminate cruelty on the fortunes of the Romans and the
> Spaniards, and ravaged with equal fury the cities and the
> open country. The progress of famine reduced the miserable
> inhabitants to feed on the flesh of their fellow-creatures ...
> Pestilence soon appeared, the inseparable companion of
> famine; a large proportion of the people was swept away; and
> the groans of the dying excited only the envy of their
> surviving friends.[5]

It does seem as though there were too many mouths to feed, and the best solution all round was for them to settle and begin farming. Maximus made them land-grants.[6] The Vandals and Suebi settled in the north-west (Galicia) and the central southern area of Spain (Andalucia – which some people have suggested is derived from 'Vandalucia'), with the Alans settling in the provinces between. The migrants became the new overlords of swathes of Spanish territory. Another Spanish chronicler, Orosius, who fled from Spain to Africa in 414, reported that the Spanish preferred 'impoverished liberty' under the Barbarians to 'taxable comfort' under Rome.[7] And Salvian shared this view of Spanish public opinion:

> What can be a greater proof of Roman injustice than that
> many worthy noblemen to whom their Roman status should
> have been the greatest source of fame and honour, have
> nevertheless been driven so far by the cruelty of Roman
> injustice that they no longer wish to be Romans? The result
> is that even those who do not take refuge with the barbarians

are yet compelled to be barbarians themselves; for this is the case with the greater part of the Spaniards.[8]

It seems likely that it was soon after the takeover of Spain that the pagan Vandals converted to Christianity. It also seems likely that the missionaries who converted them were Goths. Arian Christians and proud of it; or, from an official perspective, adherents of the dreadful heresy identified with Barbarianism.

Roman Catholicism was certainly popular among the Roman governing classes in the West, but it wasn't so obviously the Christianity of choice of ordinary people. Even Ambrose, the charismatic bishop of Milan, complained of the decline in people coming to take communion there. He said the same thing was happening in the East, but that's not too surprising given the fact that Catholicism was imposed from above on an Arian population there. The bishop of Constantinople complained: 'In vain do we stand before the altar; there is no one to partake.'[9]

There may well have been a whiff of popular discontent in people's reluctance to attend Catholic churches, possibly connected with the incorporation of Jesus into the imperial power structure. The Catholic Church emphasized not his human incarnation but his transcendent magisterial authority, his right to judge the living and the dead and to determine their fate for all eternity. Basically, the terrible power of Roman authority was presented as being derived from the even more terrible power of Jesus, a looming supreme God painted on the apse ceiling over the altar where his blood was to be drunk and his body eaten.

The Arian Church seems to have been much more popular. Their Jesus was not the same as the all-powerful God; he was rather less threatening, and wasn't identified with the state. For the Goths, Arianism was now the mark of their identity. Their churches were not Roman churches, their rituals were not Roman rituals. Not very different, but a bit different. And the Vandals too became Arian Christians.

Not that Goths and Vandals were necessarily that friendly. In 417 the new King of the Visigoths, Wallia, did a deal with Constantius that would finally give his people the Roman-endorsed homeland they had been seeking for two generations. Galla Placidia, Athaulf's widow, was returned to Rome to marry Constantius and make him part of the imperial family. Their child would be the natural heir to Honorius, who was evidently not going to father any children. And Wallia would use his army to re-establish Roman control of Spain, in exchange for a permanent land-grant in Aquitaine. His Visigoth nobles were legally established on the lands of minor Roman aristocrats, and were themselves to become the backbone of the anti-Bagaudae forces that would protect the Empire from revolution.

But Wallia did not, as things turned out, make any concentrated attack on the Vandals. His army's targets were the Alans and the Suebi. The Alans were perhaps the most curious of all immigrant peoples – Iranians from the steppes of the Caspian, whose language, religion and culture were quite unrelated to those of the Goths. They were horse-breeders who fought like Persians – knights in armour on horseback – and with oriental bowmen. Driven westward by the Huns, they had joined the Vandal migration and their support had been vital to the Vandals in the terrible battle with the Franks.

Their other distinguishing feature was that they used extraordinarily powerful dogs for hunting and cattle handling. Examples of this primitive breed survive today as working dogs in parts of Spain, and are known as Alano. The Alans' dogs are the ancestors of all the Molosser types, including bulldogs, boxers, St Bernards, mastiffs, Rhodesian ridgebacks and rottweilers. Alanos retain their original characteristics; they have never been bred for beauty, but as totally fearless and loyal pack dogs with a legendary grip using the whole jaw back to the molars. An Alano will hold any animal once seized without regard to any injury or threat to its own life, but it will reliably release the prey upon command.

The Alans were the main target of Wallia's Visigoth army, and they were totally overwhelmed. In 417, after the death of their king, they offered their crown to Guntheric, and from then on the ruler of this rather lumpy merger was called 'King of the Vandals and Alans'.

In 421 Constantius finally became co-emperor with Honorius; as a racially acceptable Roman, he had been able to move one step beyond Stilicho. But just when it looked as though the Western Empire had an effective ruler, he died and the Ravenna court fell to infighting.

That probably saved the Vandals from the next stage of Constantius' programme. A huge military force had been put together to retake Spain; it included the Visigoths from Aquitaine, the field army from Gaul and another army led by the Count of Africa, Boniface. But Boniface dropped out of the campaign. He wasn't going to get tied up in Spain when there was a power struggle in Ravenna. The Visigoths also seem to have rather lost interest, and the Gallic field army was given a bloody nose.

The Roman Empire was by this time severely dysfunctional. With no one to stop them, the Vandals conquered Cartagena in 425, and the next year they captured Seville. We know little about what happened; they supposedly sacked both cities, but that may mean little more than that they took them over. It was generally agreed among Roman authors that the Vandals were not particularly war-like. (Orosius, for example, said that Stilicho was 'descended from the unwarlike, avaricious, perfidious and crafty nation of the Vandals'.)[10]

The most significant result of these events was that the Vandals gained control of harbours full of ships. It seems unlikely that they were natural seamen themselves, especially since six years earlier the Augusti had decreed death to those 'who have handed over to the barbarians the knowledge, formerly unknown, of building ships'.[11] It must be assumed that the Spanish sailors were now under their control, just as Spanish peasants were under their control on the farms. The Vandals had acquired an entirely new (to them) resource, and they took over the Balearic Islands. Vandals first visited Ibiza in 426.

And they now had a way of leaving Europe altogether.

THE HUNS AT THE GATES OF RAVENNA

Around this time a great force of pagan Huns – 60,000 of them, according to one (perhaps unreliable) report[12] – appeared outside the capital of the Western Roman Emperor in Ravenna. Enough to blow away any force in Christendom. But – contrary to what you might be expecting – they had come not to destroy the Emperor but to save him. Actually, they were too late and the Emperor in question, a usurper called John, was later presented to the public in the hippo-drome of Aquileia with one of his hands cut off; he was then mounted on an ass, and publicly tortured by the stage performers before he was put to death. The Romans hadn't lost their flair for showbiz.

These Huns were under the leadership of a young Roman general by the name of Aetius, a man who would become celebrated for his cool judgement, military virtues and personal honour. His father had been field army commander in Gaul and had just been killed, perhaps in connection with John's usurpation. Aetius himself had grown up amongst Barbarians: he had been a hostage first in the household of Alaric the Goth, and then in that of Rugila, the King of the Huns.

The Roman imperial court in Ravenna was an extraordinary den of luxury, corruption and plotting. Honorius had died in 423. The obvious heir was the child of Honorius' sister Galla Placidia and Constantius III, a four-year-old called Valentinian. But Constantius was dead, and mother and child were at Constantinople, at the court of Galla Placidia's nephew, Theodosius II, now 22 years old. In her absence the hard men of Ravenna named John, one of the court soldiers, as the new emperor of the West. Obviously, so far as Theodosius II was concerned, his cousin Valentinian had to be emperor of the West, so he sent an army to capture John.

Theodosius' army did its business in the nick of time, before the arrival of Aetius and his Huns. Somewhere among them, almost certainly in a position of authority, was Rugila's young nephew Attila.

The curious thing about the Huns is that their first large-scale entry into the Roman world was being made not as fierce enemies but as allies of players in a Roman power-struggle. Huns had been appearing as highly valued mercenaries in Roman armies for at least 15 years, but a full-scale Hun army (even if there were really far fewer than 60,000 of them) under Roman command was something quite new. Theodosius II agreed to pay them for their military service, even though they had come to fight him, on condition that they went home quietly, and he also agreed to allow Aetius to continue in his father's old place, and the job that John had given him, as military commander in Gaul.

The court of Valentinian and his mother was a mixture of Catholic fundamentalism, sorcerers and astrologers, and Valentinian, as he grew up, 'being an extraordinarily zealous pursuer of love affairs with other men's wives, conducted himself in a most indecent manner, although he was married to a woman of exceptional beauty'.[13]

The actual management of the Western Empire was left to the court's most powerful generals, Aetius and Boniface. Naturally they were rivals, and Aetius (in Europe) convinced Placidia that Boniface (in Africa) was plotting against her. He also wrote to Boniface that Placidia wanted him dead, so Boniface refused Placidia's summons to return to Rome (convincing her, of course, that Aetius was right). Boniface then realized that she would send an army to arrest him. He decided that he needed allies, and that the Vandals were his best bet. So, according to the historian Procopius, he offered them a deal. If they would come over to his aid in Libya, he would give them land to settle there.

THE VANDALS TAKE NORTH AFRICA

Guntheric's capital was now Seville, and he was apparently sharing his rule with his illegitimate half-brother, who took the extraordinary name Gaiseric – 'Caesar-king'. Presumably that was because Guntheric was a sick man – he died in 428, the year that preparations began for the move into Africa.

According to Hydatius, bishop of Aquae Flaviae in northern Portugal, Guntheric was killed by a demon after profaning the church of Seville. It seems odd that he should ever have profaned a Christian · basilica because the Vandals were really very puritanical people who took their new religion extremely seriously. Salvian said that for God to hand the Spanish into the power of the Vandals showed how much he wanted to punish sins of the flesh, 'since the Spaniards were conspicuous for their immorality and the Vandals for their chastity'.[14] In the twenty-first-century version of the legend (in which the demon has been downgraded to a thunderbolt) the basilica is said to have contained the relics of St Vincent of Saragossa, who may be the only Christian martyr to have been tortured to death by being cruelly put into a comfy bed. (The story is that, after pain had failed to weaken his will, he was laid on a soft bed in the hope that kindness would do the trick. He promptly died, and began a new career as the patron saint of wine-makers.)

But we should also remember that, to Roman Catholic writers, an Arian Christian such as Guntheric would 'profane' a sanctuary by setting foot in it. And if they could lay claim to a divinely inspired demon to back up their position, they surely would – even if it did make God's criteria for intervention in human affairs seem pretty self-centred.

Gaiseric, now sole king of the Vandals and Alans, was nearly 40 years old and lamed after a fall from his horse. He had lived through the whole of this terrible migration from Hungary to southern Spain, and he seems to have possessed a quite extraordinary determination to take control of his own and his people's destiny. The other Germanic peoples saw themselves as Romans who needed to estab- lish themselves within the framework of the Empire. Alaric's brother Athaulf may have had more revolutionary ambitions, but had soon abandoned them. But Gaiseric had no desire to be Roman. He was determined to organize his people in a way that made them quite independent of Rome.

The Visigoth King Wallia had also been succeeded by his illegiti- mate half-brother, Theoderic, and Gaiseric evidently felt that it would be prudent to create an alliance that would protect his northern border. He married his son Huneric to Theoderic's daughter. But he would not need that alliance for long.

With or without Boniface's help, Gaiseric organized an astonish- ing migration of the whole Vandal people. He carried out a census of all males, 'from feeble old men to the babe born yesterday' – there were 80,000 men to transport.[15] If that is true, there must have been at least 40,000 men of fighting age. With their families, the migration must have consisted of around 150,000 people. Assuming that a ship could carry 100 people and their goods, that would have meant 1500 ferry crossings. There must have been a prodigious effort of boat-build- ing on the beaches, knocking together short-life hulls that would get over to Tangier and back in 24 hours. With 100 boats, the whole cross- ing could be achieved in a fortnight. Or perhaps it took fewer vessels and therefore a slightly slower pace – the embarkation and unloading of the vessels would have been a logistical nightmare, and probably required at least a month.

By the time Boniface had grasped the facts of Aetius' plot and tried to call the whole Vandal thing off, it was too late. If the landing was in Tangier, the most obvious place to go, it would have been unopposed because it was administratively outside Boniface's province. The local commander had what amounted to a police force of about 5000 men who were supposed to supervise the movements of nomads, and an effective 'army' of only about 1000 or so properly trained and equipped soldiers.[16]

And once ashore, the Vandals began walking east.

OLD ROMAN AFRICA

The new immigrants were moving into a coastal strip through what is now Libya and Tripoli, the settled area of Roman Africa. It was quite highly urbanized, with some 600 towns that had grown wealthy on selling agricultural produce to Europe, and had spent their money on buildings and conspicuous consumption. Regions that are today barely inhabited were then the sites of thriving and prosperous mini-cities. There are more Roman triumphal arches today in Africa than in any other Roman province, and more than two dozen theatres have been found. Every town had fine houses, public baths and public gardens.[17]

However, the best days of Africa were well and truly over by the time the Vandals arrived. As the income of the Empire fell and its military expenditure grew, Africa became the milch-cow that was expected to close Rome's vast fiscal gap. There had once been a time when the Empire had solved its financial problems by conquering Barbarian lands and appropriating their wealth; now, all it could do was tax its own citizens. The bitter complaints that Salvian described and that produced the Bagaudae guerrillas in western Europe were being heard in Africa too. Marginal land dropped out of cultivation, rural misery was widespread. The rich did not pay taxes, and the newly ruined abandoned their lands or became serfs. Throughout the Empire the population was falling – partly because people could not afford families so easily, and, probably, partly because wine sweetened with concentrated fruit 'must' that had been boiled in lead vessels diminished men's fertility. The fields were still well irrigated and the harvests bountiful. But the towns were abandoned by the rich, who moved out to luxurious country villas: many towns became shabby markets for the poor, conducted in the shade of the great monuments of another age.

Of course, Africa had not always been Roman. The great civilization of Carthage had been Phoenician, its language Canaanite.

Rome's original assumption of a world-ruling role had been over the dead body of Carthage, which it had not only conquered, but extirpated as completely as it could. In 146 BC the city had some 700,000 inhabitants. When it was captured, the Roman soldiers spent six days in an orgy of killing, setting fire to buildings so that their work would be illuminated at night. More than half a million people were said to have been slaughtered without any regard to age or sex.[18] Not even the most virulent anti-Barbarian propagandists ever ascribed such ruthless, inhuman savagery to anyone else. Genocide was a peculiarly Roman speciality.

Roman Carthage, founded 175 years later, was on a new site. But the ghost of old Carthage still haunted Africa. The Roman word for that civilization was 'Punic', from the Greek *Phoinikos*, Phoenician. In Latin, 'Punic' meant 'treacherous'. The Punic language and religion survived in the countryside, and when the Vandals arrived Augustine, the bishop of Hippo, was advising his fellow-clergy to learn the language so that they could speak to their flock. In the third century the future Emperor Septimius Severus had grown up in Libya speaking Punic.

AFRICAN CHRISTIANS – THE GROWTH OF DONATISM

In the early fifth century, very large numbers of poor African Romans converted to Christianity, but the Christianity they adopted had little in common with the religion of Ravenna and Constantinople. Instead, it drew directly on the buried traditions of Phoenician Carthage, the Canaanite city that had been Rome's enemy. Baal, their old god, whom many had worshipped as Saturn, was now understood to be the God of the Bible, God the Father, who was called *senex*, the Old Man. This was a religion of strict observance. The old religion had at its centre ritual and blood sacrifice; this one had ritual, penance and martyrdom.[19]

Just like seventeenth-century English Puritans who called their children Fear-the-Lord and Praise-God, the names of Libya's Catholics show that this society thought Christians should aspire to saintliness. The bishop of Carthage was What-God-Wants, his successor was Thanks-to-God, the bishop of Teluda was He-has-God.

But their ethics were regarded by many as insufficiently rigorous. As misery and poverty increased, African Christianity mutated into a particular and fiercely anti-Catholic form known as Donatism, after its leader Donatus. Its adherents believed, with a bitter conviction, that only the pure could hold office in the True Church. Any submission of the Church to secular authority was deemed to be wrong – anyone who did deals with emperors was damned, no matter what his place was said to be in the Church hierarchy.

The issue had arisen out of the persecution of Christians by the Emperor Diocletian at the start of the fourth century. Many clergymen tried to avoid martyrdom by surrendering real or pretended ecclesiastical objects. The anti-compromise party never forgave them. When a new bishop of Carthage, Caecilian, was consecrated by one of the 'guilty' bishops, these rejectionists appointed a rival bishop of their own.

When the persecution stopped and Christianity became the imperial cult under Constantine, Caecilian was recognized as bishop of Carthage, and his clergy were exempted from taxes and official duties. A Church Council endorsed his status – naturally enough, as no gathering of bishops was ever likely to say that a moral lapse means losing your bishopric. Meanwhile, the rejectionist anti-bishop of Carthage was replaced by Donatus, a Numidian crusader with a huge popular following. What followed was, literally, war.

Caecilian called in the army. The Catholic Church began martyring the Donatist Church – and African Christianity flourished in the blood of martyrs and detestation of Rome and Catholicism. The Donatist Church grew strong and built its own enormous churches – by 330 it had 270 bishops. Its enemies were the imperial administrators and the class of great landowners from which those administrators came.

The Donatists began to massacre Catholics, and guerrilla bands of Donatists began to free slaves and overthrow the social order. They were called *circumcelliones* – people who hung out round the *cellae rusticanae*, the shrines of martyrs attached to many of their churches in Numidia and where dwellings and food stores have been found. They dressed in rough habits like monks (Augustine called the female members *sanctimoniales*), had their own rituals and a battle cry, *Deo laudes* ('God be praised'). It was a deliberate separation from the Catholic formula of *Deo gratia*, 'God be thanked', a formula that suggests some sort of contractual arrangement between God and his flock.

Donatists were fanatical revolutionary martyr-terrorists, attacking landlords and money-lenders and sometimes forcing rich men to run behind their carriages while their slaves rode. And since they believed that martyrs went straight to heaven, they would reportedly challenge passers-by to kill them or would throw themselves en masse off cliffs.

ST AUGUSTINE

One of the most influential of all Christians to come out of Africa during this time – or rather to stay in Africa, because he lived in the Libyan city of Hippo Regius – was the bishop of Hippo. St Augustine, as he is known to millions of Christians, was the anti-Donatist rhetorical hit-man. By logic and authority he demonstrated that suicide was not martyrdom but a sin. (It must have been very disheartening for any Donatist, having persuaded a passing fish-paste salesman to kill him, to find that instead of entering heaven he had just bought a ticket to hell.)

Augustine also argued forcefully that God didn't care what wickedness his priests got up to – they could still validly administer the sacraments. Thanks to his unstinting efforts, and his unswerving development of a rationale of persecution, Donatism became a criminal offence in itself. Three hundred bishops and their clergy were banished. Their congregations were deprived of the rights of citizens, and fines ranging from 10 to 200 lb of silver were imposed on anyone worshipping at a Donatist service. Gaiseric was seen by thousands of Africans as their saviour from Rome, and it seems quite clear that many of the attacks on Catholic churches that were blamed on the Vandals were actually being carried out by vengeful dispossessed Romans.

The other great campaign launched by Augustine was to improve the lot of mankind by insisting that all humans were sentenced at birth to eternal damnation (the idea of eternal damnation was another of his theological platforms). This was because the act of conceiving them passed on the sinfulness of Adam and Eve. The doctrine was known by the rather snappy title of Original Sin. Human beings can only be saved by the grace of God, and then only when it is administered through the sacraments of the Church. That was the great attraction of the doctrine of Original Sin: it made the priesthood indispensable.

Augustine's leading opponent on Original Sin was a British monk, Pelagius. One of Pelagius' supporters wrote an outraged letter to Augustine:

> Babies, you say, carry the burden of another's sin … explain to me, then, who this person is who sends the innocent to punishment. You answer, God … he persecutes new born babies, he hands over babies to eternal flames … you have come so far from religious feeling, from civilized standards, so far indeed from common sense, that you think your Lord capable of committing kinds of crime which are hardly to be found among barbarian tribes.[20]

Augustine was unmoved. His correspondent was absolutely correct.

The bishop had penned a famous prayer: 'Grant what Thou commandest, and command what Thou dost desire.' At a time when the whole Empire was in turmoil, with economic collapse and political upheaval, and huge numbers of refugee Barbarians trying to find somewhere to live, often at the point of a sword, this prayer meant 'We just accept our fate; God decrees what will happen and His Church may offer pre-determined grace to us and save our wicked souls.' Pelagius was so alarmed by this that he went to Rome to point out that if man has the moral responsibility to obey the law of God, he must also have the moral ability to do it. God, he argued, provides a following wind to believers, but they still have to sail the boat themselves.

Augustine didn't agree with that. He had the political power of the Catholic Church behind him, and soon Pelagians were treated as harshly as Donatists.

THE NEW VANDAL KINGDOM IN AFRICA

Such was the state of the civilized Roman world in Africa when the Barbarian Vandals arrived under the thoughtful guidance of Gaiseric. Like the Donatists, Gaiseric hated the Catholic Church and all that it stood for. But Gaiseric was the follower of another African, Donatus' contemporary. He was an Arian Christian, and Arius himself had been from Libya.

It was, of course, a walk-over. The Vandals had come not to destroy but to settle, and to rural cultivators who had been reduced to the status of serfs with a crushing tax burden, the Vandals were obviously seen as liberators. Boniface's pathetically small forces offered no effective resistance. The Vandals took over management of the large estates and dramatically reduced taxes. The Empire lost an annual supply of about half a million tons of wheat, most of its olive oil and a huge proportion of its tax revenue. Unlike any other Barbarian leader, Gaiseric had no intention of continuing to be within the Empire at all.

With the enthusiastic support of most of the population, he removed the Catholic hierarchy from their churches and took the Church gold and plate and estates – if the local Christians, the Donatists, hadn't got to them first. Being a serious believer in old-fashioned Christianity, he installed Arian priests and bishops, and over the following decades he and his son exiled over 5000 Catholic churchmen.[21] 'Vandalizing' the churches meant replacing one orthodoxy with another, leaner, far less wealthy one.

Gaiseric's new kingdom was not part of Rome, but in many ways Rome provided the model for it. He installed his own people in place of Roman landlords (on a scale that did not happen anywhere in Europe), but established an autocracy of nobles rather than ruling through any tribal council. This was probably necessary because the Vandals were no longer a single ethnic group: on the long journey that had occupied Gaiseric's life, they had become a mixture of Suebi, Visigoths, Alans, Spaniards and probably many other peoples too. But his use of Roman norms extended to minting coins based on Ravenna designs, making Latin the official language (again possibly recognizing a situation that already existed, as the Vandals and Alans spoke completely unrelated languages and may well have used Latin as their *lingua franca*) and employing Roman engineers and architects.

Taking over the countryside was one thing; the cities were a different matter. The Vandals were not so popular there and didn't have any way of breaking in. The Count of Africa, Boniface, retreated to Hippo, which had become the walled refuge of the leaders of the Catholic Church – a Church that was dominated by Augustine.

Augustine and Gaiseric were never going to be friends. Gaiseric was an Arian, a heretic, an instrument of the Devil. Augustine had devoted his life to attacking heresy with the energy of an ideologue. Gaiseric and his 'Vandal Horde' had no way of getting into the walled city. They sat outside and waited, until they got bored and hungry and wandered off. Augustine devoted the time to writing ferocious attacks on the Pelagians and waiting for God to rescue the city. After three months he died, and a few months later a relief force arrived from Constantinople. Boniface marched out of the city, met up with his rescuers and was promptly defeated by the Vandals. He sailed back to Ravenna and Hippo surrendered. It was claimed that the Vandals burnt the city down, but apparently they managed to do that without damaging any of the books in the library. Augustine's legacy was saved for posterity.

And in 435 the Empire recognized Gaiseric's authority over all Libya except for Carthage. The treaty was signed in Hippo. There was nothing savage or alarming about the negotiation: in fact Gaiseric specifically ordered the release of the highest-ranking of his prisoners, Marcian, who later became emperor himself in Constantinople. Being a shrewd operator, Gaiseric made Marcian swear an oath that he would never take up arms against the Vandals. Marcian was as good as his word. The sixth-century Greek historian Procopius describes the treaty negotiations as follows:

> At that time Gaiseric … displayed a foresight worth
> recounting, whereby he made his good fortune most
> thoroughly secure … He made a treaty with the Emperor
> Valentinian providing that each year he should pay to the
> emperor tribute from Libya, and he delivered over one of his
> sons, Huneric, as a hostage to make this agreement binding.
> So Gaiseric both showed himself a brave man in the battle
> and guarded the victory as securely as possible, and, since
> the friendship between the two peoples increased greatly, he
> received back his son Huneric.[22]

A LEGACY OF BLOODSHED

The Vandals just don't look like Barbarians should. Procopius said that

> The Vandals, ever since they took possession of Libya, used
> to indulge in baths – all of them, every day. They enjoyed an
> abundant cuisine, the best and sweetest that sea and earth
> produce. They very commonly wore gold and dressed in silk,
> and spent their time dressed up in theatres and at the races
> and other enjoyable recreations, and above all in hunting.
> [The countryside was still forested and fairly rich in game,
> including lions – the Alans would have brought their big
> hunting dogs for that.] And they had dancers and mimes and
> other musical shows and performances which were worth
> seeing. Most of them lived in parks, well watered and shaded
> by trees, and they had great numbers of banquets.

He added that 'all manner of sexual pleasures were in great vogue
among them', but then he did have to find something to criticize about
them – they were still supposed to be Barbarians, after all.

Gaiseric's own attitude to sexual misbehaviour seems to have
been quite ruthless. It is recorded that he had his son's marriage
annulled and sent the lady back to her father with her nose cut off and
her ears cropped. This is reported by Jordanes (a historian who had
been employed by the Goths) as a personal act of cruelty 'because of
the mere suspicion that she was attempting to poison him'.[23] But this
kind of mutilation was a standard way of punishing sexual misbehaviour in the most 'civilized' circles,[24] and the implication is clearly that
Huneric's wife was being branded a slut. The lady's father, the King of
the Visigoths, was unlikely to forget the outrage. Its consequences
would be devastating.

The Vandals certainly disapproved of Roman morals, and of the
Roman lust for blood. The most characteristic expression of Roman
values was in the amphitheatre, where the great and good provided, at
their own expense, entertainment for the masses in the form of the
slaughter of animals, prisoners and gladiators. This peculiarly Roman
event had been going on for hundreds of years: in the middle of the

first century AD Seneca had described the crowd's enjoyment of the midday show in Rome's Coliseum:

> It's pure unadulterated murder. The combatants have no
> protective covering; their entire bodies are exposed to the
> blows. No blow falls in vain. This is what a lot of people
> prefer to the regular contests ... And it is obvious why.
> There is no helmet, no shield to repel the blade. Why have
> armour? Why bother with skill? All that just delays death.
> In the morning men are thrown to the lions or bears – at
> noon they are thrown to the spectators themselves. No
> sooner has a man killed than they shout for him to kill
> another or to be killed.[25]

This was the most enduring feature of Rome: forms of government could come and go, religions could be established and overthrown, but Roman-ness endured, and so long as it did, there would be crowds watching death in the arena. Augustine described the power of the blood-lust it created. He said he knew a young Carthaginian who 'had been caught in the whirl of easy morals at Carthage, with its continual round of futile entertainments, and had lost his heart and his head to the games in the amphitheatre', but who was influenced by one of his lectures. 'By a great effort of self-control he shook himself free of the dirt of the arena and never went near it again' – until one day his friends dragged him, protesting, to a show.

> They found somewhere to sit and Alypius clenched his eyes
> shut, determined to have nothing to do with the atrocities. If
> only he had been able to close his ears! Because when some
> incident in a fight drew a great roar from the crowd he could
> not contain his curiosity. Whatever had happened, he was
> sure that if he saw it he would find it repulsive and remain
> master of himself. So he opened his eyes.
> When he saw the blood, it was as though he had drunk
> a deep draught of savage passion. Instead of turning away he
> stared at what was happening and drank in all its frenzy,
> unaware of what he was doing. He revelled in the

wickedness of the fighting and was drunk with the
fascination of bloodshed. He was no longer the man who had
come to the arena, but was simply one of the crowd.

He watched and cheered and grew hot with excitement,
and when he left the arena he took with him a diseased mind
which would give him no peace until he came back again.[26]

These shows had a very overt educational purpose. One part of that
was to present the now outdated distinction between Civilization and
the Wild. Gladiators were dressed in traditional costumes, as mythic
monsters or long-forgotten Barbarians. Savage beasts and criminals
were presented and done to death to show how Rome made the world
safe. But even more fundamental was the fact that these shows were
the homage paid by the Empire to the old virtues of the Roman
Republic. The Romans believed that it was very good to watch killing.
Not just good entertainment, but morally good. It turned people into
better Romans.

Nowadays, we tend to think that compassion is one of the noblest
human virtues – that in fact you can measure the quality of a civilized
society by its level of compassion for the weak, the poor, for those who
suffer. By that standard, Rome may not deserve to be called civilized
at all, because in Rome compassion was regarded as a moral defect.
Augustine's God, who condemns babies to immolation in the eternal
fires of hell on a fine point of law, was a true Roman. Seneca, that
stern guardian of republican virtue, said in an essay for his ward and
pupil Nero that compassion was an emotion that 'belonged to the
worst sort of people – old women and silly females'.[27]

Gladiators were to be watched and admired because they went to
their deaths without flinching. Cicero said cheerily, 'If they have given
satisfaction to their masters, they are happy to die.' Pliny felt he was
watching 'an inspiring spectacle demonstrating the love of praise and
desire for victory'. These writers were excellent Romans. Unlike old
women and silly females, they felt absolutely no compassion for the
victims whose deaths entertained and educated them.

A day in the arena was a display of the power of Rome over nature
and human life. It began in the morning with the animal shows. Entire
landscapes would rise from the underground scenery docks, and then

in would come the exotic beasts – lions, tigers, leopards, crocodiles, elephants – that would be expected to tear each other to pieces. Lunch was the time for the execution of prisoners. They could be slaughtered by the wild animals, or (which was very popular) made to kill each other. Since prisoners tended not to display much heroic virtue as they met their end, the upper classes were disposed to say that they found this butchery somewhat distasteful; but it was an effective demonstration of the power and ruthlessness of the state. Then came the gladiators, in their various costumes, demonstrating in bloody fact the correct way for a man to die. This was the main event, and individual gladiators had followings like any sports star of the modern world.

It used to be said that the Christians stopped these events. Christians, after all, were supposed to show compassion; and Christians had themselves been arena victims in the early days of their religion. But the sad truth is that the Christians of Rome, being the good Romans that they were, staged gladiatorial combats themselves. At least one bishop of Rome (St Damasus) actually hired gladiators as his own bodyguard. Although Honorius explicitly forbade gladiatorial contests in 404, it seems that they continued wherever Romans wanted to demonstrate that their traditional values were still intact.

It would be the Barbarian Christians, the Vandals, who put a stop to the blood sports of Roman North Africa.

DE-ROMANIZING CARTHAGE

In 439, the Vandals finally took Carthage. Gaiseric deliberately timed his attack for 19 October, the day of the consular games, when the population – including the Catholic bishop – was gathered to watch the arena 'sport'. The Vandals walked in virtually unopposed, and put the games out of business for ever.

This was the largest city after Rome in the Western Empire, and most of what we know about it comes from a thorough depiction of the city's vices by Salvian of Marseille.[28] In Salvian's view the population spent their days in a drunken stupor, stuffing themselves with food and engaging in all possible combinations of fornication. He contrasted this with the moral uprightness of the Vandals, whom he saw as much more proper people.

Historians have tended to write off Salvian's description as the product of the fevered imagination of a Christian moralist who fantasized about the parties that he wasn't invited to attend. But a Canadian team excavating in Carthage in the 1970s discovered a massive rubbish dump near the theatre, in the entertainment sector of the city, and found that just before the Vandal conquest people were drinking an unusually high percentage of Gaza wine, famous for its quality and strength. They were also eating a lot of gourmet oysters. The archaeologists suggested that this did support Salvian's picture of the Carthaginians as people living in a continual drunken stupor, passing their time with eating, drinking and fornicating – though they did admit that there was 'no archaeological evidence which explicitly pointed to this latter sin'.[29] After the Vandals took over, the city of Carthage seems to have sobered up somewhat, and although the archaeologists found that Gaza wine did continue to be imported by them, the quantities dropped significantly.

There was very little actual persecution of Catholics by the Vandals – certainly nothing to compare with the Roman treatment of Christians before the conversion of the Empire, when Christian women were mauled to death by lions in the Carthage amphitheatre. And nothing compared to the persecution of the Donatists. In fact the worst complaints of Catholic writers are that they were forbidden to sing their hymns, even at funerals.

It is true that according to the bishop of Carthage, Quodvultdeus ('What-God-Wants'), the Vandals filled the city with so many dead that there was no one to bury them, mothers were enslaved, pregnant women slaughtered, babies torn from their nurses were left in the streets to die and, even worse, women who once ran their own households now had to work for a living.[30] But the bishop and his churchmen all survived this slaughter unharmed. Thanks to the bishop's vigorous campaign against Arianism, these Catholics were shipped off to Naples. He was eventually made a saint on the basis that it was a miracle the ship didn't sink. Two bishops seem to have been burnt by looters, but that was certainly not Gaiseric's policy – in fact he was very vocal in his determination to avoid creating Catholic martyrs.

It used to be said that the Barbarians destroyed the cities of the

Roman world, and that it is their fault that medieval Europe was a rustic continent with a few small towns. Carthage was taken as the classic example of how this happened: it was deserted by the eighth century, and that was supposedly down to the uncivilized Vandals. Modern excavations have shown that this is simply nonsense.

Carthage was certainly deserted in the eighth century, but the decline had begun under the Romans, as economic collapse led to the wealthy retreating to their country estates and the urban fabric being left to decay.[31] There's plenty of evidence of public buildings going out of use during the Vandal period. A massive judiciary basilica in the heart of the city began to collapse from about 450,[32] and a luxurious bath-house, presumably already ruinous, was demolished some time in the sixth century.[33] But this wasn't anything new, for the city was already falling apart when they got there. The Vandals demolished the performance spaces for drama, music and poetry (the theatre and the odeon), but that was because these places were regarded as immoral; and then a new building appeared on the site of the old theatre – evidence of renewal, not of destruction.[34] The circus remained a hugely popular venue for chariot racing, which went on quite unchanged. And it's clear that Vandal Carthage had a large educational establishment; there were schools of liberal arts, philosophy, languages and ethics,[35] where Romans and Barbarians sat side by side in full lecture halls.[36]

In fact, it's surprisingly hard to find any evidence at all of the non-Roman-ness of life in Vandal Africa. The Vandals lived just as the people around them did, to the extent that only eight graves in the whole continent can be confidently identified as Germanic.[37] Historians have described the Latin poets who were writing in the Vandal kingdom as a threatened minority surviving among Barbarians, but there is no reason to suppose that these poets were not Vandals themselves – apart from the determined belief, contradicted by all the evidence of lifestyles, that Vandals could not have been that sophisticated.[38]

The consensus nowadays is that 'For the city of Carthage, the Vandal occupation was largely a non-event, at least as far as the day-to-day life of its citizens was concerned.'[39]

MARE BARBARICUM

When Carthage fell, the Romans had not just lost Africa: they had lost the Western Mediterranean. The whole of the Mediterranean, every inch of its coast and every island in it, had been under Roman rule since 133 BC. Spain was still thought of as Roman, even if there was no Roman power there any more. The treaty with Gaiseric had created in Roman minds the fiction that Africa was still theirs. But now the treaty was dead, and Africa was gone. After 572 years, the geography of the world had been ripped apart. 'Mare Nostrum', 'our sea', wasn't theirs any more.

A Roman road-atlas survives from the fourth century, thanks to the copying efforts of a Rhineland monk around 1200. The Tabula Peutingeriana, as it is known, is a long, thin schematic representation of the world, 20 times longer than it is wide, depicting land stretching from Gibraltar to the Bay of Bengal. An update of an older map, it shows Pompeii, which was not rebuilt after being buried in the eruption of AD 79. At the time it was originally made, Roman rule covered more than 90 per cent of the atlas.

The Mediterranean flows through 80 per cent of the atlas like a river – not a barrier but a highway in itself, the main artery of the Roman world. The centre of the world is Rome, a golden circle within which an emperor sits in a purple toga, holding orb, sceptre and shield. Immediately below him is the port of Ostia, represented by a single semi-circular warehouse embracing the quay and the lighthouse – an open masonry mouth waiting to take in Rome's food. And exactly opposite across this narrow Mediterranean passageway is Carthage, the source of the food.

But now the Mediterranean was no longer a highway. Gaiseric, determined to break Rome's remaining power if he could, immediately started a ship-building programme. The sea was about to change sides, and become Barbarian. For the Romans, it would be as dangerous as any forest. Emergency licences were issued to Eastern traders to feed Rome; the militia were called up and the civilian population authorized to carry arms because of the danger of sudden attack by 'the enemy' from the sea.

Rome needed to strike back, and a huge fleet and army began to be assembled on Sicily from both East and West of the Empire under five commanders. But it never sailed. Instead, in 442, Rome was forced to sign a humiliating new treaty with Gaiseric, accepting the delivery of African grain from him in exchange for a non-aggression pact that recognized this former 'enemy' as 'allied King and friend', acknowledged his authority over at least part of Sicily and sealed the bargain by betrothing his son Huneric to Eudocia, the daughter of Emperor Valentinian III.

The armada that assembled in Sicily in 440 was vast, comprising 1100 ships. It could have carried an army that would have driven Gaiseric and his Vandals out of Carthage, and the Western Roman Empire would have survived. So why did it never sail?

Once again, the story of the Vandals was bound up with that of the Huns. But this time, the Huns had saved them. They had launched their first attack on the Empire.

XIV
NEMESIS

There is one name that represents raw Barbarian savagery at its most ruthless and unreasoning. At least, it does if you feed on Roman-based imagery, as warmed up for us by the Renaissance and constantly reheated ever since.

ATTILA THE HUN

Raphael's sixteenth-century painting of the Pope's meeting with Attila outside Mantua (he actually shows them meeting outside the gates of Rome) shows a confrontation between God's Holy Church, defended by saints from heaven, and the living image of the anti-Christ, whose savage followers are wreathed in the sulphurous fumes of hell itself. We'd better meet this man. Have your crucifix ready, and a clove of garlic. Oh yes, and a nice present. A middle-aged Greek historian, Priscus, accompanied an embassy to him in 449, and left a very full account of what happened.[1]

To start with, Priscus' meeting was not in the open air or in a tent, but at Attila's large, beautifully constructed wooden palace. The great man was away, and when he arrived he was met by a procession of singing maidens walking under long linen veils that were held up by attendants. As he rode along, his chief minister's wife came out of her house with refreshments on a silver table, which was held up so that Attila could reach it from horseback.

Attila was a charismatic man with a finely tuned sense of politics. He knew how to present himself and how to create an aura around himself. Self-promotion and the creation of a personal myth were things he excelled at, and he used this meeting not only to impress the Romans but to show his own people how he humbled those Romans.

After being kept waiting for several days, the ambassador was then invited to a banquet at three o'clock precisely. The guests were required to drink a toast to their host at the palace door, then went into a great hall with chairs around the sides, where Attila was reclining on a couch. Behind him was a dais with his four-poster bed, swathed in curtains. Priscus described their host as a short, dark man with a broad chest and large head, small eyes and a flat nose. He had a wispy beard, which was turning grey. Although imperious, he was not prone to violence. 'He was a very wise counsellor, merciful to those who sought it and loyal to those whom he had accepted as friends.'

There was a strict order of precedence to the seating, and a prolonged ritual of each guest individually drinking to Attila's health. Then little tables were brought in with the food, which was a rich banquet served on silver platters with gold and silver cups. Attila, though, had only a wooden cup, a wooden plate and very simple food. He wore plain clothes and no ornaments. The feast ended with minstrels and then comedians, and the ambassador went to bed while it was still going on.

It would be nice if we could say that Attila is a much misunderstood figure in history, that his aims have been misinterpreted and that he was all in all a thoroughly good egg. After all, in Hungary and Turkey he is now regarded as a great hero, a kind of Hunnic King Arthur, and Attila is a popular choice for a Hungarian boy's name. A famous Hungarian romantic novel of 1901 integrates Priscus' account with the Hungarian myth to produce a hugely sympathetic picture of a charismatic Great King.[2]

There were certainly people who actively preferred living among Huns to living among Romans. At Attila's court Priscus met a Greek, a merchant who had been captured and had made a new life for himself as a prosperous Hun. This man explained that his life now was better than it would have been in the Roman world, and the reasons he gave were very similar to those given by Salvian when talking about the Bagaudae of the West. Roman rule imposed back-breaking taxation and operated a legal system that served the rich and punished the poor, whereas among the Barbarians, certainly in peacetime, people were simply left to get on with their lives.

There's a certain amount of truth in that, especially since Attila didn't need to tax his subjects – he was taxing Constantinople. But this Great King was not out to make the world a better place for all mankind. Attila was as ruthless as any Roman, and wielded more arbitrary power: Priscus retorted that at least the Romans didn't hold their lives and property at the whim of their rulers.

A Great King from one point of view is a megalomaniac from another. According to Jordanes, quoting Priscus, the story was put about (presumably by Attila himself) that a herdsman followed the trail of blood from a limping heifer and found a half-buried sword that he took to Attila. Attila immediately recognized it as the Sword of Mars, granting him the power to win wars and signifying that he had been appointed to rule the world.[3] And like any other world-conqueror, he wasn't bothered by how much suffering and horror he caused in the process.

THE ELUSIVE HUNS

Priscus' embassy took place some 80 years after the Goths had fled in terror from the Huns' arrival in Dacia, and the Huns had long since settled down. The Renaissance vision of a rough Barbarian pagan being overwhelmed by miraculous power wielded by the Pope is obviously fantasy. But it is much closer to the way things were seen at the time than the current popular image of the Huns as a horde of wild Asiatic horseman galloping through the Empire, slaughtering its inhabitants and reducing its cities to rubble.

By the time the Vandals crossed into Africa the Huns were living in wooden houses in Dacia and Pannonia, enjoying the profits from the agriculture of the peasants who were now their subjects. The Huns themselves remain elusive; they seem to have become very like the Goths. Thousands of fifth-century burials have been excavated in Hun territory, and hardly any of them are identifiably Hunnic. On the basis of the goods buried with the bodies, most look very Germanic.[4]

We know almost nothing about the Huns – their origins, even their language, remain a mystery. Not a single word of Hunnish has survived, but that may be because it was not a distinct language. They probably spoke Turkic – one of Attila's uncles was called something like Octar, and *öktör* means 'powerful' in Turkic. Other names support the thesis – his father was Mundzuk ('pearl'), one of his wives Erekan ('beautiful queen') and his son Ernak ('hero').[5] Attila too could be a Turkic word – it is a diminutive of *atta*, 'father' in both Turkic and Goth; but it was not actually his name at all – just a way of referring to him. The title 'Little Father' survived into the twentieth century as the conventional way of speaking of the Tsar of all the Russias. So the word *attila* belongs to the language of his subjects, and most of them were not Huns at all. Attila and his brother Bleda lived in a court that spoke Gothic German, and understood Latin and Greek. One of Attila's advisers and his secretary were Romans, while another adviser had been a leading rebel in the Bagaudae rising in Gaul.

The Huns were now a complex society incorporating many other peoples. In the 420s and 430s King Rugila had engaged closely with the Empire, supplying mercenaries to it and exchanging hostages. To convince him that it was best to be a peaceful neighbour, Theodosius II, the Eastern Emperor, made him an annual payment of 350 lb of gold. This, of course, was supposed to come back to the Empire as the Huns shopped for luxuries and weapons – a bit like foreign aid today. That also had the advantage, from a Roman perspective, of drawing the Huns into the market economy.

After Rugila's death, his nephews Bleda and Attila took his place. That was shortly before Constantinople sent off huge numbers of men and ships to Sicily for the proposed attack on Gaiseric. Theodosius was anxious to keep his depleted frontier secure, so he agreed that a double kingship should get a double subsidy. At the Huns' insistence, the contract was made on horseback, to discomfit Constantinople's ambassadors. Even though the Huns were now leading more settled lives based upon agriculture, living on horseback was still the symbolic essence of Hun identity.

As part of the deal, two refugees from the brothers' rule were handed back to them – the kings were evidently nervous of any dissident plotters inside the Empire. The returnees were duly impaled. Rome's first Christian emperor had abolished the comparable punishment of crucifixion for obvious reasons in 337, and though Roman punishments were still intended to cause humiliating and long drawn-out agony (mutilation and pouring molten lead down offenders' throats),[6] this gesture showed that the Huns had their own way of doing things.

But once it was clear that Constantinople's defences had been sent away, the brothers thought the deal they had achieved could surely be improved upon. It wasn't long before they crossed the Danube with a considerable force. This Hun invasion wasn't a bunch of wild horsemen from the steppes. Their accumulation of useful tools and skills from the wider world had now supplied them with an entirely new set of instruments for making war. The Huns had acquired engineers, and those engineers had built siege engines and catapults. Forget the whooping hordes with their bows and arrows. These boys moved slowly, deliberately, and with enough muscle to knock holes in the walls of banks. They knocked over a number of forts, flattened towns and besieged Naissus (modern Niš). Using missile launchers and massive iron-tipped battering rams, protected by substantial mobile sheds, they took the city.

The Empire was stunned. For the first time ever, it was being invaded by a Barbarian army equipped with effective heavy artillery. The idea of carrying on with the war on Gaiseric was immediately abandoned. Constantinople had too much at risk on its doorstep to mount a huge campaign in Africa. In 442 the Huns were paid off with an even larger subsidy – something over 1000 lb of gold a year. And in a new treaty with Gaiseric, Rome recognized him as an ally, no longer an enemy and, humiliated, was given back access to African corn and olive oil.

But once Constantinople's army was back from Sicily, Emperor Theodosius II felt much bolder, and stopped paying the subsidy. It was around that time, in 445, that Attila found he would have to manage without his elder brother's help. Bleda died. No one knows how, but everyone's finger seems to point at Attila.

ATTILA'S NEW ORDER

No other Barbarians seemed so alien to the Romans: a profound fear pervades their writings about the Huns. This was a result of Attila's unique approach to relations with the Empire. He created a kind of Iron Curtain at the Danube, completely closing off the Hun world from Rome.

Rome had well-established ways of relating to Barbarian peoples across its borders. It allowed movement and trade, but kept a wary eye on what was going on while encouraging 'Romanization' through paying subsidies to leading Barbarians, encouraging the recruitment of mercenaries and exchanging hostages so that the children of Barbarian leaders would grow up among Roman culture and thus learn the benefits of 'civilization'.

Attila stopped all that. He understood that if he could obtain exclusive control of the subsidies and ratchet them up high enough, he could establish dominance in his own society. And if, instead of allowing free trade with the Empire, he controlled trade and movement across the frontier, then he would have a position of extraordinary power.

Monopoly control of Roman subsidies seems to be a policy he learnt from Rugila, who refused to allow the Romans to pay subsidies to anyone whom he claimed as a subject, threatening to annul his treaties with Rome otherwise.[7] And Attila copied Rugila's insistence on having fugitives returned; Huns would not be allowed to live inside the Roman Empire. Since he also abandoned Rugila's policy of supplying mercenaries to Rome, he was creating a new kind of separation between Rome and the pagan Barbarians.

It was a separation he was evidently keen to make as decisive as possible. One of the demands that Priscus' embassy was obliged to confirm was that there should be no cultivation of a belt of land 100 miles wide on the south side of the Danube. Once it had been Romans who wanted frontiers. Now it was the Barbarians.

The Huns had always had a multiplicity of rulers: nomadic peoples don't have centralization because it creates problems of oversizing. But now they were no longer nomadic, and a single dominant ruler was a real possibility. Exclusive control of Roman gold – and lots of it – was, Attila saw, the key to that position, along with a sterilization of Roman influence. He would be the fount of the money, but his subjects would not be allowed to spend much of it on Roman goods. A single marketplace was set up for Roman–Hun trade, at Margus, on the Danube near Belgrade in modern Serbia. It wasn't much of a market – the Huns bought mostly grain and sold animal products. Excavation of settlements in Hun territory show an extraordinary lack of Roman material and a preponderance of Gothic goods (and Hunnic caul-

drons). Archaeologists suggest that this indicates an anti-Roman attitude on the part of the people themselves, but they seem not to have
been allowed an entirely free choice in the matter. And then in 449,
when the market was established and presumably growing more popular, he had it uprooted to Naissus, 150 miles upriver – a city that he had
sacked seven years before. It obviously wasn't meant to prosper.

There is one startling piece of evidence that the non-Hun inhabitants did identify with the Huns, and were most definite about their
non- Roman-ness. They began binding their children's heads to make
them long and pointed, as their masters did.[8] Especially, it seems, those
of the girls – presumably to help them marry into the new ruling class.

If the people behind Attila's Iron Curtain didn't spend their
money on Roman goods, or build themselves Roman-style homes (and
none seem to have been found there), what was the gold Attila handed
out to be used for? The answer rests probably in treasure like that
found at Szilágysomlyó in Transylvania. It's a stunning collection of the
highest-quality bling, which clearly marked the high status of its
owners. This is believed to have belonged to a Gothic group. Another
treasure unearthed in 1979 in Pannonia, in modern Hungary (the
Pannonhalma treasure), must have belonged to a Hun. It includes
beautiful gold-decorated harness, swords and bow decorations, some
of which are stylistically identical to finds in the Rhineland and on the
Sea of Azov.[9]

Attila's ability to dispense gold meant that all the upper ranks of
his society depended on him for their marks of status. The kingdom
he built on this wealth was huge, dominating the Goths from the
Caspian to the North Sea. Hun remains have been found from Austria
to the Ukraine. For the first time, the Roman Empire found itself the
prey of a Barbarian kingdom that intended to feed on its flesh.

BLEEDING CONSTANTINOPLE

Attila must have realized almost from the start that Theodosius II was
a soft touch. He was 'a meek man and an excellent illuminator of
manuscripts',[10] and Attila set out to bleed him dry. The first real test of
his ability to do so came with Theodosius' bold decision to cut off the
subsidy once his troops were back home to defend the walls of

Constantinople. And what walls they were! The finest defence works in the world, little more than 30 years old. Reconstructed, they still stand today. Attackers first had to cross a moat 60 feet wide and 30 feet deep, with an elaborate hydraulic system to flood it. If they got across, they would land on a 60-foot-wide killing field that ended at a 30-foot-high wall with a roadway on top and a series of guard towers. Anyone who managed to climb that wall would find himself on another killing field, 45 feet wide, that faced another wall, 60 feet high, with a walkway on top and towers every 150 feet. All this was built with a full understanding of the power of artillery. No siege machine could possibly break this wall: that would take something much more powerful. Attila waited for his destiny to be revealed.

On 27 January 447 the walls of Constantinople collapsed. The fates had given the Hun leader an earthquake. He marched on the city, whose entire population was in a state of manic desperation. The supporters of all the circus racing teams – the equivalent of every foot-ball supporters' club – organized a top-speed rebuilding programme, and went at it day and night. And the sports fans did it! By the time Attila reached Constantinople, the walls had been rebuilt.

Ironically, had these been the Huns of old, riding fast and deliv-ering a hailstorm of powerful arrows, they would have covered the 500-odd miles to their goal in a matter of days and taken the city easily. But those days were over. Attila's army was a great wagon-towing machine designed to take towns, not to storm farms, and it rolled remorselessly towards Constantinople at an average speed of little more than 6 miles a day.

When it did arrive, it mangled the army sent against it. But Constantinople itself was once more impregnable. So, in the spirit of impressing on Constantinople that he meant business, Attila turned his army to demolishing the towns of the Balkans.

In the days when the Goths had ravaged this territory, 70 years before, the citizens had retreated to those towns and lived relatively safely behind their walls. But the story seems clear from an excavation of Nicopolis ad Istrum:[11] walled towns that had safely survived the Goths were demolished by the Huns. This town, like many others in the region, was utterly destroyed. The Huns weren't just looting and killing: it was hard work to demolish a city centre. Roman urban civilization on the Danube plain north of the Balkan mountains was ended. And Constantinople was duly impressed.

Attila's demands would be met. Apart from the money he was owed, he wanted the usual fugitives returned, a cordon sanitaire along the Danube – oh! and come to think of it, he wanted a nobly born Roman wife for his secretary … the usual things. The arrears of Theodosius' subsidy were now handed over in full – 6000 lb of gold – and the annual payment raised to 2100 lb. Great households were forced to cough up their gold and silver, and there was real distress amongst the formerly affluent. In some cases people were driven to suicide by their inability to pay the share demanded of them. New Rome had been sacked and looted without its walls ever being breached.

Priscus' embassy two years later was meant to finalize this agreement – but in a way that Priscus didn't know about. His party included an assassin, who had been hired by Theodosius' chamberlain Chrysaphius – the man who ran the imperial household – to remove the threat of Attila for ever for a fee of 50 lb of gold. That would have been a wonderful bargain, but Attila knew all about the plot. Instead of torturing and killing the assassin, he sent his secretary, Orestes, to Constantinople, to appear in front of the Emperor and his chamberlain with the 50 lb of gold in a bag tied round his neck.

Orestes, having shamed the imperial court, told Theodosius that agreeing to pay tribute had degraded him 'to the condition of a slave. It is therefore just that he should reverence the man whom fortune and merit have placed above him; instead of attempting, like a wicked slave, clandestinely to conspire against his master.' Attila demanded that his slave Theodosius should send him a new embassy, this time consisting of leading dignitaries who should bring Chrysaphius with them to be executed.

The mild Theodosius, stunned and ashamed, agreed. Attila had what he wanted from Constantinople – not territory but Respect. And the money. Priscus understood his motive to be, above all, domination: 'He ruled the islands of the Ocean [presumably the Baltic] and, in addition to the whole of Scythia, forced the Romans to pay tribute … and, in order to increase his empire further, he now wanted to attack the Persians.'[12]

But then he had a better idea.

ATTILA TURNS ON THE WEST

When the Very Grand Ambassadors duly went to Attila, they abased themselves, handed over fabulous gifts and the petrified chamberlain, and dutifully arranged Attila's secretary's marriage. And Attila pardoned everyone, even Chrysaphius. He was all sweetness and light. By the time the ambassadors left, which must have been in late spring, there were no issues outstanding between Attila and Constantinople. The Iron Curtain slammed shut behind them; it would presumably open again the following year, 451, when the next instalment of tribute arrived.

And Attila began preparing his Big Surprise. At the start of the campaigning season of 451, Attila and an unimaginably vast army thundered into northern Gaul, about 750 miles away. Some said there were half a million Huns;[13] others reported 700,000. It is still not at all clear what had happened.

It would have taken nearly two months for Attila to get men and horses to the Rhine,[14] but war-horses need grass as tanks need diesel, and there's no grass in central Europe in winter. He must have moved this entire army in great secrecy at the end of the previous summer, just after the ambassadors left. Once at the Rhine, Attila's Huns and Goths gathered winter fodder and began deforesting that part of Germany,[15] building what would become a bridge of boats when the thaw came and the new grass grew. He was obviously looking for maximum surprise impact – this was a campaign of shock and awe. His Iron Curtain made that possible. How long had he been planning it?

It certainly seems likely that he was thinking of it when Priscus' embassy arrived in 449. Priscus was told that his next target was Persia. This sounds like deliberate disinformation. Priscus didn't believe it and asked how that was possible; he was told that the Huns knew a route around the Caspian Sea.

What was Attila after? His pretexts for the attack varied wildly. For a start, he claimed half the Western Empire as the dowry for his next bride, who was to be the Western Emperor's sister, Honoria. She had, he said, asked him to marry her. She'd even sent him a ring!

Now as ridiculous as this sounds, it just might have been true.

Honoria was a pretty feisty sort of woman. In fact, she was trouble. She had had an affair with her chamberlain in Ravenna, and when she found she was pregnant she tried to have him proclaimed emperor. But he was put to death, and she was told she had to marry some boring senator whom she refused to have anything to do with. Her mother, Galla Placidia, packed her off to live a life of celibacy in Constantinople, under the supervision of her cousin Pulcheria. This was just not Honoria's idea of the good life.

She must have figured that Attila would be her knight in shining armour, so she had a letter and ring smuggled out to him. Once word got out about what she'd done, she was packed off back to her brother Valentinian's court in Ravenna.

Attila announced that he accepted Honoria's proposal and that the dowry he wanted was Gaul. It was as good as any other pretext – perhaps better than the one about the Roman banker who possessed some gold plate that Attila claimed was his by right of conquest. Maybe the banker also had weapons of mass destruction? As pretexts for war go, these seem pretty flimsy even by the standards of our own time. It looks as if Attila, ready to move on now that Constantinople had submitted, had simply decided that the West was a softer target than Persia. But it's also possible that this attack had already been financed by someone else – that Attila had, in effect, been hired to invade Gaul.

The evidence comes in a few lines in Jordanes' summary of a lost work by Cassiodorus, *The Origins and Deeds of the Goths*, written about 550. He says that when Gaiseric learnt that the Hun's 'mind was bent on the devastation of the world, he incited Attila by many gifts to make war on the Visigoths'. Rome had used Visigoths to attack the Vandals in Spain; was this the Vandal king's revenge? There had been a brief period of amity between Vandals and Visigoths when Huneric married Wallia's daughter, but that had ended when Gaiseric sent the lady back minus her nose and ears.

Knowing what we do of Attila's way of thinking, Gaiseric must have made his payments appear as the tribute of a servile subordinate. He would have had to make very substantial gifts indeed – Attila thought in terms of mountains of gold rather than baskets of trinkets. Could Gaiseric have raised that kind of money? North Africa was rich, but it has been suggested that he was acting as intermediary for some-one much richer: the ruler of Persia.[16] Instead of being his next victim, Persia had become, through Gaiseric, his paymaster.

Although there is no concrete evidence to support this specula-tion, and it has never been taken very seriously, it is not absurd. Persia would certainly have been keen to refocus Attila's mind away from the East; other groups of Hunnic nomads were already causing very seri-ous problems there.[17] Could Gaiseric have been a go-between? There were strong trade links between Carthage and the Eastern Mediterranean, and traders must have moved between Persian and Vandal territory. If the theory is true, and Persia was the hidden hand financing payments by Gaiseric to Attila, then the final disintegration of Roman power in Europe was to be the ultimate triumph of Persian diplomacy.

But more than anything else, Attila wanted to rule the world. And he expected Rome to fall over in shock when he finally crossed the Rhine in March 451. The plan was all about overwhelming force and surprise; there was no way that the Empire could assemble an army large enough to confront him before he had taken all Gaul and had Italy at his mercy.

But it did. Attila's secrecy had been blown by a piece of really bad luck. Bad luck for him – worse for his slave in Constantinople, Theodosius II. On 28 July 450, when Attila was well on his way west, the 48-year-old Theodosius was killed in a fall from his horse while hunting. His elder sister Pulcheria (Honoria's jailer) took control of the court. She married Marcian, the man who had pledged Gaiseric never to attack the Vandals, and had him installed as the new emperor. And they immediately sent an ambassador to Attila, carrying costly gifts.

This was totally unexpected. The ambassador was refused access and allowed to go away again with his undelivered gifts. The conclu-sion must have seemed obvious: there was no one at home. Attila had gone. Pulcheria and Marcian decided that the humiliation could now end. They cut off the payments that had been agreed to Attila. It was a smart move. It rescued the finances of the Eastern Empire, and by the time Attila heard about it he was in no position to do anything – his army must have been boat-building in Germany. More importantly, the most powerful man in the Western Empire must have grasped the significance of Attila's disappearance.

That man was Aetius, who had made his name by appearing at the head of a huge army of Huns in 424. He was the general in charge of the defence of the West, and more powerful even than Valentinian – he was, in effect, a new Stilicho (which did not bode well for his future, but let's not get ahead of ourselves). He had achieved his position with Hun help. At a low point in his own career he had taken refuge with Attila's uncle and been saved by his military backing – the Hun army that came back to Ravenna with him in 433 guaranteed his installation as head of the Western forces. He had rewarded them by recognizing their settlement in Pannonia in 437, and two years later brought the Visigoths to heel with the help of his Hun allies. He knew Attila better than any other Roman, had provided his secretary and had even sent his son to live at Attila's court. So he grasped the meaning of Attila's disappearance, and began hurriedly negotiating a coalition of forces to defend Gaul. He even knew where and when the strike would come because knowledge of a huge Hun presence waiting to attack had spread through Belgium, and a bishop had gone to Rome to try to get help.[18]

In the spring of 451 the Hun army ploughed a furrow of fire and blood down through Gaul. Metz was besieged in early April and destroyed. Once again, this was no lightning strike by wild horsemen but the steady march of a heavy army. Both the defence of cities and the accounts of what actually happened to them were left to the Church to arrange. The bishops did their best to organize some sort of defence, and the religious chroniclers scribbled down somewhat deranged accounts of events. The terrified monks described the Hun as a scourge sent by God to punish the wicked, and recounted various miracles that saved the deserving. For them, the defining feature of the whole situation was that the Huns were pagans – this was heaven's war being played out on earth. As a result of the triumph of this sort of intellectual authority, we actually have no idea where Attila went or what he did for several weeks.

But Aetius' forces were in the field relatively quickly. He had managed to put together his anti-Hun coalition army, backing up the Roman armies of Italy and Gaul with Burgundians and Visigoths. Attila did not have to hunt out the Visigoths: they came to meet him. Aetius' force caught up with him in June, about 1200 miles from his homeland, at Orléans. It was massive enough to drive the Huns off.

Attila hadn't expected this; he started heading back home as fast as he could. But Aetius wasn't going to leave it at that. He gave chase, and caught up with the Hun army (evidently moving quite slowly) after only about 100 miles. The exact location has never been conclusively established, but it is sometimes referred to in the sources as 'the Catalaunian fields' (the fields of Chalons). At all events, it was somewhere in the region of Troyes. There a tremendous battle was fought, with great loss of life – 165,000 men perished, according to the chief source, though no one went round counting. It was the first battle that Attila did not win.

SIGNS AND MIRACLES

Before the battle, Attila's shamans – his soothsayer-priests – had examined some sheep entrails and announced that the battle would end with the death of one of the commanders. As the day started to go against him, Attila grew distraught. Convinced that his number was up, he wanted to heap up saddles to make himself a funeral pyre – an obvious way of looking after your men if you happen to be a megalomaniac. In the end his lieutenants persuaded him that it was not a disaster and, after a stand-off, Attila was able to withdraw slowly and, tails between legs, he and his army limped back to Hungary. The leader who died on the battlefield was Theoderic, the King of the Visigoths. Attila had at least achieved what Gaiseric had asked him for.

The next year, 452, he was back, this time heading for Italy itself. And this time Aetius had no coalition to stop him. His arrival seems to have been totally unexpected. When he reached the town of Aquileia, at the head of the Adriatic, Attila laid siege to it, but was on the point of giving up when he saw a stork carrying its young, one at a time, out of the city. Omens were important to the Little Father: he understood that the prescient stork was moving home before the city was destroyed. So he decided not to abandon the siege, and very shortly afterwards Aquileia's defences collapsed. The stork's nesting place was indeed doomed, but historians now believe that Attila did little damage to this city or to the others he captured in this campaign.

City after city fell: Padua, Mantua, Vicenza, Verona, Brescia, Bergamo ... until finally Attila arrived at the gates of Milan and took that too. This was an important symbolic moment: Milan was the city where Constantine had declared the Empire to be Christian. It had also been the seat of Ambrose, who had campaigned so hard and successfully to extirpate paganism from Rome in the previous century. It had been one of the capitals of the Western Empire. Now a pagan sat on its throne.

It was while he was in Milan that a significant incident took place that shows the nature of Attila's ambition. After seeing a painting in the palace depicting Roman emperors on golden thrones, with what he took to be Huns lying dead at their feet, he commanded that the picture be repainted, with himself on a golden throne and Roman emperors not dead, but cravenly pouring out sacks of gold at his feet.[19] At least in the eyes of the tenth-century Byzantine scholar who recorded the story, and probably in his own eyes as well, Attila was seeking not the extermination of the Empire but its submission.

Valentinian had refused him Honoria, but matters were now out of Valentinian's hands. He was apparently in Rome, and scared witless – at least according to one contemporary source, Prosper of Aquitaine.[20] Aetius was evidently now unable to mount a large military force.[21] So Valentinian sent an ambassador to Attila. He sent Leo, the bishop of Rome.

Leo was a man of firm and uncomplicated views. He was also apparently completely fearless, convinced that he was living under the personal protection of the Trinity and that it was his duty, as Holy Father of the city of St Peter, to carry the authority of the Roman Imperium. Virgil, in his *Aeneid*, had spelt out Rome's vision of its own place in the world: 'Remember, Roman, your authority [*imperium*] rules the nations.' That had been at the time of Augustus, and for 450 years it had been the job of emperors to exercise that power. But now there was a vacuum, and a new kind of authority was ready to step up to the throne. The bishop of Rome.

He met up with Attila on the bank of the river Mincio in Lombardy – possibly, as one historian has suggested, almost within sight of Virgil's farm.[22] The occasion had all the makings of a mythic encounter. Both the Holy Father and the Little Father believed they had been chosen to lead the world. It was a meeting of giant egos. And yet – almost magically – where force had failed, diplomacy succeeded. Attila turned his mighty army around and headed off back to Hungary.

A thousand years later, Raphael's picture of the encounter showed Pope Leo I (actually he depicted the then current Pope, Leo X) calm and dignified, raising his hand in a gesture of peace, while above him Saints Peter and Paul brandish swords. Attila looks perplexed, while his army starts in terror and turns to flee before this oh-so-evident manifestation of the wrath of God.

So what really happened? No miracle. The Pope wasn't actually single-handed – he may not have had two saints by his side but he had two senators, one of them the ex-consul Avienus, possibly the richest man in Rome, and the other the ex-prefect of Italy, Trygetius, a diplomat who had negotiated with Gaiseric a few years before. In effect the money man, the deal-maker and a papal fig-leaf in case Attila was superstitious. Which he was, so that helped.

Jordanes makes it clear that when Attila agreed to withdraw 'he declared and avowed with threats that he would bring worse things upon Italy, unless they sent him Honoria, the sister of the Emperor Valentinian and daughter of the Augusta Placidia, with her due share of the royal wealth'.[23] So Attila had been told he would receive them. In other words, Leo and his companions had been sent by Valentinian to offer a complete surrender. Attila had been given his bride and a dowry (in gold, not land – but he much preferred that), and they would be transferred to him shortly. He had achieved the submission of the West. There was absolutely no purpose in moving on to Rome, especially if, as some people think, food was short and his army was suffering disease.

Attila retired once more to Hungary to plan the next year's campaign. While waiting for Honoria to arrive, he took another bride, and on his wedding night is reported to have got drunk, burst a blood vessel in his nose and bled to death. Given that one of the few things we know about Attila (from Priscus) is that he did not get drunk, there is room for an assassination theory here.[24] He was 50 years old. He never received Honoria, and no one knows what happened to her.

HOW ATTILA HELPED CREATE THE PAPACY

Attila had won a worthless victory. The real winner was the man we now call Pope Leo I; he came back with a tale that could be spun into Christian magic, proving that the Church had saved Rome from a sack that was never actually threatened. The Church was now, it would be said, the true power in Rome, the replacement for military authority. This was the moment when the Roman Empire lost Rome. Not to Attila, but to the Pope.

The bishop of Rome was called Pope, but that was a form of address used for nearly 2000 office-holders of the Church. The word was simply *papa*, 'father'. There was no special title for the bishop of Rome. But it was Leo's belief that, because Rome was the city of St Peter, he should be head of the Church.

Not every pope in Christendom was willing to fall into line with that. Leo had been engaged in a ferocious argument with the bishop of Arles, who was dismissing and appointing bishops in Gaul as he saw fit – just as if he ran the Church himself, for goodness' sake!

Leo, however, had the advantage of being backed by the Emperor, Valentinian, and in 445 (the year after Attila became sole ruler of the Huns) Leo extracted an astonishing letter from the great man. The Emperor formally recognized the primacy of the bishop of Rome over the whole Church, on the grounds that he was the holder of the keys of St Peter and that the dignity of the city of Rome was supreme. But more than this, it asserted that the bishop's rulings had the force of law and that any opposition to them should be treated as treason. The civil power was told that it was now in the service of the bishop of Rome; provincial governors must now forcibly extradite anyone who refused to answer his summons.

The bishop of Arles caved in and went to collect his heavenly reward in 449. Still, Leo needed something more convincing than an emperor's letter to establish his place as the new master of the *imperium*. A meeting with the greatest pagan on earth might just fit the bill. And it did.

But the truth is that it was not Leo's calm presence, nor the hand of God that intervened to turn the pagan king around. Attila never intended to stay.

THE HUNS VANISH

Ferocious and effective as it was in the short term, Attila's war machine didn't (in the parlance of modern film distribution) have legs. It simply had no way of sustaining itself over great distances and over extended lengths of time.

The Roman army had owed a lot of its success to its ability to remain in the field of battle. It could outstay any other force, partly because it was a fully paid up professional army, and not reliant on part-time recruits who needed to go home for the harvests, and also because it was supported by a vast bureaucratic service, providing logistical support in the form of rations, equipment and information. By contrast, Attila's 'bureaucracy' consisted of one secretary (supplied by the Romans) and a prisoner by the name of Rusticus, who was good at writing Greek and Latin.

Attila had no long-term strategic aims beyond conquering the world. He made no plans for supplying food and fodder. His armies lived off the land, which of course added to the awfulness of their arrival, but also meant that they had to keep moving. His kingdom, strange and frightening as it appeared, was essentially parasitic, feeding on the Empire. It had no future even if he had lived, and after his death it vanished, leaving nothing behind.

Attila the Hun didn't come anywhere near conquering Rome, no matter how close it might have appeared. The real damage he did was that he forced the Romans to abandon their reconquest of Vandal-held North Africa, and, perhaps almost more serious, made them think that the Church could save them from earthly dangers.

VANDALS IN ROME

In 450 the Emperor's daughter had asked Attila to marry her in order to rescue her from a fate of lifelong seclusion. Five years later the Roman Emperor's wife appealed to the Vandal leader Gaiseric to rescue her from Rome.

The story goes like this. There had been chaos at the head of the Western Empire. Other than Pope Leo, there was no one to take competent control. There was no effective army. The court was a catastrophe.

According to one gossipy source, John of Antioch, Valentinian had fallen for the wife of a senator called Maximus, and tricked her to come to him. He won a ring from Maximus in a game of dice, and used it to authenticate a fake summons from Maximus for her to attend the Empress at the palace. Once there, Valentinian raped her.[25]

Maximus determined to kill Valentinian, but dared not do so while Aetius was alive, so he continued to be the Emperor's good friend and convinced him that Aetius was plotting to replace him. Aetius' son was betrothed to Valentinian's daughter; the man was plainly above himself. Valentinian personally delivered the deadly sword-thrust to his greatest general, his own protector and the only capable defender of Rome. In the words of Marcellinus, 'And with him died the western empire, nor since then has it been able to recover.'[26]

Once Aetius was out of the way, Maximus arranged Valentinian's murder prior to taking over both his throne and (his own wife now having died) his widow, Eudoxia, whom he forced to marry him. This was when Eudoxia sent her appeal to Gaiseric. And Gaiseric did turn out to be a knight in shining armour.

He came to Rome from North Africa with a huge fleet and a substantial army – with the intention of making his own Arian empire rich at the expense of the dying Catholic one. Maximus, terrified of the Barbarian demon (who was in his mid-sixties), tried to run away. Rome was now in the hands of the mob, who captured the Emperor, stoned him and tore him to pieces.

Pope Leo, knowing a sequel is often as effective as the original, confronted Gaiseric as he had confronted Attila. According to Christian accounts, for what they are worth, he extracted a promise from Gaiseric that there would be no killing, no torturing to discover the location of hidden treasure and no destruction of buildings. This does look like Leo once more taking the credit for what was going to happen anyway: Gaiseric was unlikely to be responsive to a Catholic bishop, but was as ever determined to create no Catholic martyrs. And he had no desire to demolish buildings.

The city he entered was in the process of being dismantled anyway. The population of Rome had fallen to just one quarter of the size it had been in the third century. The great temples had been systematically attacked by Christian mobs, and now the inhabitants were looting the imperial structures for stone to build their own homes. The Vandals, so far as is known, did no damage at all to secular or religious buildings, apart from lifting part of a roof that they mistakenly thought to be made of gold.

Gaiseric moved into the imperial palace and ordered his men to load the fleet with the imperial treasures. Included in the inventory were the treasures of the Temple in Jerusalem, which had been looted and demolished by Vespasian in AD 70. Oddly, none of the chroniclers who describe this 'sack of Rome' seem at all interested in the fact that what was being taken had actually been brought to the city as loot in the first place. And whereas the Romans had destroyed the places from which they took their plunder, not a single building in Rome was destroyed by the Vandals.

After two weeks Gaiseric and his men returned to Libya with their loot, as well as with Eudoxia and her two daughters, as requested. It is astonishing how many writers refer to this as 'kidnapping'. One of the daughters was already betrothed to Gaiseric's son and now married him; after a brief stay in Libya, Eudoxia and her other daughter (a married woman) were sent to their family in Constantinople.

As for the Western Empire, it was essentially finished. Priscus says that after Gaiseric took Rome 'There were still other emperors in the west, but although I know their names well, I shall make no mention of them whatsoever. For it so fell out that they lived only a short time after attaining the office, and as a result of this accomplished nothing worthy of mention ...' [27]

Without money to pay its legions Rome had lost control of Spain, Gaul and Britain, and the city itself became the site of a civil war in the early 470s. The ruins of Rome were actually created by the Romans themselves, who turned from using ancient stones and statues for their new homes to using them as ammunition.

THE END OF EMPIRE

Meanwhile, Gaiseric was establishing a new kind of state in Libya. He ruled that his throne would be hereditary (instead of the Goth tradition of election by acclamation), he replaced the tribal aristocrats in his administration by place-men of his own choosing, and he reorganized his warriors into a formal army in commands of 1000 men. The Vandals were now all-powerful in the Mediterranean and continued to raid and plunder Sicily and mainland Italy. Gaiseric treated these raids as crusades, going to the support of Arian communities and reportedly believing that the divine wind would choose his victims: he told his pilot that he was sailing 'Plainly against those with whom God is angry.'[28] The help wasn't necessarily appreciated.[29] In 467 one sea-going gang even raided southern Greece. The entire Empire was being ruined by the loss not just of Africa and its vast wealth, but of the Mediterranean itself.

A new Eastern Emperor, Leo, decided that this situation must be ended no matter what the cost. In 468 he assembled a fleet of 1100 warships and a force of 100,000 men in what was undoubtedly the most expensive military expedition of the ancient world. For the first time, a single expedition was vast enough to push the Empire to the brink of bankruptcy. It included every kind of unit the Empire could hire or command, including Goths, Burgundians and Huns.

There was a genuine fleet-to-fleet sea battle, using archery, bombs filled with incendiaries, snakes and scorpions, and hand-to-hand fighting. The Roman fleet was successful, and landed in Libya. The ground troops then clashed – Vandal horse-swordsmen and camel-mounted Moors on one side, and legions supported by Hun archers on the other. Once again the Vandals were on the losing side, and the Roman forces then marched on Carthage.

Gaiseric brokered a truce with the Roman navy, which was waiting at anchor, and then sent fire-ships into the dense mass of vessels. His warships entered the chaos and the Romans fled – as did the ground forces. The expedition turned out to be a total disaster.

Eventually an Eastern Emperor, Zeno, formally recognized Gaiseric as the ruler of North Africa, the Balearic Islands, Corsica, Sardinia and Sicily. Gaiseric returned Roman prisoners (except for those who had been purchased as slaves, in which case the individual owners made their own deals), granted freedom of worship to Catholics and ceased to make raids on the Empire.

In 476 a parcel arrived at Constantinople, sent from Rome. It contained the imperial regalia, and with it was a letter saying that it was no longer needed, so perhaps the Emperor there would like to look after it. It had been sent by a German, Odovacer. He had gently deposed the last Western Roman Emperor, 13-year-old Romulus Augustulus ('little Augustus'), and packed him off to live in the country.[30] Odovacer was a new thing. He was King of Italy. And an Arian.

The following year old Gaiseric finally died. It had been an astonishing career. Between his birth in Hungary and his death in Carthage he had witnessed the complete transformation of the world. He also lived to a ripe old age, almost 80, in a world that was otherwise almost entirely run and controlled by men who would live barely half as long.

EPILOGUE

At the start of this book, we asked what the world would be like if, instead of suckling Romulus and Remus, the wolf had eaten them. What if there had been no Rome? What if there had been only Barbarians?

After the disappearance of the last Roman emperor from the West, a Barbarian empire came into being that seems to answer that question. The Eastern Goths, the Ostrogoths, whose parents and grandparents had raided with Attila and his Huns, moved back to Italy in 489, and this time they stayed there. They were no longer pagans, but as self-aware Goths they avoided the Roman Catholic Church. Like the Vandals and the Visigoths, they were Arians, and under their king Theodoric they set about building a new kind of Rome. In place of the old violent, intolerant and ruthless Roman Catholic empire, there was a gentler and more inclusive Barbarian vision.

Whereas Rome tried to make all its citizens 'Romans', and tried not to recognize nations within the Empire, Theodoric believed that it was possible to build an empire of different nationalities. He set out to establish harmony between the different kingdoms and peoples of the West, intermarrying his relatives to different royal families and guaranteeing them their own law codes. He ruled both as a Gothic king and as a patrician, paying respectful homage to Constantinople, but never calling himself emperor.

Ruling from Ravenna, where he did his own gardening, he restored Italy's broken-down cultivation systems, importing experts in well-boring from Africa and draining swamps. He opposed superstition and debauchery, banning theatres and books of magic, and he issued edicts to protect ancient monuments. A new golden age of Latin literature flourished, but without suppressing Gothic as a language of education and worship. Theodoric ruled from Sicily to the Danube, from Belgrade to the Atlantic, and Italy enjoyed 33 years of well-ordered peace. Europe had known nothing like this for centuries. He is still remembered by ordinary Germans as the greatest of all rulers – but without even a Roman name. They remember him as Dietrich. Dietrich of Berne.

A new Barbarian future? Fat chance. The Western Empire had gone, but the Romans had not, and Theodoric naturally allowed full toleration to Catholics. The Romans, passionate about their religious beliefs and their anti-Barbarian racialism, incited riots and rebellions to the point where the aged Theodoric was eventually obliged to crack down on Catholicism and become brutally repressive.

Catholicism was always strengthened by being attacked. Gaiseric's aggressive anti-Catholicism had deepened Catholic intolerance and Attila's deal with Pope Leo had established the mythic authority of the Pope as greater than that of any emperor. Between them they had actually created the power that would dominate the coming centuries, the power of the Pope-King of Rome, who inherited the authority and wore the vestments of a Roman emperor and took the old pagan title of Pontifex Maximus. The Church finally destroyed Rome and replaced it with its own form of civilization.

The final triumph of Catholicism over Arianism in western Europe began with the Vandals' old enemies, the Franks, who had done them so much damage when they first crossed the Rhine in 406. The Franks had originated in the early third century as a confederation on the German shore of the Rhine north of Mainz. The name is first mentioned by Roman historians in connection with a battle fought against them in about 241, when some of them crossed the Rhine and settled in Belgic Gaul. They evidently identified themselves as non-Roman, hence their name ('free people'). Although Rome eventually treated them as allies, they were very slow to become Romanized, and remained pagan right up until nine years after Gaiseric's death, when their king, Clovis, converted.

And when they did convert, it was not to Arianism. They became Roman Catholics. Theodoric left Catholic bishops in their posts, and one of them, Bishop Avitus of Vienne, worked very hard at converting the Germanic people of the Burgundians from Arianism to Catholicism. He did it not with threats but with wit and verve, which has been preserved in a long series of letters he wrote to the Burgundian king.[1] He was evidently quite a character. Ninety-six of his letters survive. He also wrote a rather brilliant long poem, *De spiritalis historiae gestis*, in classical hexameters, containing a summary of the Bible; it is said that Milton used it in writing *Paradise Lost*.[2]

The bishop converted several members of the Burgundian royal family, including King Gundobad's daughter Clotilda, who married Clovis, the King of the Franks. Clotilda made it her business to convert her new husband, and in 496 he decided to try out her god, in an experimental way, when he found himself losing a battle. He recited a prayer to the Christian God, pointing out that his own gods had given up on him. Whereupon the enemy suddenly turned and fled, and Clovis converted on the spot.[3]

Since the Catholic Christ was evidently a powerful battle god, Clovis now decided to make full use of him. He made up his mind to conquer the whole of Gaul, demolishing the Visigoth kingdom in the south. They were Arians. The Catholic God obviously wouldn't put up with that. 'Now Clovis the king said to his people: "I take it very hard that these Arians hold part of the Gauls. Let us go with God's help and conquer them and bring the land under our control."'[4] He smashed the Visigoths in 507 and established the Catholic kingdom of the Franks, which survived to produce Charlemagne (who created the title Holy Roman Emperor for himself) and ultimately France. And the Catholic God was established as the European Roman battle-god in whose name the Franks ultimately conquered Jerusalem, calling themselves Crusaders.

After Theodoric's death in 526, Arianism was in retreat. The Roman Empire was still alive, well and ferocious in the East, and the Vandal Kingdom of Africa outlived Gaiseric by only 58 years. In 533 a revitalized Eastern Empire launched a successful two-year campaign to expel the Vandals and restore Roman rule to North Africa. The Catholic establishment and its Pope united with Byzantium, and Italy was then reconquered by the East and the Catholic Church. After Theodoric's long peace, Italy was subjected to 30 years of war and reduced to complete ruin. Catholicism was triumphant.

And the Catholic Church gave us history. The Romans had already falsified the picture of the world they conquered. Now the Church controlled our understanding by the selective preservation of some texts, the destruction of others and the creation of new ones. Theodoric's bones were taken from his mausoleum in 540 and every effort was made to wipe out his memory. The Arian Goths became savages, the Vandals were turned into destroyers, and Attila was designated the Scourge of God.

That was the final stage in the story of how we lost our history and Europe's ancestors were transformed into savages fit for children's tales. That is how Barbarians were made.

NOTES

Full details of the books listed below can be found in the bibliography on page 274.

INTRODUCING THE GOODIES AND BADDIES
1. Caesar, *The Gallic War*, VI, 27
2. Strabo, *Geography*, XVI, 4, 10
3. Pliny the Elder, *Natural History*, VIII, 3
4. Browne, T., 'Pseudoxia Epidemica', I, 3, i
5. Livy, *History of Rome*, V, 35
6. Ibid, 36
7. Plutarch, *Lives*, 'Camillus'; Livy, VI, 1
8. Plutarch, op. cit.
9. Livy, V, 48

I UNEARTHING THE CELTS
1. James, S., *The Atlantic Celts*; Cunliffe, B., *The Celts*
2. Cunliffe, B., *Facing the Ocean*
3. Ibid
4. For a thorough discussion of the Roman and Greek view of Celts see Rankin, D., *Celts and the Classical World*
5. Diodorus Siculus, *Library of History*, XXVI, 2–3
6. Ibid
7. Ibid, XXVIII, 1–3
8. Strabo, IV, 4, 5
9. Ibid
10. Ibid
11. Ibid, 5, 2
12. Ibid, 4, 2
13. Ibid
14. Diodorus Siculus, V, 30
15. Caesar, IV, 33
16. Biel, J. (ed.), *Der Keltenfürst von Hochdorf* (Stuttgart, 1985); Krausse, D., *Hochdorf III* (Stuttgart, 1996)
17. Piggott, S., *Wagon, Chariot and Carriage*, p. 27; Alinei, M., 'The Celtic Origin of Lat. Rota and its Implications for the Prehistory of Europe', forthcoming in *Studi Celtici*
18. Clark, Prof. A.C., 'The Reappearance of the Texts of the Classics', paper presented to the Bibliographical Society, 21 February 1921
19. Ibid
20. Caesar, I, 14
21. We have selective memories even here: Polybius also said that the Romans were 'fickle, full of lawless desires, unreasoned passion, and violent anger' and that the only thing that held them in check was the official use of superstition, where government was backed up by gods who threatened

'invisible terrors and suchlike pageantry' (VI, 57). But we don't choose to include that information in our image of Rome.

22. Olmsted, G.S., *A Definitive Reconstructed Text of the Coligny Calendar*
23. Lewis, M.J.T., *Temples in Roman Britain*
24. Pliny, XVIII, 296
25. Reynolds, P.J., 'Reconstruction of the Vallus – the Celtic Reaping Machine', *Bulletin of Experimental Archaeology*, 3 (1983)

II THE LOOTING OF GAUL

1. Cauuet, B., *L'Or dans l'Antiquité*
2. Strabo, IV, 5
3. Andreau, J., *Banking and Business in the Roman World*, p.144
4. Caesar, I, 3
5. Ibid, 28
6. The number of dead comes from Plutarch, *Lives*, 'Caesar': 'of the three millions of men, who made up the gross sum of those with whom at several times he engaged, he had killed one million and taken captive a second'. It's not meant as an exact figure. Historians argue over the population figures for Gaul and the rest of the Empire – our figures are what we think are the best guesses.
7. Caesar, I, 31
8. Ibid, 29
9. Suetonius, *The Twelve Caesars*, 'Caesar', LIV
10. Caesar, IV, 15
11. Plutarch, 'Caesar'
12. Dio Cassius, *Roman History*, LX, 19
13. Caesar, I, 16
14. Ibid, 21

III CELTIC WOMEN AND THE GREAT BRITISH REVOLT

1. Dio Cassius, LXII, 1
2. Ibid, LXXVII, 16
3. Ginnell, L., *The Brehon Laws*
4. Plutarch, *Virtues of Women*, XXII
5. Evans, D. E., 'Onomaris: Name of Story and History?', in Carey, J. et al (eds.), *Ildánach Ildírech*, pp. 27–37
6. Polybius, *Histories*, II, 8
7. Plutarch, *Virtues of Women*, VI
8. Megaw, J.V. S., 'The Vix Burial', *Antiquity*, 40 (1966), pp. 157–63
9. Keller, J., *Das keltische Fürstengrab von Reinheim I* (Römisch-Germanisches Zentralmuseum, Mainz, 1965)
10. Ammianus Marcellinus, *Res Gestae*, XV, 12, tr. Beresford-Ellis, P., *A Brief History of the Celts*
11. Strabo, IV, 5, 3
12. Fulford, M., 'Calleva Atrebatum: An Interim Report on the Excavation of the Oppidum, 1980–86', *Proceedings of the Prehistoric Society*, 53 (1987), pp. 271–9

13. Fulford, M., and Timby, J., *Late Iron Age and Roman Silchester: Excavations on the Site of the Forum-Basilica 1977, 1980–86*, Britannia Monograph Series 15 (Society for the Promotion of Roman Studies, 2000)
14. Tacitus, *Annals*, XII, 37
15. Dio Cassius, LXII, 2
16. Stead, I. M., 'The Snettisham Treasure: Excavations in 1990', *Antiquity*, 65 (1991), 447–65
17. Dio Cassius, LXII, 2
18. Gregory, T., *Excavations in Thetford, 1980–1982, Fison Way*, Vol. 1 (Norfolk Museums Service, 1991)
19. Tacitus, *Annals*, XIV, 31
20. When Claudius died in AD 54, his widow could not act as guardian of the adolescent Nero – hence the appointment of Seneca
21. Crook, J.A., 'Feminine Inadequacy and the Senatusconsultum Velleianum', in Rawson, B. (ed.), *The Family in Ancient Rome*, pp. 83–92
22. Tacitus, *Annals*, XIV, 31
23. Ibid
24. Caesar, I, 13
25. Ibid
26. Suetonius, 'Claudius', XXV
27. Diodorus Siculus, V
28. Ibid
29. Tacitus, *Annals*, XIV, 30
30. Ibid
31. Ibid 33
32. Ibid
33. Dio Cassius, LXII, 3
34. Tacitus, *Annals*, XIV, 37
35. Ibid, 1
36. Tacitus, *Germania*, VI
37. ' ... urged by their general's appeals and mutual encouragements not to quail before a troop of frenzied women', Tacitus, *Annals*, XIV, 30
38. Tacitus, *Histories*, IV, 13–15
39. Webster, J., 'At the End of the World: Druidic and Other Revitalization Movements in Post-conquest Gaul and Britain', *Britannia*, 30 (1999), 1–20
40. Frere, S., *Britannia*, p.160
41. Breeze, D.J. and Dobson, B., *Hadrian's Wall*
42. Funari, P.P.A., *Dressel 20 Inscriptions from Britain and the Consumption of Spanish Olive Oil*
43. Whittaker, C.R., *Frontiers of the Roman Empire*, p. 86
44. Hong, S. et al, 'Greenland Ice Evidence of Hemispheric Lead Pollution', *Science*, 265 (1994), p. 1841; Renberg et al, 'Pre-industrial Atmospheric Lead Contamination Detected in Swedish Lake Sediments', *Nature*, 368 (1994), p. 323; Shotyk, W. et al, 'History of Atmospheric Lead Pollution from a Peat Bog, Jura Mountains, Switzerland', *Science*, 281 (1998), p. 1635; Nriagu, J.O., 'Tales Told in Lead', *Science*, 281 (1998), p. 1622
45. Tacitus, *Agricola*, 30

IV ROMANS ON TOP

1. MacMullen, R., *Romanization in the Time of Augustus*
2. '"Romanization"... encourages us to put the creation of the Roman Empire at the heart of historical investigation, and to explain change and choice in the provinces in terms of that process, seeing life in the Roman Empire only through the dialectic of colonized and colonizer', Crawley Quinn, J., 'Roman Africa?', *Digressus*, Sup.1 (2003)
3. Hingley, R., 'The "Legacy" of Rome: The Rise, Decline and Fall of the Theory of Romanization', in Webster, J. and Cooper, N. (eds.), *Roman Imperialism*
4. Caesar, VI, 17
5. *Historia Augusta*, 'Severus Alexander', 60. This source is not always reliable (see ch. XII, note 4) but significant nevertheless.
6. *Historia Augusta*, 'Aurelian', 44
7. Ibid, 'Carus', 14
8. Coşkun, A., *'Cover Names' and Nomenclature in Late Roman Gaul: The Evidence of the Bordelaise Poet Ausonius* at www.linacre.ox.ac.uk/Files/Pros/CNN.pdf (2003)
9. Tacitus, *Agricola*, 21
10. Brown, P., *The World of Late Antiquity*, p.12
11. At least, that's what most historians think. Some don't: see Jones, A.H.M., *The Roman Economy*
12. Justinian, *Digest*, quoted in Finley, M.I., *Classical Slavery*, p. 44
13. 'The slaves did not liberate the peasant farmer to take part in democratic politics, but to fight to conquer an empire.' Appian, *The Civil Wars*, 1,1
14. Duncan-Jones, R., *Structure and Scale in the Roman Economy*, p. 115
15. Bartlett, B., 'How Excessive Government Killed Rome', *Cato Journal*, 14, 2 (1994)
16. Brown, P., *The World of Late Antiquity*, p. 25
17. Bartlett, B., op. cit.
18. Salvian, *Of the Government of God*, V, 4
19. Salvian, V, 6, tr. Jones, M.E., *The End of Roman Britain*
20. Claudius Mamertinus, *Panegyrici Latini*, X, 4, 3
21. *Codex Theodosianus*, V, 17, 1
22. Ammianus Marcellinus, XXVII, 8
23. Ibid, XXVIII, 2–3
24. Claudius Mamertinus, XI, 3, 4
25. Zosimus, *History*, VI, 5
26. Gerontius, *The Life of Melania the Younger*
27. The implication drawn from the story, and the suggestion that it is evidence supporting the view of a British break with Rome, is at the suggestion of Prof. Michael E. Jones
28. Salvian, V, 4
29. Ibid, 6
30. Ibid, 5
31. Van Dam, R., 'The Pirenne Thesis and Fifth-century Gaul' in Drinkwater, J. and Elton, H., *Fifth-century Gaul*

V THE GERMANS

1. Tacitus, *Germania*, XXIV
2. Musset, L., *The Germanic Invasions*
3. Tacitus, *Germania*, VII
4. Caesar, IV, 2
5. Todd, M., *Everyday Life of Barbarians*, pp. 107–8
6. Tacitus, *Germania*, X
7. Ibid, VI
8. Todd, M., op. cit., p. 96
9. Caesar, IV, 22
10. Tacitus, *Germania*, XXV
11. Ibid, XI
12. Ibid
13. Ibid, VII
14. Caesar, I, 31
15. Ibid
16. Ibid, 33
17. Tacitus, *Germania*, V
18. Schnurbein, S., 'Augustus in Germania and His New "Town" at Waldgirmes East of the Rhine', *Journal of Roman Archaeology,* 16 (2003), pp. 93–107
19. Velleius Paterculus, *Compendium of Roman History*, II, 118
20. Tacitus, *Annals*, II, 45
21. Velleius Paterculus, II, 109
22. Tacitus, *Annals*, II, 19
23. Velleius Paterculus, II, 118
24. Ibid, 117
25. Ibid
26. Dio Cassius, VIII, 56, 18
27. Florus, *Epitome of Roman History*, II, 88
28. Josephus, *Jewish Antiquities*, X, 10
29. Velleius Paterculus, II, 118
30. Tacitus, *Annals*, I, 54
31. Velleius Paterculus, II, 118–19
32. Ibid, 119–20
33. Ibid
34. Todd, M., *The Early Germans,* pp. 50–1
35. Tacitus, *Histories*, IV
36. Dio Cassius, LVI, 23
37. Suetonius, 'Caligula', XXIV
38. For the name of Arminius' wife see Strabo, VII, 1, 4
39. Tacitus, *Annals*, I, 55
40. Ibid, 66
41. Ibid, 57
42. Ibid, 58
43. Ibid, 59
44. Ibid, 61

45. Ibid, II, 10
46. Strabo, VII, 1, 4
47. Tacitus, *Annals*, II, 42
48. Velleius Paterculus, II, 108
49. Tacitus, *Annals*, II, 45
50. Ibid, 63
51. Ibid, 84
52. Ibid, I, 9: 'The ocean and the remote rivers were the boundaries of the empire'; I, 11: 'Augustus had written with his own hand ... that the empire should be confined to its present limits.'
53. Suetonius, 'Augustus', 25

VI DACIA AND THE VANISHED WORLD
1. Julian, 'The Caesars', XXVIII, 327
2. Eutropius, *Breviarum Ab Urbe Condita*, VIII, 6, 2
3. Ibid
4. Hanson, W. S. and Haynes I. P., *Roman Dacia*
5. Vékony, G., *Dacians-Romans-Romanians*, p.50
6. Lydus, I., *Powers or the Magistracies of the Roman State*, II, 28
7. Strabo, VII, 3, 11
8. Herodotus, *The Persian Wars*, IV, 93–6
9. Strabo, VII, 3, 5
10. Plato, *Charmides*, 157
11. Vékony, op. cit., p. 50
12. Dio Cassius, LXVII, 6
13. Ibid, LXVIII, 9
14. Ibid, LXVII, 6
15. Ibid, 7
16. Ibid, 8
17. Ibid, 10
18. Ammianus Marcellinus, XXIV, 3, 9
19. Dio Cassius, LXVIII, 6
20. Ibid
21. Ibid
22. Ibid, 8
23. Ibid, 10
24. Ibid, 11
25. Ibid, 14
26. Ibid
27. There had been a canal before the Romans took over Egypt, engineered by Egyptians and Persian Barbarians, but Rome had let it silt up. All that Trajan's engineers had to do was clear it out and rename it 'Trajan's River'.
28. Whittaker, C.R., *Frontiers of the Roman Empire*

VII THE GOTHS
1. Procopius of Caesarea, *History of the Wars*, III, 2, 2
2. Philostorgius, *Ecclesiastical History*, II, 5
3. Ammianus Marcellinus, XXXI, 3, 8

4. Ibid, 4, 6, probably quoting Pindar
5. Ibid, 4, 4
6. Ibid
7. Ibid, 4, 10–11
8. Ibid, 5, 10
9. AIbid, 8, 9
10. Ibid, 13, 4
11. Ibid, 13, 6
12. Themistius, 'Oration 16', tr. Moncur, D. and Heather, P., *Translated Texts for Historians* (Liverpool, 1996)
13. Orosius, *Seven Books of History against the Pagans*, VII, 35
14. Zosimus, V, 4
15. Orosius, VII, 37
16. Claudian, *De Bello Gothico*, II, 129. Our modernization.
17. Ibid, 139
18. Zosimus, V, 37
19. Ibid, 45
20. Ibid, 47
21. Ibid
22. Ibid, 48
23. Ibid
24. Ibid
25. Ibid, 53
26. Ibid, 54
27. Ibid
28. Zosimus, VI, 8
29. Ibid, 9
30. Ibid, 10; Procopius, III, 2
31. Zosimus, VI, 11
32. Letter to Demetriades, no. 30, quoted in Brown, P., *Augustine of Hippo*, pp. 288–9
33. Orosius, VII, 39
34. Ibid
35. Zosimus, VI, 10
36. Procopius, III, 2
37. Orosius, VII, 37
38. Augustine, *City of God*, I, 1
39. Ibid, 7
40. Orosius, VII, 43

VIII HELLENES
1. Horace, *Epistles* II, 1, 156
2. Throckmorton, P., 'The Road to Gelidonya' in Throckmorton, P. (ed.), *History from the Sea*
3. Price, D. J. de Solla, 'An Ancient Greek Computer', *Scientific American* (June 1959), pp. 60–7
4. Price, D. J. de Solla, 'Gears from the Greeks'

5. The general belief that the Romans sterilized it by ploughing the site with salt is not correct. They didn't have enough salt.

6. Diels, H., *Laterculi Alexandrini aus einem Papyrus ptolemaischer Zeit*, Abhandlungen der königlich–preussischen Akademie der Wissenschaften zu Berlin, philologische-historische Klasse (1904), II, 2–16, 7.3–9

7. Vitruvius, *On Architecture*, VII, 14

8. Thucydides, *History of the Peloponnesian War*, I

9. Herodotus, *Histories*, V, 22

10. Thrasymachus, *On Behalf of the Larisaeans* – the only surviving line of the oration!

11. Demosthenes, *Third Philippic*, XXXI

12. Champion, C., 'Romans as Barbaroi: Three Polybian Speeches and the Politics of Cultural Indeterminacy', *Classical Philology*, 95, 4 (2000), pp. 425–44

13. Pliny, XXIX, 14

14. Ibid

15. Gruen, E.S., *The Hellenistic World and the Coming of Rome*, ch. 7

16. 'If the Greeks had had gunpowder, electro-magnetism, the printing press, history would need to be rewritten. Why the inquisitive Greek mind did not find out these things is a mystery.' Warner, C.D., 'Thoughts Suggested by Mr Froude's "Progress"', *Scribner's Monthly*, 7, 3 (January, 1874)

17. Plutarch, *Lives*, 'Marcellus'

18. Schramm, E., *Die antiken Geschütze der Saalburg*

19. Marsden, E.W., *Greek and Roman Artillery*

20. Diodorus Siculus, XIV, 16, 8

21. Ibid, XX, 91–6

22. Soedel, W. and Foley, V., 'Ancient Catapults', *Scientific American* (March, 1979), pp.150–60

23. Rochas d'Aiglun, E.A., *Poliorcetique des Grecs* and *La Science des Philosophes et l'Art des Thaumaturges dans l'Antiquité*

24. Middleton, W.E.K., 'Archimedes, Kircher, Buffon and the burning mirrors', *ISIS*, 52 (1961), pp. 533–43

25. By the Comte de Buffon, author of an encyclopedic *Natural History*. At 66 feet 40 mirrors ignited a creosoted plank, and at 150 feet 128 mirrors ignited a pine plank instantly. In another experiment 45 mirrors melted 6 lb of tin at 20 feet. *Supplément à l'Hist. Naturelle*, I, pp. 399–483, quarto edition

26. Stavroulis, O.N., 'Comments on: On Archimedes' Burning Glass', *Applied Optics*, 12, 10, A15 (1973)

27. The experiment was performed by Ioannis Sakkas, encouraged by historian Prof. Evanghelos Stamatis. He built 200 bronze-coated mirrors and assembled them along with some 60 men, on the pier of the Skamanga naval base near Athens, Greece (*The Times*, 11 November 1973). He argued that it would have been easier for Archimedes, as he had summer sun (the experiment was done in winter) and a more combustible enemy (cedar ships instead of plywood). The experiment was dismissed by Simms, D.L.,

'Archimedes and Burning Mirrors', *Physics Education*, 10 (1975), pp.
517–21, but then Dr Sakkas was reported to have repeated the same
positive results five times.
28. Lucian was evidently referring to a well-known story: ' ... at the siege of
Syracuse, he reduced by a singular contrivance, the Roman ships to ashes',
Hippia, chapter 2
29. Archimedes is said to have set on fire the enemy's triremes by means of
'pyreia', Galen, *De Temperamentis*, I, iii. The meaning of 'pyreia' is uncertain.
30. Zonaras, *Annales*, I, 9
31. Eustathios, *ad Iliad*
32. Dio Cassius, IX, 4
33. Rashed, R., *Les Catoptriciens Grecs, I: Les Miroirs Ardents* (Les Belles
Lettres, 2000)
34. Tzetzes, *Book of Histories* (Chiliades), 2, 118–28, in Thomas, I., *Greek
Mathematical Works*
35. Zonaras, I, 11
36. Toomer, G.J., *Diocles on Burning Mirrors*
37. Its most recent manifestation was in a TV programme (Discovery
Channel, *Mythbusters*). Filmed in October 2005, on a cloudy day with a
maximum temperature of 20°C, an array of mirrors set fire to an old wooden
fishing vessel at 75 feet, but the fire went out. Syracuse in July and August
commonly has clear skies and temperatures of over 30°C. The leader of the
MIT team involved, Prof. David Wallace, said it showed the weapon was a
technical possibility, but not that it was used (*San Francisco Chronicle*, 22
October 2005).
38. Simms, op. cit.
39. Idem, 'Archimedes' weapons of war and Leonardo', *The British Journal
for the History of Science*, 21.6 (June 1988), pp. 195–210
40. Livy, XXV, 31
41. Cicero, *De Re Publica*, I, 14, 21
42. Plutarch, 'Caesar'
43. Appian, IV, 9
44. Suetonius, 'Vespasian', XVIII
45. Russo, L., *The Forgotten Revolution*, p.133
46. Heron of Alexandria, 'Automata', I, 7, 340–2

IX PERSIA — THE EARLY DYNASTIES

1. Tr. Oppenheim, A.L., in Pritchard, J.B., *Ancient Near Eastern Texts
Relating to the Old Testament* (Princeton, 1950)
2. Isaiah, 45.1
3. The inscription from Persepolis is known as the *daiva* (demons)
inscription because it includes 'there was a place where previously demons
[*daiva*] were worshipped. Afterwards, by the grace of Ahuramazda I
destroyed that sanctuary of demons, and I proclaimed: "The demons shall
not be worshipped!"' Historians have had a lot of fun guessing who got the
short end of that stick.
4. Plutarch, 'Crassus'
5. Ibid

6. Ibid
7. Dio Cassius, XL, 27
8. Pliny, VI, 47
9. 'Has Crassus' soldier ta'en to wife/ A base barbarian, and grown grey/ (Woe, for a nation's tainted life!)/ Earning his foemen-kinsmen's pay', *The Odes and Carmen Saeculare of Horace*, III, 5, 5–8, tr. Conington, J. (London, 1882)
10. Dubs, H.H., *A Roman City in Ancient China*
11. There is a lack of sources for the Parthian period, but it is believed that there was little significant difference from education in the following dynasty. Information that follows is based on Tafazzoli, A., 'Education Under The Parthian and Sassanian Dynasties' in *Encyclopedia Iranica*
12. Gray, W.F.M., 'Batteries B.C.', *The Laboratory*, 25, 4 (1956)
13. Eggert, G., 'The Enigma of the Battery of Baghdad', *Proceedings: 7th European Skeptics Conference*, pp. 42–6, GWUP, Rossdorf (1995)
14. Dio Cassius, LXXVI, 9
15. Euripides, *Bacchae*, final chorus

X SASSANIANS
1. Dio Cassius, LXXX, 13–16
2. Herodian, *History of the Empire*, VI, 4, 4
3. Zonaras, XII
4. ´Onsor-al-Ma´âlî Kaykâvûs b. Eskandar, *Qâbûs-nâma*, ed. Gh.-H. Yûsofî, Tehran, 1345 Š. [1966], pp. 77, 89, 95, cited in Khaleqi-Motlaq, D., 'Iranian Culture, Iranian Etiquette in the Sasanian Period' in *Encyclopedia Iranica*, from which the material in this section is drawn.
5. 2 Chronicles, 8.4
6. 'Vopiscus', *Historia Augusta*, III. This mysterious text, which is now believed to have its origins in the fourth century, contains much that is untrue – which is a shame, as it is our main source on the lady. The admirable Bill Thayer, whose website at the University of Chicago is one of the most valuable electronic sources of primary texts, says 'even this cesspit of lies has patches of truth to it here and there, and this looks like one of them. Maybe Zenobia was indeed descended from Cleopatra.'
7. Ibid
8. Heather, P., *Fall of the Roman Empire*, p. 62

XI BEHIND THE MYTHS
1. Heather, P., *Fall of the Roman Empire*, p. 328, guesstimating that the Hungarian plains could hold 150,000 horses and every Hun warrior needed ten of them
2. H.G. Wells, *The Outline of History*, 28, 4
3. *The Times*, 30 July 1900
4. 'So then – the Vandals of our isle/ Sworn foes to sense and law,/ Have burnt to dust a nobler pile/ Than ever Roman saw!'
5. Gregoire, H.B. (Abbot of Blois), *Convention Nationale. Instruction publique. Rapport sur les destructions opérées par le Vandalisme, et sur les moyens de le réprimer. Suivi du Décret de la Convention Nationale* (Imprimerie Nationale, Paris, 14 Fructidor, an II [1793])

6. ' ... a species of infidelity in men who, having professed the faith of Christ, corrupt its dogmas'; Thomas Aquinas, II–II, 11, 1

XII THE CHRISTIANIZATION OF THE EMPIRE
1. Namatianus, 'De reditu suo', II, 41 sqq.
2. Livy, XX, 1
3. Appian, *History of Rome*, LVI–LXI. There is an obvious connection with the black stone of the *Ka 'bah* at Mecca, which is believed to have fallen as a meteorite and, in pre-Islamic times, was worshipped as the seat of a goddess with similar attributes to Hecate.
4. *Historia Augusta*, 'Aurelian', 20. The reliability of the source is more questionable than most (and that's saying something!), as it seems the text may have been written to 'prove' the superiority of paganism over Christianity and does include some blatant fiction. But the Sibylline Books were certainly used on occasion.
5. Gibbon, E., *Decline and Fall of the Roman Empire*, IX, 2
6. Jordanes, *The Origins and Deeds of the Goths*, XXIV
7. Herzfeld, E., *Zoroaster and His World*
8. ' ... that is, they had deliberately deformed skulls as the Huns are described to have had': personal communication, Dr Jeannine Davis-Kimball, Center for the Study of Eurasian Nomads
9. The treaty of 'fifty years of peace' signed in 562, under which Byzantium pledged an annual payment in gold for defence of the Caucasus (see fragments 11 f. in Blockley, R.C., *The History of Menander the Guardsman* and Guterbock, K., *Byzanz and Persien in ihren diplomatisch-völkerrechtlichen Beziehungen im Zeitalter Iustinians*, pp. 57 ff.), is shown to be intended as defence of the eastern frontier against the Huns in Göbl, R., *Die Münzen der Sasaniden im Königlichen Münzkabinett*, p. 5
10. Quoted in Publius Fabius Scipio (pseud.), 'Who Were the Huns and How Did They Make Such an Impact in Europe?', www.ancientworlds.net/
11. Heather P., *Fall of the Roman Empire*, p.156
12. Blockley, R.C. (ed.), *The Fragmentary Classicising Historians of the Later Roman Empire*
13. Ammianus Marcellinus, XXII, 5
14. Aquinas, Ia, 3c, 1c
15. Deferrai, R.J. (tr.), *Saint Ambrose: Theological and Dogmatic Works* (Fathers of the Church, 44 Washington DC, 1963), praef.
16. Dio Cassius, LI, 22
17. Gibbon, op. cit., 3, 27, i
18. Gregory of Nyssa, *De Deitate Filii et Spiritus Sancti*, Gregorii Nysseni Opera X, 2 (Leiden)
19. Guenther, O. (ed.), *Epistolae Imperatores: Corpus Scriptorum Ecclesiasticorum Latinarum*, 35, 1–2 (Vienna, 1895); Roberts, W.E., 'Magnus Maximus: Portrait of a Usurper', MA thesis (University of South Carolina, 1997), pp. 99–102
20. Theoderet, *Ecclesiasticae Historiae*, 5, 25 in *Patrologiae Graecae* 82, ed. J.P. Migne (Paris, 1864)

21. From the time of Antoninus Pius, c. AD 100, emperors had halos on their coin portraits
22. Ambrose, *De Fide*, II, 16
23. Rufinus of Aquileia, *Church History*, II, 23
24. These apocryphal quotations are in tune with the only biographical information we have, from the Byzantine encyclopedia, taken in turn from a *Life of Isodore* by the sixth-century Greek philosopher Damascius. This asserts that 'Those who were appointed at each time as rulers of the city at first attended her lectures, as also it used to happen at Athens. For if the reality had perished, yet the name of philosophy still seemed magnificent and admirable to those who held the highest offices in the community.'
25. Socrates Scholasticus, *Ecclesiastical History*, VII, 15
26. John, Bishop of Nikiu, *Chronicle*, 84, 87

XIII VANDALS
1. Heather, P., *Fall of the Roman Empire*, p.194
2. Gibbon, E., *Decline and Fall of the Roman Empire*, III, 14
3. Orientus, *Commonitorium*, II, 184
4. Prosper of Aquitaine, *Epigramma*, 17
5. Mariana, *de Rebus Hispanicis*, I, p. 148 (Hagae Comitum, 1733), quoted in Gibbon, XXXI, who concedes that it is 'perhaps exaggerated' by a desire on the part of the contemporary chronicler Hydatius, on whom this is based, to make the invasion fit apocalyptic Biblical prophecies
6. Collins, R., *Visigothic Spain*
7. Orosius, VII, 41
8. Salvian, V, 5
9. Jungman, J.A., *The Early Liturgy to the Time of the Gregory the Great*
10. Orosius, VII, 38
11. *Codex Theodosianus*, IX, 40, 24
12. Prosper of Aquitaine, *Chronicle*, 425
13. Procopius, III, 3
14. Salvian, VII,7
15. Procopius, I, 5
16. Heather, op. cit., p. 270
17. Raven, S., *Rome in Africa*, ch. 7
18. UNESCO excavations begun in 1972 established that the city was not, as had been believed, completely razed. That did not happen until Augustus flattened the ruins to build a new city.
19. Raven, op. cit., p. 168
20. Quoted in Kirwan, C., *Augustine*, p. 134
21. Victor of Tunnunna, *Chronicon*, n.d. 479; Ferrandus, *Vita Fulgentii*, XX, 40
22. Procopius, III
23. Jordanes, XXXVI
24. Tirnanic, G., 'The Mutilated Nose: Rhinokopia as a Visual Mark of Sexual Offence', a paper presented at the Byzantine Studies Conference (2003). It remains a popular attitude in part at least of the old Byzantine

Empire: a survey in Diyarbakir, Turkey, in 2005 found that 21 per cent of respondents believed an adulterous woman should have her nose or ears cut off (BBC News 19 October 2005).

25. Seneca, *Letters*, 7, 2–5
26. Augustine, *Confessions*, VI, 8
27. Seneca, *On Clemency*
28. Salvian, VII, 15 f.
29. Neuru, L.L., 'Salvian, Sin and Ceramics', *Byzantine Studies Conference Abstracts*, 7 (1981), 39–40
30. Quodvultdeus, *De Tempore Barbarico*, tr. Kalkman R., dissertation (Catholic University of America, 1963)
31. Jones, A.H.M., *The Later Roman Empire 284–602*, p. 758
32. Ennabli, L., 'Results of the International Save Carthage Campaign: The Christian Monuments', *World Archaeology*, 18 (1986–7), p. 304
33. Wells, C.M. and Wightman, E.M., 'Canadian Excavations at Carthage, 1976 and 1978: The Theodosian Wall, Northern Sector', *Journal of Field Archaeology*, 7 (1980), 57–9
34. Clover, F.M., 'Carthage and the Vandals', in Humphrey, J.H. (ed.), *Excavations at Carthage*, 7, 9
35. Salvian, VII, 16
36. Dracontius, *Praef. Romulea* I, 12–15, in *Oeuvres*, III, ed. Bouquet, J. and Wolff, E. (Les Belles Lettres, 1995)
37. Merrills, A.H. (ed.), *Vandals, Romans and Berbers*, p. 12
38. George, J.W., 'Vandal Poets in their Context', in Merrills, op. cit.
39. Kuhlmann, K., *Enemies of Souls and Bodies*

XIV NEMESIS

1. Bury, J.B., *History of the Later Roman Empire*, pp. 279–88
2. Gárdonyi, G., *Slave of the Huns*, tr. Feldmar, A. (Dent, 1969)
3. Jordanes, XXXV
4. Heather, P., *Fall of the Roman Empire*, pp. 331–2
5. Man, J., *Attila*
6. MacMullen, R., 'Judicial Savagery in the Roman Empire', in MacMullen, R., *Romanization in the Time of Augustus*, pp. 204–17
7. Hodgkin, T., *The Barbarian Invasions of the Roman Empire*, II, p. 25
8. Fóthi, E., 'Anthropological Conclusions of the Study of Roman and Migration Periods', *Acta Biologica Szegediensis*, 44, 1–4 (2000), pp. 87–94
9. Tomka, P., 'Der Hunnische Fürstenfund von Pannonhalma', *Acta Arcaeologica Academiae Scientiarum Hungaricae*, 38 (1986)
10. Hodgkin, op. cit., p.25
11. Poulter, A.G., Falkner, R.F. and Shepherd, J.D., *Nicopolis ad Istrum*
12. Priscus, fragment 11, 2, p. 277, quoted in Heather, op. cit., p. 334
13. Jordanes, XXXIII, 182. It's obviously a huge exaggeration – modern historians who have their own ways of counting think there might have been a tenth of the number – but shows how frightened people were.
14. Many thanks to Peter Heather for helping us explore the logistics
15. Apollinaris Sidonius, *Panegyric of Avitus*, 325–6

16. Güldenpenning, A., *Geschichte des oströmischen Reiches unter den Kaisern Arcadius und Theodosius II* (Halle, 1985), p. 340

17. Heather, op. cit., p. 387

18. Gregory of Tours, II, 5

19. Suda mu, 405, tr. Whitehead, D.

20. Prosper of Aquitaine, *Chronicle*, 452

21. There is one source that tells a completely different story. Hydatius, the bishop in Portugal who reported that Gaiseric's brother was killed by a demon when he acted sacrilegiously, wrote a *Chronicon* intended to show the workings of God as the world approaches the apocalypse. He says (Olymp. CCCVIII) that 300,000 were killed at the battle of the Catalaunian fields (!), and that the Huns went from Gaul to Italy, where they were visited by divine punishments, plague and famine and were 'slaughtered' by Aetius (Eus. MMCCCCLXI). He doesn't mention Leo or any meeting at all. This was used by later writers to inflict a plague on the Huns (perhaps there was one?) and, more recently, to give Aetius a role in their withdrawal, which Prosper denies. Hydatius seems muddled.

22. Hodgkin, op. cit., ch. 4

23. Jordanes, LXIII. Prosper of Aquitaine simply said that Attila 'was so impressed by the presence of the high priest' that he decided to go home – Robinson, J.H., *Readings in European History* (Boston, 1905), p. 49 – but Prosper was working in Leo's service as a secretary

24. Babcock, M.A., *The Night Attila Died*

25. John of Antioch, fragment 200, 1, tr. Gordon, C.D., *The Age of Attila*, p. 51

26. Ammianus Marcellinus, XXXI, 4

27. Priscus, *Bellum Vandalicum*, 7, 15–17, tr. Dewing, in Blockley, R.C. (ed.), *The Fragmentary Classicising Historians of the Later Roman Empire*, p. 69

28. Procopius, III, 5

29. Mathisen, R.W., 'Sigisvult the Patrician, Maximinus the Arian, and Political Strategems in the Western Roman Empire *c.* 425–40', *Early Medieval Europe*, 8, 2 (July 1999), pp. 173–96

30. This was actually a takeover by Attila's men. Romulus' father was Orestes, Attila's secretary. After Attila's death he resumed his original Roman identity, in 475 became Master of Soldiers in the West and then installed his son as emperor. Odovacer's father was Attila's lieutenant Edecon.

EPILOGUE

1. Shanzer, D., 'Bishops, Letters, Fast, Food, and Feast' in Mathisen, R.W., and Shanzer, D., *Society and Culture in Late Antique Gaul*

2. Shanzer, D. and Wood, I. (tr.), *Avitus of Vienne*

3. Gregory of Tours, II, 30

4. Ibid, 37

BIBLIOGRAPHY

There is not really much point in giving anything approaching a full list of printed books in the age of the Internet, especially as there are thousands of relevant titles. Up-to-date bibliographies are easily created with search engines, and so much material is now more easily accessed and searched online – especially when it comes to primary sources and up-to-date archaeological information. Of course, the big difficulty with giving URLs is that they quickly become outdated, so really the best tool for research is Google or one of its competitors.

The obvious problem is that the most extensive resources are shaped around a Roman-centred view of what's interesting. But there are some websites that really should be mentioned.

TEXTS
www.perseus.tufts.edu
Tufts University's Classics Department started this with a website on ancient Greece; it has now expanded to include Rome and is the most extensive online archive of classic texts – at the time of writing there were 489 of them, and 112 secondary sources.

http://classics.mit.edu
The home of the Internet Classics Archive, another wonderful library, with a current selection of over 440 works of classical literature.

www.fordham.edu/halsall
Paul Halsall's extensive collection of web resources relating to all aspects of ancient Roman society and culture up to the end of the second century AD.

http://penelope.uchicago.edu/Thayer/E/Roman/home.html
The astonishing work of Bill Thayer, in transcribing (rather than scanning) a steady flow of Greek and Latin texts with helpful commentaries, has our admiration and heartfelt thanks.

www.tertullian.org/fathers
This contains several relevant texts, including Ambrose, Jerome, Salvian, Gildas, John of Nikiu, Julian the Apostate and Zosimus.

www.iranica.com/
Columbia University's project, run by its Center for Iranian Studies, provides an on-line and bound hard copy of on-going work, the *Encyclopedia Iranica*, which offers the fullest treatment in English of Persian history.

www.sasanika.com
A California State University site devoted to Sassanian studies.

http://archnet.asu.edu/topical/Selected_Topics/Classical%20Archaeology/general.php
A starting-point for on-line archaeology, it offers links to resources that make it relatively easy to stay up-to-date with what is going on.

www.ccel.org
This site, devoted to Christian classics, offers translations that include Augustine's *City of God* and Gibbon's *Decline and Fall of the Roman Empire*, among many, many others.

www.stoa.org/sol
An astonishing project in which over 100 scholars are collaborating to place on-line the first English translation of the *Suda*, a tenth-century Byzantine encyclopedia.

www.livius.org/rome.html
Dutch historian Jona Lendering's collection of hyperlinked articles on Roman subjects.

www.stoa.org/diotima/anthology/wlgr
Mary Lefkowitz and Maureen Fant post texts illustrating the social role of women in antiquity.

JOURNALS
www.indiana.edu/~classics/research/journals.shtml
A useful list of journals available online, maintained by Indiana University.

http://ccat.sas.upenn.edu/bmcr
Of the numerous online journals that now exist, we have been particularly helped by the *Bryn Mawr Classical Review* at the above address, which includes magisterial and detailed book reviews – occasionally along the line of 'This is a poor book', which does make us shudder.

www.nottingham.ac.uk/classics/digressus
Digressus, Nottingham University's 'Internet Journal for the Classical World' is at the above address. But even though this is a refereed journal, the ususal warnings about Internet articles apply – it's unlikely that a printed scholarly journal would claim to be about 'Archeaology'! (Of course, spelling mistakes matter more online, as they mess up searches.)

REFERENCES

Ambrose, *De Fide*, tr. de Romestin, H., *Select Library of Nicene and Post-Nicene Fathers*, second series, vol.10 (New York, 1896)

Ammianus Marcellinus, *Rerum Gestarum*, tr. Hamilton, W., *The Later Roman Empire*: AD 354–378 (Penguin, 1986)

Andreau, J., *Banking and Business in the Roman World* (Cambridge, 1999)

Appian, *The Civil Wars*, tr. Carter, J. (Penguin, 1996)

Augustine, *Arianism and Other Heresies*, tr. Hill, E., *The Works of Saint Augustine: A Translation for the 21st Century*, part.1, vol.18 (New City Press, 1990)

Idem, *City of God*, 7 vols. (Loeb, 1957–72)

Idem, *Confessions*, tr. Watts, W., 2 vols. (Loeb, 1912)

Aquinas, T., *Summa Theologica*, tr. Fathers of the English Dominican Province Christian Classics (1981)

Babcock, M.A., *The Night Attila Died: Solving the Murder of Attila the Hun* (Berkeley, 2005)

Beresford Ellis, P., *A Brief History of the Celts* (Robinson, 2003)

Blockley, R.C., *The History of Menander the Guardsman* (Cairns, 1985)
    Idem (ed.), *The Fragmentary Classicising Historians of the Later Roman Empire: Eunapius, Olympiodorus, Priscus and Malchus* (Cairns, 1981–3)

Breeze, D.J. and Dobson, B., *Hadrian's Wall* (Allen Lane, 1976)

Brown, P., *The World of Late Antiquity: From Marcus Aurelius to Muhammad* (Thames & Hudson, 1971)
    Idem, *Augustine of Hippo: A Biography* (Faber, 2000)

Browne, P.R.L., 'Parthians and Sasanians' in Boyle, J.A. (ed.), *Persia: History and Heritage* (British Institute of Persian Studies, 1978)

Browne, T., 'Pseudoxia Epidemica', Keynes, G. (ed.), *The Works of Sir Thomas Browne* (Faber, 1964)

Browning, I., *Palmyra* (Chatto & Windus, 1979)

Bury, J.B., *History of the Later Roman Empire* (London, 1923)

Butcher, K., *Roman Syria and the Near East* (British Museum, 2003)

Caesar, *The Gallic War*, tr. Edwards, H.J. (Loeb, 1917)

Carey, J. et al (eds.), *Ildánach Ildírech: A Festschrift for Proinsias Mac Cana* (Celtic Studies, 1999)

Cauuet, B., *L'Or dans l'Antiquité, de la Mine à l'Objet* (Toulouse, 1999)

Cicero, *De Re Publica*, tr. Keyes, C.W. (Heinemann, 1961)

Claudian, *De Bello Gothico*, tr. Platnauer, M. (Heinemann, 1922)

Claudius Mamertinus, *Panegyrici Latini: In Praise of Later Roman Emperors* (California, 1994)

Codex Theodosianus, tr. Thatcher, O.J., *The Library of Original Sources: Volume IV – Early Mediaeval Age* (Hawaii, 2004)

Collins, R., *Visigothic Spain 409–711* (Blackwell, 2004)

Cunliffe, B., *Facing the Ocean – The Atlantic and its People* (Oxford, 2004)
    Idem, *The Celts: A Very Short Introduction* (Oxford, 2003)
    Idem, *The Ancient Celts* (Oxford, 1997)

Daryaee, T., 'The Political History of Eran in the Sasanian Period' at www.sasanika.com (and the forthcoming *History of Sasanian Persia*, I.B. Tauris)

Demosthenes, 'Third Philippic', tr. Leland, T., *All the Orations of Demosthenes* (London, 1851)

Dio Cassius, *Roman History*, tr. Cary, E. and Foster, H.B., 9 vols. (Loeb, 1914–27)

Diodorus Siculus, *Library of History*, tr. Geer, R.M. (Loeb, 1947)

Drinkwater, J. and Elton, H. (eds.), *Fifth-century Gaul: A Crisis of Identity?* (Cambridge, 1992)

Dubs, H.H., *A Roman City in Ancient China* (China Society, 1957)

Duncan-Jones, R., *Money and Government in the Roman Empire* (Cambridge, 1994)
    Idem, *Structure and Scale in the Roman Economy* (Cambridge, 1990)

Encyclopedia Iranica (Routledge, 1982)

Eutropius, *Breviarum Ab Urbe Condita*, tr. Bird, H.W. (Liverpool, 1993)

Ferrandus, *Vita Fulgentii*, Patrologiae cursus completus, Series Latina, 67 (1844)

Finley, M.I., *Classical Slavery* (Frank Cass, 1987)

Florus, Lucius Annaeus, *Epitome of Roman History* (Loeb, 1929)

Frank, T., *An Economic History of Rome* (New York, 1962)

Freeman, C., *The Closing of the Western Mind* (Heinemann, 1998)

Freeman, P., *War, Women and Druids* (Texas, 2002)

Frere, S., *Britannia* (Routledge & Kegan Paul, 1973)

Frye, R.N., *The Heritage of Persia* (Cardinal, 1976)

Funari, P.P.A., *Dressel 20 Inscriptions from Britain and the Consumption of Spanish Olive Oil*, BAR British Series 250 (1996)

Gerontius, *The Life of Melania the Younger*, tr. Clark, E.A. (New York, 1984)

Ghirsman, R., *Iran: Parthians and Sassanians*, tr. Gilbert, S. and Emmons, J. (Thames & Hudson, 1962)

Ghirsman, R. et al, *Persia, the Immortal Kingdom* (Transorient, 1971)

Gibbon, E., *Decline and Fall of the Roman Empire* (London, 1782)

Ginnell, L., *The Brehon Laws: A Legal Handbook* (Littleton, 1993)

Göbl, R., *Die Münzen der Sasaniden im Königlichen Münzkabinett* (The Hague, 1962)

Gordon, C.D., *The Age of Attila: Fifth-Century Byzantium and the Barbarians* (Ann Arbor, 1960)

Gregory of Tours, *History of the Franks*, tr. Brehaut, E. (Columbia, 1916)

Gruen, E.S., *The Hellenistic World and the Coming of Rome*, 2 vols. (California, 1984)

Guterbock, K., *Byzanz und Persien in ihren diplomatisch-völkerrechtlichen Beziehungen im Zeitalter Iustinians: Ein Beitrag zur Geschichte des Völkerrechts* (Berlin, 1906)

Hanson, W.S. and Haynes I.P., *Roman Dacia: The Making of a Provincial Society* (Journal of Roman Archaeology, 2004)

Heather, P., *The Goths* (Blackwell, 1996)

Idem, *Fall of the Roman Empire* (Macmillan, 2005)

Herodian, *History of the Empire*, tr. Echols, E.G. (California, 1961)

Herodotus, *The Persian Wars*, tr. Godley, A.D., 4 vols. (Loeb, 1920–5)

Heron of Alexandria, 'Automata', *Greek Mathematical Works*, II, tr. Thomas, I. (Loeb, 1941)

Historia Augusta, tr. Magie, D., 3 vols. (Loeb, 1921, 1924, 1932)

Herzfeld, E., *Zoroaster and His World*, II (Princeton, 1947)

Hodgkin, T., *The Barbarian Invasions of the Roman Empire*, 6 vols. (Folio Society, 2001–3)

Horace, *Satires. Epistles. The Art of Poetry*, tr. Rushton Fairclough, H. (Loeb, 1926)

Humphrey, J.H. (ed.), *Excavations at Carthage Conducted by the University of Michigan*, 7 vols. (Ann Arbor, 1976–82)

Irving, C., *Crossroads of Civilisation* (Weidenfeld & Nicholson, 1979)

Isaac, B., *The Limits of Empire: The Roman Army in the East* (Oxford, 1990)

James, S., *The Atlantic Celts: Ancient People or Modern Invention?* (British Museum, 1999)

John, Bishop of Nikiu, *Chronicle*, tr. Charles, R.H. (Oxford, 1916)

Jones, A.H.M., *The Later Roman Empire 284–602* (Blackwell, 1986)
  Idem, *The Roman Economy* (Oxford, 1974)
Jones, M.E., *The End of Roman Britain* (Cornell, 1996)
Jones, S., *Archaeology of Ethnicity: Constructing Identities in the Past and Present* (Routledge, 1997)
Jordanes, *The Origin and Deeds of the Goths*, tr. Mierow, C.C. (Princeton, 1915)
Josephus, *Jewish Antiquities*, 9 vols. (Loeb, 1930–65)
Julian, 'The Caesars', *Julian: Orations 6–8*, tr. Wright, W.C. (Loeb, 1913)
Jungman, J.A., *The Early Liturgy to the Time of the Gregory the Great* (Indiana, 1959)
Kirwan C., *Augustine* (Routledge, 1989)
Kuhlmann, K., *Enemies of Souls and Bodies: Vandal Rule and Urban Decline in Carthage, AD 439–533* (Warhorse Simulations, 1998)
Kurkjian, Vahan M., *A History of Armenia* (Armenian General Benevolent Union of America, 1958)
Lewis, M.J.T., *Temples in Roman Britain* (Cambridge, 1966)
Livy, *History of Rome*, 14 vols. (Loeb, 1919–59)
Lydus, I., *Powers or the Magistracies of the Roman State* (American Philosophical Society, 1983)
MacMullen, R., *Romanization in the Time of Augustus* (Yale, 2000)
  Idem, *Changes in the Roman Empire: Essays in the Ordinary* (Princeton, 1990)
Man, J., *Attila* (Transworld, 2005)
Marsden, E.W., *Greek and Roman Artillery; Historical Development* (Clarendon, 1969)
Mathisen, R.W. and Shanzer, D., *Society and Culture in Late Antique Gaul: Revisiting the Sources* (Ashgate, 2001)
Merrills, A.H. (ed.), *Vandals, Romans and Berbers* (London, 2004)
Musset, L., *The Germanic Invasions* (London, 1975)
Namatianus, Rutilius, 'De reditu suo', *Minor Latin Poets II*, tr. Duff, J.W. and Duff, A.M. (Loeb, 1934)
Olmsted, G.S., *A Definitive Reconstructed Text of the Coligny Calendar* (Washington, 2001)
Orientus, *Commonitorium*, tr. Tobin, D.M. (Catholic University of America, 1945)
Orosius, *Seven Books of History against the Pagans*, tr. Raymond, I.W. (Columbia, 1936)
Philostorgius, *Ecclesiastical History*, tr. Walford, E. (London, 1851)
Piggott, S., *Wagon, Chariot and Carriage: Symbol and Status in the History of Transport* (Thames & Hudson, 1992)
Plato, *Charmides*, tr. Lamb, W.R.M. (Loeb, 1927)
Pliny the Elder, *Natural History*, tr. Rackham, H. (Loeb, 1942)
Plutarch, *Lives*, tr. Dryden, J. (Random House, 2001)
  Idem, *Virtues of Women*, tr. Babbit, F.R. (Loeb, 1931)
Pohl, W., *Kingdoms of the Empire: The Integration of Barbarians in Late Antiquity* (Brill, 1997)

Polybius, *Histories*, tr. Paton, W.R., 6 vols. (Loeb, 1922–7)

Poulter, A.G., Falkner, R.F. and Shepherd, J.D., *Nicopolis ad Istrum: A Roman to Early Byzantine City* (Leicester, 1999)

Price, D.J. de Solla, 'Gears from the Greeks: The Antikythera Mechanism – a Calendar Computer from *ca.* 80 BC' in *Transactions of the American Philosophical Society*, vol. 64, part 7 (1974)

Procopius of Caesarea, *History of the Wars*, tr. Dewing, H.B. (Loeb,1916)

Prosper of Aquitaine, *Epitoma Chronicon*, ed. Mommsen, T., in *Chronica Minora Saec. IV, V, VI, VII*, vol. I (Berlin, 1961)
Idem, *Epigramma* in *Sancti Prosperi Aquitani Opera Omnia*, Patrologiae cursus completus, Series Latina 51, pp. 497–532

Rankin, D., *Celts and the Classical World* (Routledge, 1996)

Raven, S., *Rome in Africa* (Routledge, 1993)

Rawson, B. (ed.), *The Family in Ancient Rome: New Perspectives* (Routledge, 1992)

Rochas d'Aiglun, E.A., *Poliorcètique des Grecs* (Paris, 1872)
Idem, *La Science des Philosophes et l'Art des Thaumaturges dans l'Antiquité* (Paris, 1882)

Rufinus of Aquileia (Rufinus Tyrannius), *Church History*, tr. Amidon, P.R. (Oxford, 1997)

Russo, L., *The Forgotten Revolution* (Springer, 2003)

Salvian, *Of the Government of God*, tr. Sanford, E.M. (Octagon Books, 1966)

Schramm, E., *Die antiken Geschütze der Saalburg* (Berlin, 1918)

Seneca, Lucius Annaeus, *Dialogues and Letters*, tr. Costa, C.D.N. (Penguin, 1997)
Idem, *Minor Dialogues, Together with the Dialogue on Clemency*, tr. Stewart, A. (Bell, 1902)

Shanzer, D. and Wood, I. (tr.), *Avitus of Vienne: Selected Letters and Prose* (Liverpool, 2002)

Socrates Scholasticus, *Ecclesiastical History*, tr. Bright, W. (Wipf & Stock, 2003)

Strabo, *Geography*, tr. Jones, H.L., 8 vols. (Loeb, 1949)

Suetonius, *The Twelve Caesars* (Penguin, 2003)

Tacitus, *Agricola*, tr. Church, A.J. and Brodribb, W.J. (Macmillan, 1877)
Idem, *Annals*, tr. Church, A.J. and Brodribb, W.J. (New English Library, 1966)
Idem, *Germania*, tr. Church, A.J. and Brodribb, W.J. (Macmillan, 1877)
Idem, *The Histories* (Penguin, 1995)

Tenney, F., *An Economic History of Rome* (Jonathan Cape, 1927)

Thomas, I., *Greek Mathematical Works*, II (Loeb, 1941)

Thompson, E.A., *The Huns* (Blackwell, 1996)
Idem, *Romans and Barbarians: The Decline of the Roman Empire* (Wisconsin, 1982)

Throckmorton, P. (ed.), *History from the Sea: Shipwrecks and Archaeology* (Mitchell Beazley, 1987)

Thucydides, *History of the Peloponnesian War*, tr. Warner, R. (Penguin, 1970)

Todd, M., *Everyday Life of Barbarians* (Batsford, 1972)
    Idem, *The Early Germans* (Blackwell, 2004)
Toomer, G.J., *Diocles on Burning Mirrors* (Springer, 1976)
Vékony, G., *Dacians-Romans-Romanians* (Matthias Corvinus, 2000)
Velleius Paterculus, *Compendium of Roman History: Res Gestae Divi Augusti*,
    tr. Shipley, F.W. (Loeb, 1924)
Victor of Tunnunna, *Chronicon*, Corpus Christianorum, Series Latina, 173a
    (Turnhout, 2001)
Vitruvius, *On Architecture*, tr. Granger, F., 2 vols. (Loeb, 1931, 1934)
Webster, J. and Cooper, N. (eds.), *Roman Imperialism: Post-colonial
    Perspectives* (Leicester, 1996)
Wells, H.G., *The Outline of History* (Cassell, 1972)
Wells, P.S., *The Barbarians Speak: How the Conquered Peoples Shaped
    Roman Europe* (Princeton, 1999)
    Idem, *Beyond Celts, Germans and Scythians: Archeology and Identity in
    Iron Age Europe* (Duckworth, 2001)
    Idem, *The Battle that Stopped Rome* (W.W. Norton and Co, 2003)
Whittaker, C.R., *Frontiers of the Roman Empire: A Social and Economic
    Study* (John Hopkins, 1994)
Wilkes, J.J., *The Illyrians* (Blackwell, 1992)
Zonaras, *Annales*, ed. Buettner-Wobst, T., 3 vols. (Bonn, 1841–97)
Zosimus, *History*, tr. Ridley, R.T. (Canberra, 1982)

PICTURE CREDITS

PLATE SECTION 1

Page 1 *top* private collection; 1 *bottom* Department of the Environment, Heritage and Local Government; 2 *top* The Art Archive/Musée de la Civilisation Gallo-Romaine, Lyons/Dagli Orti; 2 *bottom* The Art Archive/Museo Capitolino, Rome/Dagli Orti; 3 *top* Collection Musées Gaumais, Virton, Belgium; 3 *bottom* E. Rabeisen, Musée Alesia, Société des Sciences de Semur-en-Auxois; 4 *top* Bibliothèque Nationale de France; 4 *bottom* Photo Scala, Florence/Heritage Image Partnership/British Museum; 5 *top* © The Trustees of The British Museum; 5 *bottom* The Art Archive/Rheinischeslandesmuseum, Bonn/Dagli Orti; 6 *top* akg-images; 6 *bottom* Oxford Film and Television Ltd; 7 *top* © Römerkastell Saalburg, photo: Peter Knierriem; 7 *bottom* Photo Scala, Florence; 8 *top* The Art Archive/National Museum, Bucharest/ Dagli Orti; 8 *bottom* Hervé Champollion/akg-images

PLATE SECTION 2

Page 1 *top* Mihai Ciocarlie; 1 *bottom* © The Trustees of The British Museum; 2 *top* Andre Durenceau/National Geographic Image Collection; 2 *bottom* Uppsala Universitetsbibliotek; 3 *top* John Gleave; 3 *bottom* Bayerische Staatsbibliothek, Munich, Clm 534; 4 *top* Adam Hart-Davis; 4 *bottom* Adam Hart-Davis; 5 *top* Livius.org; 5 *bottom* Michael Holford; 6 *top* The Bridgeman Art Library/National Museum of Iran, Tehran; 6 *bottom* © Brian A. Vikander/Corbis; 7 *top* © Roger Wood/Corbis; 7 *bottom* akg-images/Gérard Degeorge; 8 The Art Archive/National Museum, Damascus/Dagli Orti

PLATE SECTION 3

Page 1 *top* akg-images; 1 *bottom* The Bridgeman Art Library; 2 *top* akg-images; 2 *bottom* Sonia Halliday Photographs, photo by F.H.C. Birch; 3 *top* akg-images/ Erich Lessing; 3 *bottom* Photo Scala, Florence; 4 The Art Archive/Galleria Borghese, Rome/Dagli Orti; 5 *top* Michael Holford; 5 *bottom left* The Art Archive/Jan Vinchon Numismatist, Paris/Dagli Orti; 5 *bottom centre* & *bottom right* © The Trustees of The British Museum; 6 *top* ÖNB/Vienna Cod. 324; 6–7 *bottom* Photo Scala, Florence; 7 *top* Birney Lettick/National Geographic Image Collection; 8 *top* © Chris Hellier/Corbis; 8 *bottom* Mary Evans Picture Library

INDEX

Page numbers in *italics*
refer to illustrations